*Christian Science*

---

*A Sourcebook of*
*Contemporary Materials*

# Christian Science

## A SOURCEBOOK OF
## Contemporary Materials

Boston, Massachusetts

ISBN: 0-87510-224-7
Library of Congress Catalog Card No. 89-082094

Printed in the United States of America

Designed by Joyce C. Weston

# Acknowledgments

For permission to reprint copyright material, grateful acknowledgment is made to the following:

Macmillan Publishing Company for the article "Christian Science" by Stephen Gottschalk in *The Encyclopedia of Religion,* Mircea Eliade, ed., copyright © 1987; Charles Scribner's Sons for the article "Christian Science and Harmonialism" by Stephen Gottschalk in *The Encyclopedia of the American Religious Experience,* Charles H. Lippy and Peter W. Williams, eds., copyright © 1988; Passionist Missions, Inc., for excerpts from an article in *Sign* magazine titled "Mary Baker Eddy's Christian Science" by Pam Robbins and Robley Whitson, copyright © 1980; Faculty of Arts, Lancashire Polytechnic, Preston, England, for the article "Christian Science—A Time for Reappraisal" by Richard J. V. Robinson in *Four Elements,* copyright © 1979; Christian Century Foundation for excerpts from the article "Christian Science Today: Resuming the Dialogue" by Stephen Gottschalk in *The Christian Century,* copyright © 1986; Pelham Books for a piece by R. Graham Phaup in *My God,* Hayley Mills and Marcus Maclaine, eds., copyright © 1988; Dialogcentret, Denmark, for a letter in *Update: A Quarterly Journal on New Religious Movements* by Stig K. Christiansen, copyright © 1985; Scholars Press for excerpts from the article "Mary Baker Eddy and the Nineteenth-Century 'Public' Woman: A Feminist Reappraisal" by Jean A. McDonald in *Journal of Feminist Studies in Religion,* copyright © 1986; The New England Quarterly, Inc., for the article "Historical Consensus and Christian Science: The Career of a Manuscript Controversy" by Thomas C. Johnsen in *The New England Quarterly,* copyright © 1980; *U.S. News & World Report* for the letter "Prayer's Not a Gamble" by Lois O'Brien, copyright © 1986; University of California Press for excerpts from *The Emergence of Christian Science in American Religious Life* by Stephen Gottschalk, copyright © 1973; *The New England Journal of Medicine* for the article "The Position of the Christian Science Church" by Nathan A. Talbot, copyright © 1983.

# Contents

# *Preface*

$S$everal years ago a Christian Scientist attended a talk by one of the more vocal and well-known critics of churches that aren't considered mainstream. The talk that night was on Christian Science, and the remarks, by anyone's standards, were stinging.

While leaving the church auditorium, the Christian Scientist accidentally bumped into the speaker. Extending a warm handshake, he said to him, "I want you to know that I'm a Christian Scientist. I didn't come here to argue or debate. I just came here to offer my unconditional love to you." A member of the audience, overhearing this brief encounter, asked the Christian Scientist if he'd be willing to talk to him and a few others. Twenty-five to thirty people had gathered outside, standing in the rain. They began to ask questions about Christian Science. Not hostile or vitriolic questions, but questions that showed a desire to understand. [1]

This book was compiled with those people in mind, gathered in the autumn rain that evening, wanting to hear directly from a Christian Scientist about his faith. It's unlikely anyone there was on the verge of leaving his or her own church to become a Christian Scientist. Many had concerns and doubts about Christian Science, having heard it criticized so vehemently for the last several hours. But they felt the need to go a step beyond outside sources and critics—to hear a Christian Scientist explain for himself exactly what he believes and what he doesn't believe. This book was compiled not only for that group but for any reader who would like to have been there—even those who would have insisted on standing beneath the eaves, out from under the rain!

When it became apparent that night that there was no end to

the discussion, the Christian Scientist encouraged the group to find answers to their questions in literature written by others of his church. "Or you can do as I did when I wasn't a Christian Scientist," he said. "I read *Science and Health* for myself."

*Science and Health with Key to the Scriptures* by Mary Baker Eddy is the "textbook" of Christian Science and the primary source for any understanding of the subject. It's the book for those who want to examine the whole of the theology as it speaks to both head and heart—for those who want to experience the theology for themselves.

The materials in this book are sources of a somewhat different sort. Although they differ widely in character and content, they are all reliable expressions of what Christian Scientists actually believe. Further, they are "contemporary" in that they are drawn from material published over the previous few decades. They include both expressions by Christian Scientists of their faith and scholarly discussions of Christian Science that relate its beliefs and practices to differing theological currents and opinions.

This sourcebook, then, is a collection of primary and secondary sources, of simple statements of faith as well as analytical writing that has met academic requirements. Some of the selections have been abridged. Since the originals are readily available, elisions are not used except where necessary for the sake of continuity, nor are footnotes from the original sources incorporated in the text. Many of the sources are distinctly academic (Mircea Eliade's *Encyclopedia of Religion, The New England Journal of Medicine*), others are popular in nature (*U.S. News & World Report*), while still others are church-published (*The Christian Science Journal, A Century of Christian Science Healing*). In spite of the variety of sources and authors, several basic assumptions underlie this collection.

One of the most significant is that the lives of Christian Scientists and their experiences of healing speak for themselves. In this spirit the Christian Scientist mentioned earlier told the group: "I didn't come here to debate or argue, and we don't proselytize. We don't try to convert. Converting in our religion is strictly left up to God—that's solely God's business."

Christian Scientists, of course, make information available about their religious experience and convictions—where it's wanted. And they do respond when their experience and convictions have been misrepresented. But in a manner consistent with the spirit of the teachings of Christian Science, each of the articles published here presents the facts as accurately as possible and allows others to draw their own conclusions.

A second assumption underlying this collection is that our world is better off with minorities than without them. Specifically, Christianity benefits from a variety of views and positions. If Christendom, including Christian Scientists, were more closely approximating the spirituality of Jesus and doing the works that he did with similar precision and consistency, the religious landscape undoubtedly would be more unified (not to mention more luminous). But as it is, all of us benefit from the exchange of religious ideas and the challenge to live one's own convictions more fully.

It is not expected that readers will agree with every point made in this collection, or even with every point in a single selection. In fact, an effort has been made to choose material that states very clearly the differences between orthodox Christian doctrines and Christian Science, as well as to clarify convictions that are shared in common. It is hoped, however, that by gaining a more accurate understanding of Christian Science, readers will be challenged to think more deeply about their own religious views and contribution to Christianity—and to live more of the life of Christ according to their own light.

This book has been organized so that it can be approached in several ways. Some may wish to investigate particular issues selectively, according to their own interests and needs, relying on the table of contents and index as guides. Others may want to read the book straight through, taking advantage of its structure, which builds more or less from general to specific to present-day issues.

The kind of dialogue referred to at the beginning of this preface—between a Christian Scientist and a group who had gathered to ask questions—is not unusual (although the circumstances surrounding that particular occasion were unique). Conversations between Christian Scientists and their neighbors about their respective religious convictions occur frequently, informally over "backyard fences" as well as in more organized settings, such as informational talks to church and school groups or correspondence with the church.

We've included short excerpts from a few of these conversations at the end of most chapters in sections appropriately titled "Further Exchanges." In some cases these thumbnail exchanges serve as a summary of points already made, while at other times they hint at additional insights as to how a Christian Scientist might view a subject. They are not definitive church statements—actually, the Church of Christ, Scientist, does not spell out "official" positions on each and every subject or try to dictate its members' social and political views—but simply a brief glimpse into what was said on a given occasion. As such, these exchanges offer at least an inkling of how Christian Scientists have shared their convictions with others. In so doing, they illustrate the kind of ongoing dialogue that is vital to an understanding of the religious landscape.

One final comment. The real value of the words in this book is that they represent, at least to some extent, actual experience. Christian Science began with experience. It began with Mary Baker Eddy, the Church's Founder, being healed of the severe effects of an accident as a result of spiritual light flooding into her consciousness while she read an account of healing in the Gospels. She spent the next three years practically in solitude, poring over the Bible, writing extensively, trying to grasp what had brought about this healing and what was enabling her to begin to heal other people.

The demand for Christian experience ran through her life and her writings just as it runs through the following passage from *Science and Health with Key to the Scriptures:*

> While we adore Jesus, and the heart overflows with gratitude for what he did for mortals,—treading alone his loving pathway up to the throne of glory, in speechless agony exploring the way for us,—yet Jesus spares us not one individual experience, if we follow his commands faithfully; and all have the cup of sorrow-

ful effort to drink in proportion to their demonstration of his love, till all are redeemed through divine Love.[2]

The spiritual commitment that comes from the heart or that is inherent in the writings of a religious leader such as Mrs. Eddy often isn't conveyed by academic writing. But the following selections were chosen with the hope that something of the deeply religious impulse that motivates Christian Scientists— something of the love they have for the Bible and specifically for Jesus, for the sober demands and light-filled promise of his life— will be felt, making it possible to better understand their convictions, whether or not one agrees with them.

This book has been prepared under the supervision of the Manager of Christian Science Committees on Publication.

---

1. See "Love: The Best Response of All," *Christian Science Sentinel,* May 19, 1986, pp. 903–907.

2. Mary Baker Eddy, *Science and Health with Key to the Scriptures* (Boston: The First Church of Christ, Scientist, 1906), p. 26.

# 1

# Four Overviews

This sourcebook begins with four very different overviews of Christian Science. The first, "Christian Science," is drawn from *The Encyclopedia of Religion,* edited by the distinguished scholar Mircea Eliade. The entry on Christian Science in this extensive reference work takes account of scholarship of the last several decades, while relating Mary Baker Eddy's theology to some of the broader currents in recent religious thought.

It is followed by "Mary Baker Eddy's Christian Science," an article from the Roman Catholic periodical *Sign,* which illustrates one of the premises of this book: that it is possible to understand other people's convictions and report them with reasonable accuracy without having to agree with them.

Two concluding items give brief statements of these convictions. "Focus on Christian Science," a sketch especially adapted for young people, is taken from the magazine *Catalyst for Youth,* published by the Disciples of Christ. It is followed by "My God," a statement of faith by a British Christian Scientist written for a book in which various public figures expressed their religious views in capsule form.

# Christian Science

Christian Science is a religious movement emphasizing Christian healing as proof of the supremacy of spiritual over physical power. Founded by Mary Baker Eddy, a New Englander of predominantly Calvinistic background, Christian Science emerged as a distinct phenomenon in American religious life during a period of both social and religious crisis. The dramatic conflict between science and faith, as witnessed in battles over Darwinism and critical biblical scholarship, was only the most obvious aspect of a developing breakdown in a Christian cosmology that pictured experience as split between a natural and a supernatural order. Christian Science, however, rejected traditional cosmology and was therefore free to address religious issues in a way that was limited neither by creedal formulas nor by assumptions based on nineteenth-century natural science.

Mary Baker Eddy from her earliest years showed a deep-seated longing for the divine that was broadly characteristic of the Christian tradition and especially prominent in Puritanism. She found it impossible, however, to reconcile her deepest religious feelings with the theology of a then decadent Calvinism. Yet while other revolts against Calvinism, such as those of Unitarianism and Transcendentalism, led to an attenuation or even an abandonment of Christian convictions, Eddy's Christianity was so deeply ingrained that she found it impossible to think of any ultimate answer to what she called the "problem of being" outside of a theistic, biblical context. In her own words, "From

Stephen Gottschalk, in *The Encyclopedia of Religion,* ed. Mircea Eliade (New York: Macmillan, 1987), vol. 3, pp. 442–446.

my very childhood I was impelled, by a hunger and thirst after divine things,—a desire for something higher and better than matter, and apart from it,—to seek diligently for the knowledge of God as the one great and ever-present relief from human woe."[1] STUDENT TRAINED TO FIND OUT THINGS / HIMSELF

Running parallel to this search, and contributing <u>heuristically</u> to it, was Eddy's own long quest for health. She had exhausted the healing methods of the time, including homeopathy, and the techniques of the Maine healer Phineas Quimby, to whom she turned in 1862, and although she found useful hints concerning the mental causes of disease, she never found the permanent health for which she was looking. Her growing disenchantment with all curative methods returned her to her spiritual quest, which led to a radically different perception of God and creation from that held by Quimby, namely, that reality is, in truth, wholly spiritual.

Eddy identified the advent of this conviction with her "instantaneous" recovery in 1866 from the effects of a severe accident while reading an account of one of Jesus' healings. She described the event as follows: "That short experience included a glimpse of the great fact that I have since tried to make plain to others, namely, Life in and of Spirit; this Life being the sole reality of existence."[2] This passage is reminiscent of much mystical writing, but Eddy saw the experience as the point at which she discovered a spiritual truth so concrete that it would be "scientifically" provable in the experience of others.

There can be no doubt that this moment of recovery marked an important turning point in Eddy's life, impelling the development of the theology and metaphysics to which she gave expression in her major book, *Science and Health with Key to the Scriptures,* first published in 1875. The primary purpose of the book was not to set forth a new systematic theology, but rather to serve as a textbook for religious practice. The focus throughout was on awakening the capacity of its readers to experience the presence of God directly; the "honest seekers for Truth," to whom the book was dedicated, were invited to explore the saving and physically healing effects of that experience.

A key point of Christian Science is that the understanding of

God must include a changed view of reality itself. In effect, *Science and Health* challenged the traditional Christian view of God as the creator of a material world—not on philosophic grounds, even though Eddy's conclusions are partially articulated in philosophic terms—but on the grounds of a radical reinterpretation of the meaning of the gospel. Christian Science takes the works of Jesus, culminating in his resurrection and final ascension above all things material, as pointing to the essential spiritual nature of being. Accordingly, his life exemplifies the possibility of action outside of and contrary to the limits of a finite, material sense of existence. From the standpoint of traditional Christianity, Jesus' works constituted supernatural interruptions of natural process and law; from the standpoint of Christian Science, they resulted from the operation of divine power comprehended as spiritual law. In biblical terms this meant the breaking through of the kingdom of heaven—of the divine order of things—into ordinary sense-bound experience.

Nineteenth-century Protestant orthodoxy associated the kingdom of heaven with a realm in the beyond and the hereafter; Christian Science, however, views it as the spiritual potential of present experience to be actualized once sinning mortals cease to identify their own limited, erring perceptions as reality. Regeneration or spiritual awakening occurs as one sees through sense appearance to what Eddy called "the spiritual fact of whatever the material senses behold."[3] The spiritual fact for her was not an otherworldly phenomenon, but a transforming power—a reality drastically obscured by the misconceived sense of life, substance, and intelligence, apart from God. So great is this error of misconceiving, or fundamental sin, that a revelatory breakthrough from outside material existence is required in order to manifest the true spiritual nature of creation. The advent of Jesus, according to Christian Science, constitutes the decisive spiritual event that makes possible the salvation of humanity from the flesh.

Christian Science does not deify Jesus, a point that its severest critics have sometimes said separates it conclusively from traditional Christianity. Yet Jesus' actual role in the achievement of humanity's salvation is as important to its theology as for traditional Christianity. His life of obedience and sacrifice is understood as the means through which the reality of being for humankind has broken through in the midst of ordinary human experience. This true spiritual selfhood is identified as the eternal Christ, as distinct from Jesus, although uniquely and fully incarnated in him. His mission is viewed as opening up the possibility for all men and women to make actual their own spiritual union with God. He did this by proving practically that neither sin nor suffering is part of authentic spiritual selfhood, or Christ.

While Christian Science holds that evil has no God-derived existence and therefore can be regarded ontologically as not real, it strongly emphasizes the need for healing rather than ignoring the manifold manifestations of the carnal mind, defined by the apostle Paul as "enmity against God,"[4] and as operating with hypnotic intensity in human experience. Such healing is to be accomplished not through personal will or effort but through yielding to the action of the divine Mind. Salvation, while seen as the effect of the divine grace, requires prayer, self-renunciation, and radical, unremitting warfare against the evils of the mortal condition.

Salvation includes obedience to Jesus' command to heal the sick. Sickness is one expression of the fundamental error of the mortal mind that accepts existence as something separate from God. Healing, therefore, must be predicated on the action of the divine Mind or power outside of human thought. In Eddy's words, ". . . erring, finite, human mind has an absolute need of something beyond itself for its redemption and healing."[5] Healing is regarded not merely as a bodily change, but as a phase of full salvation from the flesh as well. It is the normalization of bodily function and formation through the divine government of the human mentality and of the bodily system that that mentality governs.

The emphasis in Christian Science upon healing—primarily of sin, secondarily disease—is based on the concrete issues of everyday lived experience. The healing emphasis differentiates Christian Science from philosophies of idealism with which it is often carelessly identified, including the Emersonian transcendentalism that was part of its immediate cultural background. Indeed, departures from Eddy's teaching within the Christian Science movement itself have tended generally toward metaphysical abstraction, wherein her statements almost completely lose their bearings on daily experience.

In the context of Eddy's writings, however, such statements almost always point to the demand and possibility of demonstrating in actual experience what she understood as spiritual fact. Her abstract statement that "God is All,"[6] for instance, taken by itself could imply a pantheistic identification of humankind and the universe with God. Taken in the full context of her teachings, it indicates that God's infinitude and omnipotence rule out the legitimacy, permanence, and substantiality of anything contrary to God's nature as Principle, Mind, Spirit, Soul, Life, Truth, and Love, an assertion that is taken to be demonstrably practical in concrete situations, to some degree at least.

The radical claim as to the ultimate unreality of matter is to be assessed in these terms. Christian Science asserts that matter is not the objective substance it appears to be, but is rather a concept of substance shaped by the limitations of the human mind. This assertion no more denies the existence of humankind or natural objects than the challenge posed in physics to conventional views of perception and to the substantiality of matter denies the existence of the universe. But it does point to the necessity of bringing the true spiritual nature of humanity and the universe to light through progressive demonstration.

With this emphasis on practical regeneration and healing, one sees the clearest link between Christian Science and the American Puritan tradition. An undue emphasis on the practical aspect of Christian Science by some followers has sometimes led to a secularization of its teaching, with healing regarded as an end in itself rather than as one element of a full salvation. This tendency clearly characterizes the mind-cure and New Thought movements. These movements, in some respects akin to Christian Science, use similar terms, which, however, bear a notably different meaning.

As with any religious movement, the motives of those who call themselves Christian Scientists vary. Of the 350,000–450,000 who might so identify themselves, it is likely that a majority are not formal members of the Christian Science denomination. While many have made Christian Science a way of life and joined, others have sought it, sometimes intermittently, for comfort and support. There may be limited truth, too, to the hypothesis that activity in the Christian Science movement, in which women have been numerically predominant, has provided an outlet for women in a society that has otherwise restricted their role—particularly in the religious world. On the other hand, such an argument may reflect an unconscious male stereotyping that seeks reductionist explanations when women advance or espouse ideas.

Evidence of the religious experiences of long-term, committed adherents of Christian Science suggests that it may have survived for more than a century because it has met a more basic religious need. Disaffected Protestants, particularly, have seen in it a release not just from bodily suffering but also from spiritual malaise—an alternative to the attitude that accepts with Christian resignation the tragedies of present life in hope of compensation either in a life beyond or according to some transcendent scale of eternal values. Christian Science, however, regards the ultimate spiritual victory over evil prophesied in the Bible as requiring confrontation with all aspects of evil and imperfection in present experience.

Although Christian Science is explicitly committed to universal salvation, it focuses initially and primarily on the potential for transformation and healing within the individual. This focus, deviant as it has often seemed to conservative Christians, tends to associate it with the traditional Protestant concern over individual salvation, giving it a conservative cast in the eyes of more liberal Christians who wish to transform the social order. The identification of Christian Science with a conservative, well-to-do, middle-class ideology may be as misleading in a sociological sense as it is theologically. In fact, a greater segment of the movement comes from rural or lower-middle-class backgrounds than most outside accounts would suggest.

On the whole, the church does not share the social activism of many mainstream denominations, but its purpose in publishing

*The Christian Science Monitor*—an international newspaper of recognized excellence—indicates a substantial commitment to an interest in the public good. Eddy founded the *Monitor* in 1908 as the most appropriate vehicle for the political and social expression of the practical idealism of her teaching. In addition, it was intended to educate Christian Scientists about the need for the healing of society at large, not just the individual.

The character of the *Monitor,* to a degree, reflects the educational purpose of the church that publishes it. Eddy, surprisingly sensitive to the dangers of institutionalized religion, conceived of the church in instrumental rather than ecclesiastical terms, shaping it to provide practical means for the study, communication, and teaching of Christian Science as a way of life. It was not part of her original purpose to found a separate denomination; rather, she and a group of her students founded the Church of Christ, Scientist, in 1879, when it became clear that other Christian churches were not disposed to accept her teaching. The overall structure of the church was laid out in a document of skeletal simplicity, the *Manual of The Mother Church,* which Eddy first published in 1895 and continued to develop until her death.

The central administrative functions of this "mother" church, The First Church of Christ, Scientist, in Boston, are presided over by a five-member, self-perpetuating Board of Directors. The Mother Church with its branches, including some 3,000 congregations in fifty countries, constitute the Church of Christ, Scientist; the congregations are self-governing within the framework provided by the *Manual.*

Taken as a whole, the church's activities can best be understood as vehicles for disciplined spiritual education. These include the Bible Lesson-Sermons consisting of passages from the Bible and the Christian Science textbook studied by members during the week; the religious periodicals published by the church; and Christian Science lectures, Sunday Schools, the intensive two-week course of class instruction, and follow-up refresher meetings attended by those seriously committed to the religion.

The absence of an ordained clergy, ritualistically observed

sacraments, and all but the most spare symbols point to the almost Quaker-like simplicity of the Christian Science concept of worship, in which silent prayer has an important role and the sacraments are conceived of as a process of continuing purification and quiet communion with God. Spontaneous sharing of experiences of healing and spiritual guidance marks the Wednesday "testimony meetings."

Christian Science practitioners, listed monthly in *The Christian Science Journal,* are members who devote themselves full time to the ministry of spiritual healing, and a significant body of testimonies of healing—amounting to some 50,000 published accounts—has been amassed in Christian Science periodicals over the years. There is good evidence that this sustained commitment of an entire denomination over more than a century to the practice of spiritual healing has been a significant factor in the reawakening of interest in Christian healing among many denominations in the 1960s and 1970s.

By the 1979 centennial of the founding of the church, the Christian Science movement found itself experiencing greater challenges from the currents of secular materialism than it had encountered since the early days of its founding. The increasing secularization of Western society worked against the kind of radical Christian commitment it required, while at the same time its healing practices encountered new challenges in an increasingly medically oriented society.

The history of the church, however, confirms that it is no exception to the general tendency of religious movements to grow or decline according to inner vitality rather than external pressure. Nor are external signs of growth in themselves altogether valid indicators of spiritual strength; indeed, it was because of this that Mary Baker Eddy forbade the publication of church membership statistics at a time when the movement was growing rapidly. The great numerical growth of the movement in the decades after Eddy's death may well have been attributable more to sociocultural factors unrelated to and, in some respects, opposed to the specific religious and redemptive purposes of the church itself.

It is too soon to assess the long-term significance of some

signs of decline of the Christian Science movement. Indeed, these signs must be qualified by other factors, among them the erosion of the insularity and complacency evident to some degree in the church's posture in earlier decades, the maturing of the movement, its willingness to position itself in relation to the rest of the Christian world, and the significant growth it has experienced in some developing nations.

---

1. Mary Baker Eddy, *Retrospection and Introspection* (Boston: The First Church of Christ, Scientist, 1891), p. 31.

2. Mary Baker Eddy, *Miscellaneous Writings* (Boston: The First Church of Christ, Scientist, 1896), p. 24.

3. Mary Baker Eddy, *Science and Health with Key to the Scriptures* (Boston: The First Church of Christ, Scientist, 1906), p. 585.

4. James 4:4.

5. Eddy, *Science and Health*, p. 151.

6. *Ibid.*, p. 366.

# Mary Baker Eddy's
# Christian Science

For those who stand outside it, Christian Science is a religion shrouded by mysterious metaphysics and obscured by two major misconceptions: that it is a faith-healing cult and/or that it is one more branch on the tree of Protestantism.

In reality, it is neither. And while it is radically different from Catholicism (and from Protestantism as well) in both form and content, it can teach us much about the endless possibilities that exist for human beings who seek—and find—God.

Ecumenical dialogue is usually undertaken by those traditions which are closest and whose divisions are therefore less radical (such as the current, very fruitful Catholic-Lutheran and Catholic-Anglican dialogues). It is easy for those in the mainstream to relate to each other, since they begin with so much already in common.

It is a far greater challenge to attempt to discover the bases for dialogue with the very unusual forms of Christianity. Upon examination, we find the unusual churches have unusual gifts of great potential value for us all. This very introductory look at Christian Science is a simple beginning response to the very demanding challenge of the potential ecumenical interrelation of Science with the other churches.

With her initial realization of Christian Science in 1866, Mary Baker Eddy synthesized many and varied elements in her life to formulate a religion, eventually so well integrated that it has stood virtually unaltered since her death in 1910. Its survival is

Pam Robbins and Robley Whitson, in *Sign,* vol. 59, no. 10 (July–August 1980), pp. 16–21.

especially noteworthy in light of the controversy and opposition it engendered from its inception. People often mistrust what they do not understand, and Christian Science, with its emphasis on the spiritual and negation of the physical, its patent refusal to rely on medicine, and its departure from traditional Christian positions, seemed to some an enigma and a threat.

Over the past century, Christian Science has earned respect, first by sheer longevity (time tends to lend respectability to the most radical movements and philosophies), by the journalistic world leadership exercised by Mrs. Eddy's best known undertaking, *The Christian Science Monitor,* and by the simple, quiet dignity of its churches, its publications and its members' lives.

Still, it is fair to say that, across the board, Christian Science is little understood and, worse, often misunderstood. Its truths are neither easily synopsized nor quickly communicated. Yet, Mrs. Eddy's scientific system of faith is precisely a *system,* capable of being intellectually grasped. A Scientist, or active member, is always thought of as a *student,* and reads and studies daily, confident that God is knowable, as revealed through the Bible as interpreted by Mrs. Eddy's textbook, *Science and Health with Key to the Scriptures. . . .*

For non-Scientists, any attempt to understand the system is, in a sense, hampered by its very cohesion. Just as one does not expect to find options in nuclear physics, one cannot expect to find them here. The structure of this religion, aptly called Science, parallels the structure of any other science; it lacks flexibility because each piece is closely linked to others and makes sense only in conjunction with the other pieces.

A New Hampshire native, raised by strict Congregationalist parents, the young Mary Baker was never a stranger to spiritual interests or physical distress. Shortly after marriage, she lost her husband while expecting their first child and was so ill after the baby's birth that his care had to be undertaken by another woman who subsequently raised him as her own. Acquainted with grief and disappointments and prone to chronic ailments, Mrs. Eddy sought physical healing through various channels, including the then-popular homeopathic medicine. But when she was spontaneously healed following a serious fall in 1866, she constructed a religious system based on an understanding of healing unlike any other. Christian Science regards healing not as a cure for bodily ills, but as spiritual regeneration, a setting aright of man's relationship with God.

This view of healing has nothing to do with *faith* as we commonly think of it. It has to do with *understanding,* and living, the truth.

"Truth is immortal," writes Mrs. Eddy, "error is mortal. Truth is limitless; error is limited. Truth is intelligent; error is non-intelligent. Moreover, Truth is real, and error is unreal. This last statement contains the point you will most reluctantly admit, although first and last it is the most important to understand."[1]

The entire issue of reality versus unreality is the crux of Christian Science, and the root of its confusion for those outside it. It is important to understand that Scientists do not close their eyes to what *is,* but see beyond it. They believe that there is a vast difference between "God's man and Adam's man"; that human nature can be improved, evil is not inevitable, spiritual resources are boundless; that the "real man" as God created him is perfect, upright and free, and need only arrive at and live out that realization of spiritual selfhood.

Mrs. Eddy taught that God is Spirit and his creation is spiritual. He made us in his own image and likeness, as Genesis recounts. The Genesis story also refers to Adam's deep sleep, a reference, Mrs. Eddy says, to our false concept of creation, that of sinful mortals in a matter world, not "real" man as made by God. Scientists point out that nowhere is it mentioned that Adam awoke, and perhaps we are all still dreaming the "Adam-dream"[2] and will until awakened by the Christ, the living Truth!

Mrs. Eddy also taught that it is not possible to ascribe anything of disharmony to the author of harmony, who is God. Everything that comes forth from God, the one and only Cause, is directly reflective of God. Nothing comes from God which is not Godlike. Divine Mind produces divine idea; a true human being is a divine idea and must reflect in all things appropriately human only that which is appropriate to God.

Evil, sickness, death and deceit are not products of a perfect God. If he did not create them, if they cannot be ascribed to him, it follows that they do not exist, for he created everything that is. But, Mrs. Eddy stressed, this is not to say that they do not seem real. The "only reality of sin, sickness, or death," she writes, "is the awful fact that unrealities seem real to human, erring belief, until God strips off their disguise."[3]

We tend to see aspects of humanness that are erroneous, she claims, such as three-dimensional reality. St. Paul himself said, perhaps with exasperation, "Flesh and blood have no part in that Kingdom."[4] When the error ceases—imagining that flesh and blood are the human condition—we can glimpse man as the immortal image of God. When early Christians were fed to the lions, it hurt. The romanticized Bible-movie versions of such events are absurd: it takes *x* number of minutes to die in such a way and it is agony. But on a deeper level of perception, the Christians transcended merely physical death, for they knew they were even then coming into the fullness of their resurrected life.

The people who seek Christian Science healing do so because they experience pain; but the pain is not reality, and when they recognize its unreality, it ceases to hurt them. This is not auto-suggestion, they maintain. This is understanding that God created man minus a capacity for sickness and when one fully grasps that, he is exempt from it.

As the Scientist principle of healing sets it apart from faith healing, so does its fundamental theology set it apart from main-stream Christianity. Indeed, Christian Science does not even fit comfortably under the wide umbrella of Protestantism, for it conflicts with tenets shared by most denominations.

Christian orthodoxy generally holds that God created man; man fell from grace, but was redeemed by Jesus Christ and can now work out salvation and attain eternal life.

Christian Science teaches that God created man, not as body and soul, but as eternal spirit. "Adam's man," mortal man liv-ing in a matter world, is a misapprehension of this real man, who is incapable of sinning. Mrs. Eddy was convinced God would not create man capable of sinning, then punish him for doing so.

Mrs. Eddy rejected the idea of a trinitarian God (at least as popularly misunderstood as three separate entities), but ascribed to Divine Principle three offices—Life, Truth and Love. As Catholics, we might equate those with belief in Father, Son and Holy Spirit, but they are not identical viewpoints. Mrs. Eddy defined God as "incorporeal, divine, supreme, infinite Mind, Spirit, Soul, Principle, Life, Truth, Love."[5] For her, the Christ was the Truth, always present to us, needing only to be recognized and tapped. Jesus of Nazareth best exemplified the Christ, so well, in fact, that the names are linked forever, but Jesus was not divine, she said.

Mrs. Eddy taught that he was a man, born of a virgin, "the offspring of Mary's self-conscious communion with God." He was "born of a woman" and "partook partly of Mary's earthly condition, although he was endowed with the Christ, the divine Spirit, without measure. This accounts for his struggles in Gethsemane and on Calvary, and this enabled him to be the mediator or *way-shower,* between God and men."[6]

Mrs. Eddy also stressed that it was not what Jesus said, but what he did that challenges us to emulate him. Christian Scientists emphasize the works of Jesus, because they believe his triumph is possible to all.

"Jesus," writes Mrs. Eddy, "walked on the waves, fed the multitude, healed the sick, and raised the dead in direct opposition to material laws. His acts were the demonstration of Science, overcoming the false claims of material sense or law."[7]

She rejects the belief that Jesus lived, suffered and died as a surrogate or delegate, a sacrificial lamb who ransomed us. Each person must "take up the cross" and follow Christ, she maintained, finding his own spiritual selfhood and doing what Jesus did.

"Christianity as Jesus taught it," Mrs. Eddy points out, "was not a creed, not a system of ceremonies, nor a special gift from a ritualistic Jehovah; but it was the demonstration of divine Love casting out error and healing the sick, not merely in the *name* of Christ, or Truth, but in demonstration of Truth. . . ."[8] These words are significant when we consider the religion she founded and the organized church she finally, reluctantly, formed.

Hesitant to institutionalize Christian Science, she did so only because it was necessary for its survival; but she felt strongly that the institution must serve the ideal.

She defined church as "the structure of Truth and Love; whatever rests upon and proceeds from divine Principle." The Church, she said further, "is that institution, which affords proof of its utility and is found elevating the race, rousing the dormant understanding from material beliefs to the apprehension of spiritual ideas and the demonstration of divine Science, thereby casting out devils, or error, and healing the sick."[9]

Elsewhere she observed, somewhat tartly, "Our proper reason for church edifices is, that in them Christians may worship God,—not that Christians may worship church edifices!"[10]

Reluctant though she was to organize Christian Science into a denomination, once she decided it was necessary, she did it so thoroughly that it continues to function seventy years after she herself "passed to realms of higher understanding." It is governed by a Board of Directors which fills its own ranks. Membership numbers are impossible to obtain, for no public statistics are made available, but the ranks of Scientists remain strong enough to support such major undertakings as *The Christian Science Monitor.*

Christian Science has no ordained ministry, no ritual, no ceremony. We might think of it as a very austere form of worship. The active Scientist daily reads and prayerfully considers a Lesson-Sermon (set forth from selections from the Bible and correlated portions of *Science and Health* by Mrs. Eddy)— human mind reflecting Divine Mind. On Sunday mornings, in simple but handsome churches, Scientists come together for a solemn reading aloud of the materials in which they have immersed themselves. There is no personal preaching and but a modicum of group prayer. Mrs. Eddy believed that communion takes place in the heart and that baptism is an ongoing process of regeneration. "Healing is the best sermon, the best lecture, and the entire demonstration of Christian Science," she wrote at one point.[11] At another, she said, "To my sense the Sermon on the Mount, read each Sunday without comment and obeyed throughout the week, would be enough for Christian practice."[12]

There is in Science a rigid prohibition against proliferating church organizations, which serves to "keep the church lean" and to draw Scientists into active participation in appropriate social movements outside the Church. Sunday School children learn the Lord's Prayer (and its meaning according to Christian Science) and the Ten Commandments, but they then go straight into children's versions of the Lesson-Sermon. There is thus no traumatic transition from the child's faith-world to that of the adult.

Despite her steadfast opposition to any personal devotion to her, Christian Scientists still adhere to the rules and regulations laid down by Mrs. Eddy, a testimony to her organizational skill and her influence. Yet, as in anything human, there must be continuing progress and development or stagnation. Mrs. Eddy herself was revising her textbook to the very end, but today's Scientists must grapple with the question: How to authentically enhance the tight coherence of Science, yet find ways for reaching out and updating?

The first century of its existence has indicated that Christian Science is not a universal call, and its adherents must explore ways in which they can leaven society and maximize their influence and impact. It is important for us as Catholics (and, ecumenically, to all Christians) that they do, lest we be deprived of what they have to offer—and they have much to offer us.

First of all, as with all other religious systems, there is the gift of heightened perspective that comes from taking a long look at something different. Regardless of how unexpected some stances are, at the very least they help us to see what divergent possibilities exist. A system like Christian Science, so pragmatic, so scientific—and so fascinatingly American—can prod us to re-think what we believe, not that we might reject or revise it, but that we might invest it with richer meanings, and see it in new dimensions.

All of that would be true, even if it were discovered that there was nothing directly pertinent in Christian Science, nothing we could relate to our own experience. But, in fact, there are areas in which there are positive points of contact between Science and Catholicism. One is the perspective on mysticism which Science provides us. The word itself too often connotates a nebulous subjectivity (and so Mrs. Eddy rejected the word lest it be misleading); but Christian Science offers a mysticism devoid of mistiness. Scientists build their spiritual life on a foundation of faith as the derivative of experience. Many Christians tend to confuse faith with trust; they trust that the *apostles experienced* what they said they did and told the truth about it. Scientists test themselves to see if they are in the faith by whether they *experience* Christ in themselves (as St. Paul insists, II Cor. 13:5). For them, faith is not to be a security blanket; it does not mean there are no questions, but rather that there is a solid rock of experience beneath their feet. Faith is not a jump into the dark, with fingers crossed and the hope somebody is going to be there; it is grounded on experience. They measure their growth in faith by how well they demonstrate what they understand.

Interestingly, if a medieval monk were to meet a modern Christian Scientist as the latter studied his weekly Lesson-Sermon, the monk would identify immediately with him. The Scientist's daily reflective study resembles that of the monk's daily meditation of sacred texts, called *lectio divina* ("divine study"). Both meditate on the words, hoping to reach beyond them to the reality they signify. This is a point of contact historically, perhaps; but it is also a reminder that for a Christian in search of God, intellect is a tool not to be feared or exalted, for beyond intellectual knowledge there is the insight that comes with prayer. While Mrs. Eddy called her system Science, and organized it in a logical, coherent fashion, it is first of all a religion, and as such, it affords another valuable view of prayer.

The Scientist prays in willing dependence on God, seeking not to change God's mind but to bring human mind into accord with divine Mind, to reach an understanding of Truth. He prays in a spirit of surrender, never asking for specific things or solutions. Even in healing, the Scientist does not pray for a "cure" but, rather, recognizes and acknowledges the will of God, that all be in harmony, and embraces it. If their prayers are "answered," then it is no surprise, no oddity, but only the natural order of things. "Miracles," as Mrs. Eddy points out, "are no infraction of God's laws; on the contrary, they fulfil His laws;

for they are the signs following Christianity, whereby matter is proven powerless and subordinate to Mind."[13]

In addition to these insights into mysticism and prayer, Christian Scientists offer us their example, as people living out their beliefs in a difficult setting. Active members shun alcohol and tobacco, seeking to free themselves from all forms of materialism. They reject gambling, believing in a divine law in which accidents or "chance" are unknown. They strive daily to grow in knowledge of God.

One of the difficulties with Christian Science today is some of its vocabulary. Essentially it is the English used at a particular period in time and, as such, its meanings are sometimes not evident.

The fact is that Mrs. Eddy was known to spend hours, even days, seeking to phrase a point precisely; and she was endlessly revising the textbook, which went through numerous editions. Yet, this same vocabulary enriches us in our understanding of our own faith, as in the use of the phrase—"Father-Mother God." Designed to express the tenderness of God, the term reminds us in the twentieth century that we cannot cling to the image of a purely paternalistic deity. (Mrs. Eddy also notes that "God made them, *male and female*," and they were "in his image and likeness.")

For Catholics, who weigh celibacy against marriage, Mrs. Eddy's teaching offers more food for thought. She called marriage "the legal and moral provision for generation among human kind"[14] and viewed it as a human, not a spiritual institution. Marriages are not performed by the Christian Science church, since there are no ordained ministers; but she did stipulate that members be wed by ordained clergymen of other denominations. She recognized the potential of marriage for enriching human experience, and she never said or implied that celibates were in any way "superior" to their married counterparts. In this she reminds us of the Catholic position that both states are holy. But Jesus said that in the resurrection there would be neither marrying nor giving in marriage; there would be a life different from the one we have now. Those who embrace celibacy here and now (chosen celibacy, not sim-

ple bachelorhood or spinsterhood) are supposed to be doing so
for everyone, not just themselves. Their unusual gift is to
witness to the fullness of resurrected life. Mrs. Eddy recognized that, and her views on marriage offer a provocative look
at the issue of how to relate different levels of spirituality to
life, sexuality, death and transfiguration.

Whatever else a religion offers its people, perhaps its greatest
measure is how it equips and prepares them to meet life's final
crisis—*death*. Cynics might ask how Scientists can persist in
their belief that they can overcome sickness and death, when
even their foundress died. But Mrs. Eddy never expected that
she would not pass through the transition we call death. She felt
that mankind collectively had not achieved sufficient spiritual
perfection to conquer that ultimate enemy, although that is not
to say it will never be conquered. Indeed, she taught that the
person lives on, continuing to strive for perfection after "death"
and that what appears to be an ending is merely a passing, ascend-
ing to a realm of higher understanding.

"Life is deathless," she wrote. "Life is the origin and ultimate
of man, never attainable through death, but gained by walking
in the pathway of Truth both before and after that which is
called death."[15]

No sketchy analysis of Christian Science, however respectful
or well-intentioned, can communicate it adequately, any more
than the nuances of Catholicism could be captured for non-
Catholics in a single written effort. But even an overview can
suggest some of the uniqueness of the faith and an awareness of
the amazing gift that was Mary Baker Eddy's. A simple New
Englander of eclectic education, she set forth truths she believed
were divinely revealed to her through intense study and reflection, and articulated them with such care and thoroughness that
they bear fruit a century later.

Much maligned in her lifetime, she is remembered today for
the words she wrote and the Church she founded. Whatever the
present and future state of Christian Science, Mrs. Eddy's contributions cannot be underestimated. If she changed a single life,
she may have changed thousands of lives, and in either case,
who can say she did not change the world? As she said herself,

"It is of comparatively little importance what a man thinks or believes he knows; the good that a man does is the . . . sole proof of rightness."[16]

---

1. Mary Baker Eddy, *Science and Health with Key to the Scriptures* (Boston: The First Church of Christ, Scientist, 1906), p. 466.

2. *Ibid.,* p. 282.

3. *Ibid.,* p. 472.

4. I Cor. 15:50.

5. Eddy, *Science and Health,* p. 465.

6. *Ibid.,* pp. 29, 30.

7. *Ibid.,* p. 273.

8. *Ibid.,* p. 135.

9. *Ibid.,* p. 583.

10. Mary Baker Eddy, *The First Church of Christ, Scientist, and Miscellany* (Boston: The First Church of Christ, Scientist, 1913), p. 162.

11. Quoted in Robert Peel, *Mary Baker Eddy: The Years of Authority* (New York: Holt, Rinehart and Winston, 1977), p. 98.

12. Mary Baker Eddy, *Message to The Mother Church for 1901* (Boston: The First Church of Christ, Scientist, 1901), p. 11.

13. Mary Baker Eddy, *Miscellaneous Writings* (Boston: The First Church of Christ, Scientist, 1896), p. 29.

14. Eddy, *Science and Health,* p. 56.

15. *Ibid.,* p. 487.

16. Eddy, *Miscellany,* p. 271.

# Focus on Christian Science

Some say it's just a theory; others say it's another sect. Followers of Christian Science talk about lives reformed and bodies restored to health. Critics of Christian Science seem not to know exactly what to think—about its healings or its theology.

Perhaps by examining a bit of its history, looking into the life of its founder, noting something of its organization and membership, and trying to catch at least the essence of its spirit, Christian Science will come a bit more sharply into focus as religion, way of life, and church structure.

Mary Baker Eddy founded the Church of Christ, Scientist, and wrote the textbook which sets forth the basic religious teachings of the denomination. There are more than three thousand branches of The Mother Church in Boston. Each of these local churches found in fifty-seven countries is democratically self-governed, but is organized in line with fundamental provisions of the *Church Manual* governing the denomination as a whole.

Christian Science history is rooted in the New England of pilgrims, puritans, revolutionaries, poets, philosophers, and those orderly stone-upon-stone walls which endlessly organize the landscape.

Mrs. Eddy (Mary Baker) was born in Bow, New Hampshire, in 1821. She first began to discern the pattern of Christian Science at the age of forty-five, in 1866. She published the textbook on the subject (*Science and Health*) in 1875. The church was launched in 1879, reorganized in 1892. Religious periodicals, an

---

Robert Nelson, in *Catalyst for Youth,* vol. 4, no. 9 (May 1973), pp. 2–6.

expanded church organization, and a structured headquarters operation for worldwide service were founded in 1898.

In 1908, at the age of eighty-seven, two years before her death, Mrs. Eddy established a newspaper, *The Christian Science Monitor.* "The object of the *Monitor,*" she stated, "is to injure no man, but to bless all mankind."[1]

In her early years there were few signs of the events to come. Between 1821 and 1866, she faced personal tragedy, conflict, and illness. Bible studies had always been basic in the Baker family, but the Christianity within the modest New England farm home wore smile and frown. Her mother was warm and patient; her father, his kindness well guarded, was iron-willed and severely religious.

Biographer Robert Peel speaks of Abigail Baker as "the summer to Mark's winter, the New Testament to his Old."[2] Young Mary was caught in between.

Year after year, troubles seemed to cling to her life like the storms that some days brood hour after hour among the White Mountains of New Hampshire. Illness sapped her strength; her mother's and first husband's deaths, and a miserable second marriage added their special pain; assorted treatments offered only sporadic relief.

Thus, on February 1, 1866, when she was insensible after a hard fall on an icy street in Lynn, Massachusetts, her hopes seemed to have crashed with new finality.

And yet, it was into this dark hour, we are told, that healing inspiration flashed. For three days she lay in unchanging physical condition—a doctor said it was very serious. Then she asked for her Bible and, according to the record, after turning to one of Jesus' healings, the Master's words flooded her thought: "I am the way, the truth, and the life."[3]

Years later she recalled the experience: "As I read, the healing Truth dawned upon my sense; and the result was that I rose, dressed myself, and ever after was in better health than I had before enjoyed. That short experience," she continued, "included a glimpse of the great fact that I have since tried to make plain to others, namely, Life in and of Spirit; this Life being the sole reality of existence."[4]

Between healing and explanation, however, there were many months of study, testing, and writing before what she was to call the "divine Principle of scientific mental healing"[5] could be spelled out for others.

The crux of her conviction was just this: that the allness and goodness of God is as available to mankind today as it was to mankind when the Master walked in Galilee.

In "precept upon precept" fashion, she detailed this concept in *Science and Health,* which she was to refine and revise through the years. In 1883, she added, both to the title and the contents, a "Key to the Scriptures."

Her steady devotion to the teachings and demonstrations of Christ Jesus was underscored when The First Church of Christ, Scientist, was founded in Boston in 1879. Under her leadership that first small congregation voted to form a church designed to "commemorate the word and works of our Master" and to "reinstate primitive Christianity and its lost element of healing."[6]

"What we most need," she emphasized, "is the prayer of fervent desire for growth in grace, expressed in patience, meekness, love, and good deeds. To keep the commandments of our Master and follow his example, is our proper debt to him and the only worthy evidence of our gratitude for all that he has done."[7]

There is no clergy in the Church of Christ, Scientist. Instead, by Mrs. Eddy's designation, the Bible and *Science and Health* are the "pastor" and two members of the congregation read from the books during Sunday services. Midweek testimony meetings include briefer readings. A Christian Science practitioner is a member of the church who gives full time to a public ministry of healing through prayer as understood in Christian Science.

Christian Scientists today come from a great variety of the world's neighborhoods, careers, and homes. Many have been drawn toward Christian Science for a healing of some problem, but they say they soon begin to realize that outward correction is merely the evidence of inner spiritual inspiration.

To their way of thinking, Jesus had this in mind when he told his followers: "Seek ye first the kingdom of God, and his righteousness; and all these things shall be added unto you."[8] And when one realizes, they add, that the kingdom is neither "lo here" nor "lo there," as the Master said, but "is within you," the blessings of early Christianity seem very close indeed.

The basic convictions of Christian Scientists are called the "Tenets" of The Mother Church. They are stated in both the *Church Manual* (pp. 15–16) and in *Science and Health with Key to the Scriptures* by Mary Baker Eddy (p. 497), which is the denominational textbook, as follows:

1.  As adherents of Truth, we take the inspired Word of the Bible as our sufficient guide to eternal Life.
2.  We acknowledge and adore one supreme and infinite God. We acknowledge His Son, one Christ; the Holy Ghost or divine Comforter; and man in God's image and likeness.
3.  We acknowledge God's forgiveness of sin in the destruction of sin and the spiritual understanding that casts out evil as unreal. But the belief in sin is punished so long as the belief lasts.
4.  We acknowledge Jesus' atonement as the evidence of divine, efficacious Love, unfolding man's unity with God through Christ Jesus the Way-shower; and we acknowledge that man is saved through Christ, through Truth, Life, and Love as demonstrated by the Galilean Prophet in healing the sick and overcoming sin and death.
5.  We acknowledge that the crucifixion of Jesus and his resurrection served to uplift faith to understand eternal Life, even the allness of Soul, Spirit, and the nothingness of matter.
6.  And we solemnly promise to watch, and pray for that Mind to be in us which was also in Christ Jesus; to do unto others as we would have them do unto us; and to be merciful, just, and pure.

1. Mary Baker Eddy, *The First Church of Christ, Scientist, and Miscellany* (Boston: The First Church of Christ, Scientist, 1913), p. 353.

2. Robert Peel, *Mary Baker Eddy: The Years of Discovery* (New York: Holt, Rinehart and Winston, 1966), p. 6.

3. John 14:6.

4. Mary Baker Eddy, *Miscellaneous Writings* (Boston: The First Church of Christ, Scientist, 1896), p. 24.

5. Mary Baker Eddy, *Science and Health with Key to the Scriptures* (Boston: The First Church of Christ, Scientist, 1906), p. 107.

6. Eddy, *Miscellany,* p. 46.

7. Eddy, *Science and Health,* p. 4.

8. Matt. 6:33.

# My God

The Bible tells us that God is Love and this is my highest concept of Him. I think of God as entirely good, infinitely strong and tender—a loving and caring Father-Mother, who cherishes and nurtures His children. I believe this loving bond between the Father and His universal family is unbreakable throughout eternity. Even a glimpse of His ever-presence—full of light and glory—fills me with awe and wonder.

I think of God also as infinite Spirit, the perfect creator of a perfect, spiritual universe, including man in His image and likeness, which forever expresses His own nature. I believe that God's will for man is good, always for innocence, wholeness and freedom. The material, mortal man and the universe which appear to the physical senses—with all the sin, disease and misery they include—I see as limited and mistaken concepts of God's creation which need to be outgrown through spiritual rebirth and regeneration.

It's evident that a completely good God never created evil, and I see this as the basis for challenging and overcoming the evils we encounter in the world. The light of God's presence dispels the darkness and His saving grace offers redemption to humanity, lifting us out of the depths of ignorance, sin and suffering and restoring us to our natural state of purity and innocence.

Through prayer, we can all commune with God—hear His voice and increasingly bring our thoughts and lives into obedi-

---

R. Graham Phaup, in *My God*, ed. Hayley Mills and Marcus Maclaine (London: Pelham Books, 1988), pp. 56–57.

ence to Him. The Bible is of priceless value in enabling us to draw closer to God. The Scriptures teach us who we are and how we should live. I look especially to Jesus Christ as the Son of God and the Saviour of the world, whose life and healing ministry, redeeming the sinner, restoring the sick and bringing joy to human existence, has opened up a radically different way of living.

Jesus taught us to love God supremely and our neighbour as ourselves. I believe that through studying his teachings and striving to follow his example, we can increasingly recognize our eternal relationship to God as His beloved children, and feel His love and power in our lives.

# 2

# Christian Science
# and the Bible

Christian faith of every kind is inescapably tied to the Bible. One of the first questions a devout Christian unfamiliar with Christian Science might ask about it is: Where does it stand in relation to the Scriptures? The answer given by Mary Baker Eddy in *Science and Health with Key to the Scriptures* is succinct but decisive. The first of the six basic tenets of Christian Science presented in that book reads: "As adherents of Truth, we take the inspired Word of the Bible as our sufficient guide to eternal Life."[1]

What that means to students of Christian Science is the subject of this chapter. The chapter doesn't approach the topic through either detailed academic analyses or partisan polemics. Rather, it begins with two simple human documents clearly drawn from the writers' diverse experiences.

The selection "Searching and *Finding* the Scriptures" was written by a young third-generation Christian Scientist who had attended a United Methodist seminary as part of the requirement for his service as a Protestant chaplain in the armed forces. Originally published in a Christian Science church periodical, it conveys something of the freshness and depth of the search for a more meaningful encounter with the Bible. The next selection, "Spirituality and the Demands of Christian Discipleship: A Conversation"—a published interview with a young woman who found Christian Science for herself—comes at the same sort of questions from a very different background.

---

1. Mary Baker Eddy, *Science and Health with Key to the Scriptures* (Boston: The First Church of Christ, Scientist, 1906), p. 497.

# Searching and *Finding* the Scriptures

During the hottest days of summer, who doesn't enjoy the prospect of a refreshing swim in a pool, lake, or ocean? The cool water can change a hot, oppressive day into one of sheer delight.

But have you ever noticed something funny that most of us do? Even though we know just how invigorating the water will be, we hesitate getting in. The contrast between the heat of the day and the coolness of the water is so great, we begin to have second thoughts. Will the shock be too great? It's almost as if the water, which we came to for a reprieve from the heat, is repelling us. But with the heat of the sun beating down on our face and shoulders, we finally dive into the water and ahhhhhh!! The day is transformed. Instantly, we feel alive and rejuvenated. Of course the water never was preventing us from diving in. It was our own fear and resistance all along.

Odd as it sounds, I was recently struck by the similarities between this experience and that of reading the Bible. The Bible, not unlike the cool swim in the heat of the day, promises invigoration. We come to it because we're aware of how it has transformed the lives of others. In fact, we may have had numerous occasions ourselves when we found renewal in the Bible's powerful message. Yet there are times when it almost seems as if something tries to repel us from actively reading it—from seeing its promise fulfilled.

I once had an occasion to study the Bible formally at a seminary. During this time a friend asked me, "Now that you've had

---

Scott F. Preller, in Preller et al., *The Bible: Our Fountain of Living Water* (Boston: The Christian Science Publishing Society, 1987), pp. 1–5.

a chance to take so many Bible courses, is there any one book you would recommend for understanding the Bible better?" Without taking the time to consider her question thoughtfully, I responded off the top of my head, "Yes, the Bible." We both suddenly broke out into laughter. We both realized the irony of the question, which revealed a willingness shared by many of us to read all sorts of books *about* the Bible, but a great reluctance to come face to face with Scripture itself.

Of course, this feeling of being repelled can happen on several different levels. There are many prescribed formulas for encountering the Bible, which can have the effect of making us wade only ankle deep in a source of refreshment capable of renewing our entire being. One respected scholar puts it this way: "Apart from sheer neglect, the other way in which human beings can protect themselves from the rather frightening vitality of the New Testament is by carefully dismembering it. It is obviously right that we should have New Testament scholars—indeed I owe much to them—but it is horribly possible so to dissect your subject that you remove its life."[1]

An assumption that we cannot understand the Bible's deepest meaning, or that Scripture cannot be lived but only approached intellectually, or that only scholarly commentaries can adequately explain it—all of these amount to nothing but sheer conventionalism! They would keep us from really getting wet, from soaking up and living the Bible's transforming spiritual message. Of course, this is nothing new. People were perfectly willing to allow Jesus to talk about the Scriptures, but when he began to fulfill Scriptural promises, they were quick to oppose him (see, for example, Luke 4:16–30).

It just doesn't make sense to assume the Bible can only be talked about. The Bible has a spiritual meaning—renewing and transforming—that must be lived. The very reason the Bible came into being was that people had experienced the reality of God's presence so powerfully that these experiences absolutely had to be written down so that others could understand and even share them.

Mary Baker Eddy, the Discoverer and Founder of Christian Science, was utterly convinced of the provable nature of Biblical experience, certain that there was a Science of Christianity. The events in the life of Christ Jesus, which appear miraculous to the human mind, she recognized as evidence of divine, demonstrable Principle, operating through spiritual laws. As she writes, "Jesus gave his disciples (students) power over all manner of diseases; and the Bible was written in order that all peoples, in all ages, should have the same opportunity to become students of the Christ, Truth, and thus become God-endued with power (knowledge of divine law) and with 'signs following.' "[2]

She could write such a statement because her own discipleship had revealed exactly this kind of Biblical experience. As she searched the Scriptures, the revelation of its divine power opened up before her eyes, bringing healing and regeneration. For her the Bible was no longer authoritative just because it was "the Bible," but because it was *provable,* illustrating the divine Principle, God. In writing the Christian Science textbook, *Science and Health with Key to the Scriptures,* Mrs. Eddy never intended to *add* anything to the Word of God contained in the Bible, but rather to *open* it up in a way that proved with scientific certainty that the Christ could be lived, demonstrated, and experienced here and now. How often passages in the Bible become illumined when studied hand in hand with *Science and Health!* In the section Key to the Scriptures there is a glossary that gives a metaphysical interpretation of Bible terms. And two chapters deal specifically with the books of Genesis and Revelation. The entire textbook is filled with Bible quotations and allusions that shed new light on the Scriptures.

A searching of the Scriptures that results in our lives being increasingly animated by the light of Christ involves both a spiritual understanding of the Bible and an overcoming of all resistance to gaining such an understanding. And this spiritual understanding is exactly what *Science and Health* fosters and nurtures. By "spiritual understanding" we mean a degree of knowing that goes beyond a comprehension of the words on the page, to seeing the very light of Truth that impelled the words in the first place. As we understand the spiritual meaning of the Bible, our seeking becomes our finding; we discover something of the nature of divine reality, the kingdom of God at hand.

So how do we go about searching the Scriptures and finding this transforming, spiritual meaning?

The simple and reliable way is to begin by realizing that it is God's nature to reveal Himself, that He is understandable. There's such a difference between an approach to life that assumes God to be distant and unknowable and one that is aware that God is continually communicating His nature to us. An understanding that God can be known opens the way for His grace to enter our hearts and acquaint us with Him. In Jeremiah, we read, "For I know the thoughts that I think toward you, saith the Lord, thoughts of peace, and not of evil, to give you an expected end." The text goes on to give an indication of how we can experience this "expected end." It reads, "And ye shall seek me, and find me, when ye shall search for me with all your heart."[3]

Searching with all our heart means humbly reaching out to God with an honest desire to follow Christ's leadings and put aside all human preconceptions of God. Mrs. Eddy gives a clear explanation of what is required:

> The spiritual sense of truth must be gained before Truth can be understood. This sense is assimilated only as we are honest, unselfish, loving, and meek. In the soil of an 'honest and good heart' the seed must be sown; else it beareth not much fruit, for the swinish element in human nature uproots it. Jesus said: 'Ye do err, not knowing the Scriptures.' The spiritual sense of the Scriptures brings out the scientific sense, and is the new tongue referred to in the last chapter of Mark's Gospel.[4]

Such an approach to searching ensures that all hearts are being directed by the very same God we seek to know more of. And what we find is inevitably a clearer view of God as Spirit and of man as spiritual—a view that transforms each moment of living.

But what if we feel we really are being loving and unselfish, and yet we just don't feel we're finding the inspiration we're searching for in the Bible? Then we have a choice. We can give up. Or we can become even more insistent on unmasking the resistance we encounter!

Jesus never accepted failure or limits. The words he spoke

were accompanied by proofs. Mrs. Eddy clearly shows how our own Biblical proofs must come:

> Through understanding, dearly sought,
> With fierce heart-beats. . . .[5]

We read in Genesis about Jacob wrestling with an opponent all night. Even as the dawn breaks, he continues to struggle. He simply will not give up the fight until he has gained a victory. He says to this angel, "I will not let thee go, except thou bless me."[6] And the blessing he receives is so great that his very identity is permanently changed. From then on he is called "Israel."

This story is tremendously helpful in thinking about how we engage the Bible. It isn't expecting too much to say that every honest effort to search deeply into the Scriptures can have the same kind of transforming effect in our lives. We too can insist on not letting go of what we're studying until we receive the blessing it holds for us—until we clearly see the spiritual meaning that transforms and regenerates our experience. A willingness to search—in fact, an insistence on searching deeply into Biblical texts—takes us beyond mere comprehension to the point of spiritual understanding. We arrive at the point where word and deed, profession and demonstration, become one. This is the searching that is finding.

None of us can claim always to embody the humility and yearning that go into finding this spiritual meaning. And we all realize we have more to learn of God than we now know. But we do have moments! And these moments encourage us and make us struggle and work to experience this light more consistently.

My wife and I shared just such a moment not long ago when she woke up in the middle of the night feeling quite ill. We both began praying about the situation—reaching out to God to feel and prove His love, a love that transcends the realm of mortality.

As I read—and truly searched—the Bible, I realized the necessity of total reliance on the presence and power of divine Love. Any resistance—in the form of sleepiness, unpreparedness, or inadequacy—was shattered by Love, which at that moment was nurturing me through the Bible's crisp message. I became calmly conscious that God was indeed right there loving and caring for my wife. I saw that she was in fact the very utterance of Love itself. I was reading chapters and verses, but mainly I was understanding more clearly the healing light of Christ, which presents man's sinless selfhood. This dawning awareness immediately transformed the experience. My wife called me back to bed and slept comfortably through the night. This was a glorious moment—when the resistance to really reading the Bible was overcome by divine Love and the accompanying spiritual understanding was experienced as healing.

As we search for this deeper, Christianly scientific meaning of the Bible, we find not only its spiritual intent but our own spirituality as God's beloved child. This is why such moments feel so much like coming home. As we search we find out what we really are—and ahhhhhh! Like one who takes the plunge into bracing waters, we are refreshed.

1. J. B. Phillips, *Ring of Truth: A Translator's Testimony* (Wheaton, IL: Harold Shaw Publishers, 1981), p. 24.

2. Mary Baker Eddy, *The First Church of Christ, Scientist, and Miscellany* (Boston: The First Church of Christ, Scientist, 1913), p. 190.

3. Jer. 29:11, 13.

4. Mary Baker Eddy, *Science and Health with Key to the Scriptures* (Boston: The First Church of Christ, Scientist, 1906), p. 272.

5. Mary Baker Eddy, *Christ and Christmas* (Boston: The First Church of Christ, Scientist, 1893), p. 15.

6. Gen. 32:26.

# Spirituality and the Demands of Christian Discipleship: A Conversation

As a Christian, I certainly wasn't looking for a faith to *replace* Christianity, but for a deeper sense of God, which would help me understand and live more of Christ Jesus' original teachings. I was quite sick at the time. The real problem, though, was that deep down I felt—a little like the Apostle Paul—that I was fighting against what God meant me to be. Yet in the midst of struggle, I had intuitions of a very different sense of reality. There were times when I could just feel God's presence. Something shifted for a time; so that instead of pushing or struggling I lived in the flow of God's love.

*Was this before or after you knew of Christian Science?*

Before. In fact, it was just before I left my job, moved to another part of the country, and took a less demanding job so I'd have more time to study and pray. Then the first day I was in the new city I met a man who was a mathematics teacher. As I got to know him, I could tell he was a Christian by the way he lived. But he seemed very different, more one with God. This individual rarely spoke of God. But you could sense the deep spirituality that permeated his life—a buoyancy, peace, and love that seemed to draw out the best in those around him. I wanted to know what it was that made him the way he was. One day I saw a *Christian Science Quarterly* on his desk, and I decided to find out about Christian Science. I thought that might explain what was different about him. So I borrowed from the library a

---

In Scott F. Preller et al., *The Bible: Our Fountain of Living Water* (Boston: The Christian Science Publishing Society, 1987), pp. 8–12.

copy of the Christian Science textbook, *Science and Health with Key to the Scriptures* by Mary Baker Eddy.

I guess you could say that I glimpsed in this man's life—and in the lives of several other Christian Scientists I met later—the same "original beauty of holiness" that Mrs. Eddy says she loved so dearly in the Christian ministers who taught her in her youth.[1] As I studied and worked with *Science and Health,* I began to find that Christian Science wasn't some heretical addition to Scripture. Rather, it opened up the Bible's teachings about spirituality and showed more of their practical and solid basis.

### What do you mean?

First of all, Christian Science has given me a deeper sense of prayer—one that never includes the admission that evil is God's will. This prayer begins with the assurance that His will is always good, that it can be trusted, that it doesn't cause or sanction suffering. Before, "yielding to God" had equaled "Christian resignation"—almost a kind of martyrdom in some cases. Believing God permits sickness or war or suffering of any kind subtly undermines one's trust in God's love and one's willingness to obey. Now, yielding is agreeing with a fuller sense of God—a God who is completely Love.

As a Christian I already sensed that spirituality was what I yearned for, but I didn't know divine law was *this* practical. Jesus assured us that God's kingdom really is "at hand" now. Christian Science has shown me this is a provable fact—even if uninspired human perception is blind to it. It shows that God *is* the All and Only—infinite, all-embracing—in other words *really* God. I am gaining a fresh understanding of the God who has been God all along.

Like Martha, or the older son in the parable of the prodigal son, I had felt committed to God, but burdened too. The older son had remained working and living in his father's house and undoubtedly loved him. But, it wasn't until his father spoke to him—"Son, thou art ever with me, and all that I have is thine"[2]—that he began to understand more of the total goodness and grace and limitless possibilities of the father's love. Christian

Science has shown me the God revealed in the Bible, without the veneer of limitations and misunderstandings we have imposed.

*So what's the difference between this sense of God and that which you previously entertained?*

I began to discover the God I had always worshiped and yearned to know better but couldn't fully or wholeheartedly embrace in my daily life. Earlier I felt a bridge missing. I wanted to yield my life fully to God, and yet something held me back. I felt unable fully to trust a God who I knew always *could* answer but who I wasn't sure always *would* answer—or who seemed to bring or allow very difficult times for His followers.

There always seemed to be a gap between the Biblical sense of God's complete sovereignty and goodness and my own experience of God. I became more and more aware of the aching needs of the world and very frustrated that I couldn't even consistently trust God in my own life, much less in serving others. This is why the idea of a *Science* of Christianity means so much to me—it made God's goodness and government real and realizable.

*Could you develop this point—Christianity as a Science?*

*Science* makes clear the fact that prayer is based on unvarying truths and divine law. It gives a sense of God as unvarying good, to be trusted absolutely. I had a turning point in my experience on this very idea of absolute trust.

One afternoon I was feeling slightly ill; it was really minor, but I left my office and went to another room to pray. And it suddenly occurred to me that trusting God for this need was really an encouragement to discipleship and a wonderful gift. The challenge was really a little thing, but that was why the gift was so wonderful. I saw that everything gives you an opportunity to trust God more. Trusting God for every little thing lets you know God more, and as you know God more, every little thing transforms you. And that's what you are looking for as a Christian, a way to be a better disciple in the everyday things.

I realized that the demand of Science—to rely on God, to be obedient to God in every area of life—helped one trust more fully rather than compartmentalize one's faith by applying it to some things and not others. It made Christian discipleship more concrete. I saw that true healing could not be separated from obedience—that all flows from this growing love for God and recognition of man's oneness with Him. It's looking at a bigger view of God and striving to hold on in obedience to that. This unlimited view of God began to transform my whole outlook.

*How did it transform your outlook?*

For one thing, it gradually transformed my sense of man. It's still transforming it! When you see God as limitless, you start feeling less limited. You start appealing to a God—and even companioning with a God—who loves and acts out of the total goodness that He is. You feel closer to God and glimpse more of what it means to be the child of God right now. And how to express this spirituality in practical ways.

I remember one evening when a friend shared a healing of a sprained ankle he'd just had. I wasn't particularly surprised. I had seen a number of wonderful healings in response to prayer over the years. But what did surprise me was his quiet certainty that we can *expect* God to heal because it is in keeping with His very nature. I had been sick for several years, but maybe, just maybe—although my friend's certainty confused and angered me a bit at the time—God could be like this.

In the next few months I read and reread the Bible and *Science and Health* as if I'd never read them before, trying to discover what God was actually like.

For the most part, I was so absorbed in this "new world" that was opening up that I forgot about the sickness. Sometime in June that year—nine months after I'd started studying *Science and Health*—I had to go through a series of medical tests. They showed what I'd already gradually begun to accept: I was indeed absolutely whole with no trace of the previous difficulties. But the more lasting change has been an expanding sense of God's presence and goodness. A sense that He could and would free me and *everyone* who turned to Him.

Now, I find myself more willing to face difficult things as I see that God didn't bring them. Difficulties come not from God, but from resistance to the basic fact that God's kingdom is here and is good.

I'm also less willing to accept limits from the past that try to carry over into the present—temperament, heredity, and so on. Accepting this Science of Christianity is not a one-time decision but an ongoing quest! You start asking God about who you are and who He is. You question everything you had assumed was true in light of what the Bible says actually is true.

### *Where do you find the answers?*

In the Bible. Studying *Science and Health* has helped me to go back to the Gospel itself, and I see both the questions and the answers in a new light. You realize that as you get to know God, it is not just history—"His-story"—or biography, it can be your story too. I'm beginning to see that through this transformation, through redemption, this becomes our autobiography to the degree we accept our spiritual heritage.

### *You don't mean to be claiming equality with Jesus, do you?*

No, not at all. It's similar to what Mrs. Eddy expresses when she speaks of ". . . not claiming equality with, but growing into, that altitude of Mind which was in Christ Jesus."[3] This gives more meaning to Jesus' life. It makes *more* of his sacrifice and gives an ongoing sense of it. It shows the tremendous consequences of his life in what happens to our lives as we become real disciples. I really feel closer to Jesus by not putting his example so far beyond reach that it becomes impossible to follow. His instruction—"Be ye therefore perfect, even as your Father which is in heaven is perfect"[4]—no longer seems a futile burden as one glimpses one's inseparability from God. We can begin to walk where he walked.

### *How much of this do you feel is really possible today, given the tremendous materialistic and secular currents of our time?*

That seems to be a crucial question right now. This Science of Christianity really meets materialism head-on. It shows that realizing Christian promises isn't dependent on outer circumstances but on having the Mind of Christ. It brings fresh insight into what the whole Bible really means. *Science and Health* states, "The central fact of the Bible is the superiority of spiritual over physical power."[5] It's tremendously freeing to glimpse that we can begin to realize the Bible promises about the ultimate triumph over materialism now.

And many people are already yearning for and receiving more spiritual light. As we follow God, Truth, where He leads us, we don't have to fear that we'll be misled.

---

1. See Mary Baker Eddy, *Message to The Mother Church for 1901* (Boston: The First Church of Christ, Scientist, 1901), pp. 31–35.

2. Luke 15:31.

3. Mary Baker Eddy, *Miscellaneous Writings* (Boston: The First Church of Christ, Scientist, 1896), p. 255.

4. Matt. 5:48.

5. Mary Baker Eddy, *Science and Health with Key to the Scriptures* (Boston: The First Church of Christ, Scientist, 1906), p. 131.

One of Mary Baker Eddy's most pungent critics, British historian H. A. L. Fisher, remarked of her in his 1930 book *Our New Religion:* "Prayer, meditation, eager and puzzled interrogation of the Bible, had claimed from childhood much of her energy. . . . The great ideas of God, of immortality, of the soul, of a life penetrated by Christianity, were never far from her mind."[1] Nor was the Bible ever far from her hand, to the last day of her life.

Because *Science and Health with Key to the Scriptures* is sometimes described erroneously as "the Christian Science Bible," the following excerpt from "*Science and Health* and the Bible," an essay on Mrs. Eddy's book in a 1988 scholarly work, *The Bible and Bibles in America,* is included to set the record straight. The volume is one of the Bible in American Culture series published by Scholars Press for the Society of Biblical Literature. The essay from which this brief excerpt is taken was written by Robert Peel, historian and biographer of Mrs. Eddy, and is described by the publishers as a study of "the connection between biblical and extrabiblical forms of scripture."

1. H. A. L. Fisher, *Our New Religion: An Examination of Christian Science* (New York: Jonathan Cape and Harrison Smith, 1930), pp. 41, 60.

EXCERPT FROM

# *Science and Health and the Bible*

Christian Science is first of all a study, and *Science and Health* remains its authoritative textbook. Christian Scientists are apt to speak of themselves as "students of Christian Science," and normally they devote time each day to studying the Bible and the textbook which they believe helps them to relate the "inspired Word of the Bible" more practically—more "scientifically" even—to their lives.

Thus Christian Science is also a "practice"—a way of life as well as a way of thinking and praying. In one sense every Christian Scientist is expected to be a "practitioner" of his faith, although the term is ordinarily reserved for those who are devoting themselves full-time to the ministry of healing. Truth is to be practically "demonstrated" through the regeneration and healing of human lives and bodies. Inspiration is to be validated by experience.

It was with this practical purpose that Mary Baker Eddy and a small group of her students voted in 1879 "to organize a church designed to commemorate the word and works of our Master, which should reinstate primitive Christianity and its lost element of healing."[1] In its final form the resulting organization consisted of The Mother Church, The First Church of Christ, Scientist, in Boston, Massachusetts, together with its branch churches and societies around the world.

In 1895 Mrs. Eddy ordained the Bible and *Science and Health with Key to the Scriptures* as "pastor" of The Mother Church and

Robert Peel, in *The Bible and Bibles in America,* ed. Ernest S. Frerichs (Atlanta: Scholars Press, 1988), pp. 193–213.

its branches. She also instituted a system of weekly Bible Lessons covering twenty-six topics and composed of correlative passages from the Bible and the denominational textbook. The topics of these "Lesson-Sermons" recur twice a year; the passages to illustrate them are chosen afresh each time by a committee.

Thus, every Sunday, Christian Scientists who have been individually and daily studying a given lesson during the preceding week meet together as a congregation to hear it read as a sermon by two lay Readers. In every Christian Science church service throughout the world the same lesson is read on the same day and is introduced by the same Explanatory Note from the *Christian Science Quarterly:* "The Bible and the Christian Science textbook are our only preachers. We shall now read Scriptural texts, and their correlative passages from our denominational textbook; these comprise our sermon."

The rationale of this system of combined study and worship is clear, if unusual. Pulpit eloquence was to give way to spiritual education; ritual to shared understanding; outward sacraments to inner commitment; audible to silent prayer.

The Sunday service in a Christian Science church mingles something of the bare simplicity of the New England church services that Mrs. Eddy knew as a girl with a touch of the Quaker quietism and the Unitarian rationalism with which she came in friendly contact later. The midweek meeting, for which the First Reader in each church prepares a lesson composed of passages from the Bible and *Science and Health* on a topic of his own choosing, is chiefly known for the spontaneous "testimonies of healing" given by members of the congregation—and in this respect at least bears some resemblance to a Methodist testimony meeting. For Christian Scientists the midweek meeting is, in some sense, a witness to—and a test of—the spiritual effectiveness of the Sunday service. In the age-old controversy in regard to salvation by faith or by works, Mrs. Eddy committed her followers squarely to the position of James 2:18, "Shew me thy faith without thy works, and I will shew thee my faith by my works."

The central place of the Bible in this worship system is notable, although often overlooked because of its linkage with *Sci-*

*ence and Health.* In few if any other churches is one-half of the sermon composed of readings from the Bible and preceded by an additional Scriptural reading. On the other hand, the authority given to *Science and Health* is also unmistakable and raises a question as to whether Christian Scientists give it equal authority with the Bible.

Certainly it has for them an authority at least equal to that which traditional Christians give the great historic creeds. But like those creeds it claims only to be making explicit what is inherent in the Scriptures—and to derive its authority directly from the Scriptures. *Science and Health* itself contains more than seven hundred quotations from the Bible, plus innumerable other references to Scriptural teachings, events, characters, figures of speech, textual and theological problems. Verbal echoes from the Bible abound throughout the book, often missed entirely by secular critics looking for influences on Mrs. Eddy's writing. *Science and Health* without the Bible would be, in its author's eyes, as anomalous as a key without a door to unlock.

In her 1902 revision of the textbook, Mrs. Eddy made two major changes. In the first place, she moved two chapters— "Prayer" and "Atonement and Eucharist"—up to the front of the book, thereby establishing at once the Christian spirit and theology which she considered essential to an understanding of the metaphysics that followed. The spirit is well illustrated in the following typical passage from the second chapter:

> While we adore Jesus, and the heart overflows with gratitude for what he did for mortals,—treading alone his loving pathway up to the throne of glory, in speechless agony exploring the way for us,—yet Jesus spares us not one individual experience, if we follow his commands faithfully; and all have the cup of sorrowful effort to drink in proportion to their demonstration of his love, till all are redeemed through divine Love.[2]

Characteristically, the sentences immediately preceding and following this passage introduce in an almost casual way a crucial theological point that is elaborated in various other contexts later in the book: "The divinity of the Christ was made manifest in the humanity of Jesus. . . . The Christ was the Spirit which

Jesus implied in his own statements: 'I am the way, the truth, and the life;' 'I and my Father are one.' This Christ, or divinity of the man Jesus, was his divine nature, the godliness which animated him."[3]

In a later chapter entitled "Science of Being" this point is amplified, with the addition of metaphysical terms which further extend its meaning:

> The advent of Jesus of Nazareth marked the first century of the Christian era, but the Christ is without beginning of years or end of days. Throughout all generations both before and after the Christian era, the Christ, as the spiritual idea,—the reflection of God,—has come with some measure of power and grace to all prepared to receive Christ, Truth. Abraham, Jacob, Moses, and the prophets caught glorious glimpses of the Messiah, or Christ, which baptized these seers in the divine nature, the essence of Love. The divine image, idea, or Christ was, is, and ever will be inseparable from the divine Principle, God.[4]

This in turn gains a further dimension from the answer to the question "What is God?" in the chapter "Recapitulation": "God is incorporeal, divine, supreme, infinite Mind, Spirit, Soul, Principle, Life, Truth, Love."[5]

The second change made in the 1902 revision was the addition of a final 100-page chapter entitled "Fruitage" and introduced by the words of Jesus: "Wherefore by their fruits ye shall know them" (Matt. 7:20). This was made up entirely of testimonials from people who had been healed simply by reading or studying *Science and Health*. The chapter includes healings of cancer, tuberculosis, heart disease, kidney ailments, broken bones, cataracts, eczema, alcoholism, insanity, and a host of other ills. They are not unlike the testimonials that have been published in the Christian Science periodicals monthly and weekly during the past one hundred years, except for the fact that *Science and Health* itself appears to have been the sole "practitioner" in each of these cases.

What is likely to strike the reader of this chapter, however, is how often the physical healing is presented as subordinate to an influx of light, a "new birth" or awakening to a fresh sense of life and its possibilities. Very often the chief gratitude expressed is for a higher understanding of God—and a deeper appreciation of the Bible. A frequent refrain is that the Bible is now a new book to the testifier. One woman writes that after her healing through her "illumined" study of *Science and Health,* the Bible became "my constant study, my joy, and my guide," and she continues: "The copy which I bought at the time of my healing is marked from Genesis to Revelation. It was so constantly in my hands for three years that the cover became worn and the leaves loose, so it has been laid away for a new one. Two and three o'clock in the morning often found me poring over its pages, which grew more and more sacred to me every day, and the help I received therefrom was wonderful, for which I can find no words to express my gratitude."[6]

---

1. Mary Baker Eddy, *The First Church of Christ, Scientist, and Miscellany* (Boston: The First Church of Christ, Scientist, 1913), p. 46.

2. Mary Baker Eddy, *Science and Health with Key to the Scriptures* (Boston: The First Church of Christ, Scientist, 1906), p. 26.

3. *Ibid.,* pp. 25, 26.

4. *Ibid.,* p. 333.

5. *Ibid.,* p. 465.

6. *Ibid.,* p. 691.

As mentioned in the preface, most chapters of this sourcebook conclude with a series of pertinent exchanges that have taken place in the course of Christian Scientists' ongoing contact with the general public. They are by no means intended to be definitive statements, nor do they represent the only turns a conversation or explanation might have taken. These exchanges do, however, give brief glimpses into the way Christian Scientists have shared their convictions on particular occasions. They provide an opportunity to "listen in" for a moment on part of a Christian Scientist's response to an inquiry by someone who is not a Christian Scientist.

# Further Exchanges

*How do Christian Scientists view the Holy Bible?*

I think you would find that Christian Scientists *use* their Bible as much as devoted Christians from any denomination. And I think that's important. The Bible to us isn't just a nice display piece to remind us that we're supposed to be religious. It's a working tool in daily life. It shows us how to actually be followers of the Master, Jesus Christ, not just in word but in deeds.

For instance, this morning, as I often do every morning, I read from our weekly Bible Lesson, which is made up of related passages selected from the Bible and our denominational textbook, *Science and Health with Key to the Scriptures* by Mary Baker Eddy. The passage that really stood out to me was from II Corinthians 2:14: "Now thanks be unto God, which always causeth us to triumph in Christ, and maketh manifest the savour of his knowledge by us in every place." That was just what I needed for my day—to know that it was God that was at work in my life, rather than me just struggling along on my own. So I wrote that passage down, carried it along with me during my day, and referred to it several times in the many situations I had to face.

Now, that's probably not something that would sound strange to other Christians who study the Bible and rely on its Word. But I just want to convey that Christian Scientists view the Bible in that way, as a living power that is directly applicable to daily life.

. . .

*Do we have what we need in the Bible for our salvation, or do we need something beyond it?*

We see the Bible as sufficient, in that the revelation it contains—specifically the life of Jesus Christ—fully sets forth through actual experience God's nature and man's relation to Him. On the other hand, Christian Scientists do feel that the meaning of Biblical revelation needs to be grasped in its full spiritual significance today and that a beam of spiritual light, as it were, had to be cast on it. This is for them the significance of the discovery of Christian Science.

. . .

### Do Christian Scientists take the Bible literally or figuratively?

I think your question is more complex than it might seem to be or than is often recognized in debates over Biblical inerrancy. There are very few, if any, groups that take every verse of the Bible literally. Certain Bible passages such as Jesus' statement "I am the door" simply wouldn't mean too much literally. On the other hand, to take the whole Bible figuratively would be to fly in the face of historical and textual evidence and to rob the Bible of its real power and meaning for our age. So the real question should be, Which parts of the Bible do you take literally and which figuratively? Without any attempting to go through the Bible verse by verse, let me say that Christian Scientists regard the events recorded in the Gospels as literal, historical fact, as do most Christians.

We believe, however, that the story of Adam and Eve, for example, is an allegory with profound implications for our spiritual progress today. Martin Luther once likened the text of the Bible to the "manger" in which the baby—the Christ or Word—lies. And he acknowledged that the manger has some straw in it! Christian Scientists take a similar view. We, too, feel the real need is not to be consumed by debates over literalism but to approach the Bible in a way that will transform one's life. The Bible takes on more and more profound import, particularly as one tries to live its message moment by moment. Sometimes a passage that hasn't meant too much to us might take on new meaning at a time of need or a time of prayer. Overall I would say Christian Scientists take the Bible *seriously;* they study it daily and strive to live close to its teachings. To them, studying the Bible is a lifetime pursuit, in which the very meaning of the Bible—found in both its historical events and its parables— deepens as one grows; it's not so much a basis for dogmatic argument.

. . .

**Don't Christian Scientists really elevate Mary Baker Eddy to the same plane as Jesus Christ and even substitute her for him?**

No, they don't—and if they did they would most definitely not be her followers, for nothing could be more contrary to her own teaching. Again and again, critics quote partial statements or sentences out of context. Mrs. Eddy herself, though, drew a categorical distinction between her own role as the individual who discovered Christian Science and the uniqueness of Jesus as the Saviour of mankind, the very embodiment of the Christ.

An honest, thorough appraisal of her references on this sub-ject can leave no doubt of her clear position. Asked in a newspa-per dispatch if she considered herself a "second Christ," she replied characteristically, "Even the question shocks me," and went on to state that "to think or speak of me in any manner as a Christ, is sacrilegious."[1] And in her dignified reply to Mark Twain on this matter she explained: "I stand in relation to this century as a Christian Discoverer, Founder, and Leader. I regard self-deification as blasphemous."[2]

. . .

**Do you believe what's in Mrs. Eddy's book _Science and Health_ was kind of a divine revelation?**

Yes, but not in some sort of mystical sense. Not in terms of angels or tablets down from heaven. It was a revealing or uncov-ering of all that God really is, and so a throwing of great light on the Scriptures. Christian Scientists feel that *Science and Health* helps them see the fullness of what Scripture means—to fulfill its demands and enter into the new life it opens for us.

· · ·

*But how about the way Mrs. Eddy and her followers use the Bible? Some say that they take Biblical quotations out of context and use them to support beliefs that are really unscriptural.*

Mrs. Eddy searched for and felt she found the living, practical meaning of the Bible for daily life. She makes constant and natural reference to the Bible, discusses many Biblical stories and passages, and often cites Biblical texts in making a point. But her whole teaching is aimed at conveying the spiritual meaning of the Bible, the scientific or permanent spiritual laws that underlie it. It isn't characteristic of her to single out a Biblical text, take it out of context, then build a whole theological argument upon it.

---

1. Mary Baker Eddy, *Pulpit and Press* (Boston: The First Church of Christ, Scientist, 1895), pp. 74, 75.

2. Mary Baker Eddy, *The First Church of Christ, Scientist, and Miscellany* (Boston: The First Church of Christ, Scientist, 1913), p. 302.

# 3

# Theological Dialogue

In a pluralist world of varying and often competing ideologies and belief systems, the need to understand better "where others are coming from" has become painfully obvious. This doesn't mean that all positions are reconcilable, in the religious world any more than in social and political matters. Yet clearly the ethic embraced by liberal and conservative Christians alike repudiates the tactics of "disinformation" that have become so commonplace in current politics. Christians are rightly held to a higher standard of honesty toward the faiths of their neighbors, even when they disagree with them!

A similar conviction lay behind much of the theological dialogue impelled by the ecumenical movement in the 1960s and 1970s. Christian Scientists welcomed the opportunities for genuine interfaith fellowship that opened up during the period, but their perspective on such fellowship was and is reflected in Mary Baker Eddy's words: "Our unity with churches of other denominations must rest on the spirit of Christ calling us together. It cannot come from any other source. Popularity, self-aggrandizement, aught that can darken in any degree our spirituality, must be set aside."[1]

In the late 1960s representatives of several Protestant denominations, including the Church of Christ, Scientist, met in two series of theological discussions. For some of these occasions the Christian Scientist representatives prepared position papers that served as a basis for lively but clarifying dialogue. Later these statements were published in a booklet entitled *Ecumenical Papers.* Three of these papers reprinted here focus on key questions defining the relationship of Christian Science to traditional Christianity: the Person of God, the significance of the resurrection, and the nature of sin and grace.

---

1. Mary Baker Eddy, *Pulpit and Press* (Boston: The First Church of Christ, Scientist, 1895), p. 21.

# Who Is God?

The first book of Kings records how the Syrians were once defeated by the Israelites on high ground. Obviously, the Syrians concluded, the gods of Israel were gods of the hills; so they would try their fortune again, this time on the plains. Another failure resulted. Israel's God was God both of hills and valleys.[1]

In general a Christian Scientist's first meaningful encounter with God has taken place in some valley. He is likely to recall a moment of moral anguish, of physical extremity, of bitter grief or overwhelming disappointment. In this situation he has come face to face with God; he has glimpsed God and his own relationship to God in a new light.

Then he has felt God's power lay hold of his experience. A moral imperative has become clear; a long-standing disease has vanished; new hope, new purposefulness have lifted him from the pit. His life-journey still stretches before him, but it has new direction, new motivation.

God, as we understand Him, is God of both valleys and hills. He cares for us intimately in the traffic of everyday living and He is also "the high and lofty One that inhabiteth eternity, whose name is Holy."[2] He is both transcendent and immanent. We worship Him with reverence and humility, as the God "whose name is Holy," but we also encounter Him in the home or street, the office or the factory, confidently face to face, as His beloved sons and daughters.

Faced with the wonder and majesty of God, human thought

*Ecumenical Papers: Contributions to Interfaith Dialogue* (Boston: Christian Science Committee on Publication, 1969), pp. 26–35.

must acknowledge in all humility its own inadequacy to grasp the fullness of divinity. But it has before it the experiences of the patriarchs and prophets as recorded in Hebrew Scripture, most particularly the life of Christ Jesus as recorded in the Gospels, and finally the workings of the Holy Spirit in all periods. We recognize that in these God has been continuously revealing Himself to mankind and that He has accompanied this self-revelation with acts of saving, redeeming, and healing power which have still further defined His nature. It would be immodest for any of us to claim that we personally know all the answers concerning God; but equally we should feel it the reverse of humility to reject or underestimate any part of God's revelation of Himself, given to humanity down the long millennia of history.

Christian Scientists acknowledge the paramountcy of the Bible in leading humanity to that knowledge of God and of His creation which is eternal Life. Paul Tillich describes the Bible as a record both of the divine self-manifestation and of the way in which human beings have received it. We, too, find in the Bible God's revelation of Himself, as received and responded to by men. We therefore look first to the Bible—and especially to the gospel record of the words and works of Jesus—to define for us the identity and nature of God.

The opening verse of Genesis puts God at the very beginning of all things (*in principio*); it acknowledges Him as creator. To Abraham He revealed Himself through Melchizedek as "the most high God, possessor of heaven and earth."[3] Moses recognized Him in Exodus as I AM. Leviticus speaks of "the mind of the Lord."[4] Deuteronomy says of God, "He is thy life."[5] The Psalms see Him as Shepherd and as the great Physician, "who healeth all thy diseases."[6] First Isaiah recognizes in God all three branches of government: "The Lord is our judge, the Lord is our lawgiver, the Lord is our king."[7] Second Isaiah calls Him "the God of truth."[8]

In the New Testament, Christ Jesus says that God is Spirit and good. But the name for God most frequently on his lips is Father; and this Father appraises Jesus as "my beloved Son, in whom I am well pleased."[9] John writes simply: "God is love."[10]

Two definitions of God familiar to Christian Scientists are these, given in *Science and Health with Key to the Scriptures*:

God is incorporeal, divine, supreme, infinite Mind, Spirit, Soul, Principle, Life, Truth, Love.[11]

GOD. The great I AM; the all-knowing, all-seeing, all-acting, all-wise, all-loving, and eternal; Principle; Mind; Soul; Spirit; Life; Truth; Love; all substance; intelligence.[12]

Mrs. Eddy also writes: "Love, the divine Principle, is the Father and Mother of the universe, including man."[13]

These answers to the question "Who is God?" satisfy our reason and our spiritual insights. We feel, too, that they meet the pragmatic test, to which Jesus appealed when the Baptist's disciples came to inquire whether he was the expected one. We feel that in some degree, however imperfectly, however incompletely, we are enabled through this understanding of God's nature to do some of those works which Jesus said his followers would do—to find our prayers answered in terms of spiritual and moral enlightenment, physical healing, and increased effectiveness as individuals and as citizens.

Four of our terms for God may perhaps usefully be commented on: Mind, Mother, Soul, and Principle.

The use of Mind by theologians as a term for God is not unusual. The Bible has countless references to God's wisdom and knowledge. It is hard to imagine the creator of all purposeful being as without intelligence, as not being all that the name *Mind* implies. In traditional theological discourse the characterization of God as Mind is often allied with the "argument from design." Christian Science, recognizing the entropy, fortuity, and disaster inherent in the material universe, turns rather to the universe of enduring spiritual values for the evidence of Mind's design.

Motherhood, as an aspect of the divine nature, is discussed by Dr. F. W. Dillstone, a theological writer with pastoral and teaching experience in the Episcopal Church. In his book *The Christian Faith* he notes that Christian doctrine has virtually excluded "the mother-figure from its total imagery of family relation-ships as applied to God." Then he remarks:

> Adoption of the masculine appellation led in some aspects of the Hebrew religion . . . to an extreme concentration on masculine qualities. But this was not the case in the Old Testament taken as a whole and certainly not in the New Testament. Fatherhood includes qualities of mercy and forgiveness, tenderness and gen-tleness, care and sustenance, concern for safety and comfort and renewal of life.[14]

This writer concludes that fatherhood provides an adequate im-age for the relationship of God to His creation, but he fully recognizes what we may call the feminine qualities in the divine nature.

We feel that specific recognition of God as Mother as well as Father is important. The divine name *Mother* emphasizes how completely man has his true origin in God. In his eternal nature man is wholly the offspring of heaven, calling no man on earth his father and no woman on earth his mother.

Soul in ordinary thought is closely connected with human identity and individuality. To employ it as a name for God may suggest a pantheistic containment of God within His creation or, alternatively, a swallowing up of all identity and individual-ity in some single Oversoul. The recognition of God as Soul has for us the opposite connotation. It points to Him as the continu-ing source and sustainer of identity and individuality; it makes these more definite and distinct; it ensures them a survival and continuity beyond the finite limits of the space-time continuum.

Christians agree that God is Love. But if Christianity is to be recognized as a practical, systematic, demonstrable way of life, then surely the God who is Love can be identified also as Princi-ple. The name Principle does not subtract from the divine na-ture as Father, Love, Life, the I AM: it includes all these. And it indicates God as the origin of all things—"In the beginning God . . . ," "*In principio deus. . . .*" It also points to His govern-ment of the universe not as a benevolent despot, but by univer-sal law maintaining universal order. This law is infinitely warm, adaptable, intelligent. It is the law of divine Life and Love, perfectly adjusting itself with tenderness and wisdom alike to the wheeling of galaxies and to the sparrow's fall.

To conceive of God as Principle does not mean the total denial to Him of personal being. God is certainly not a finite human person on a superhuman scale; no Christian would think of the infinite as person in that sense. C. S. Lewis writes of God: "He must not be thought of as a featureless generality. . . . He is the most concrete thing there is, the most individual. . . . Body and personality as we know them are the real negatives—they are what is left of positive being when it is sufficiently diluted to appear in temporal or finite forms."[15]

Dr. Robert F. Evans in his book *Making Sense of the Creeds* makes this point: "Metaphorical language is the indispensable verbal medium by which we approach the finally ineffable yet commanding mystery of God and his love."[16] This is true at one level, but in a more profound sense the names we give to human thoughts and objects are but types and shadows of the spiritual. Mr. Lewis, further discussing God's nature, writes:

> He is unspeakable not by being indefinite, but by being too definite for the unavoidable vagueness of language. . . . Our physical and psychic energies are mere metaphors of the real Life which is God. Divine Sonship is, so to speak, the solid of which biological sonship is merely a diagrammatic representation on the flat.[17]

We feel that "personal" is too limited an epithet for God, unless we call Him infinite Person. As infinite Person and divine Principle, God lives and loves with the fullest intensity, caring intimately for His whole creation, with every identity precious in His sight.

For its most complete example of the divine nature humanity turns to the life of Christ Jesus. Here God has revealed Himself as completely as it is possible for the infinite and eternal to reveal itself in a single human life-span. In Jesus the Word, or Christ, was made flesh; its saving presence and power appeared in the world as "the Lamb of God, which taketh away the sin of the world."[18] Jesus was tempted as other men are, yet he was without sin. At every point in his earthly career, from his conception by the power of the Holy Spirit to his ascension with the promise that the power of the Holy Spirit would come upon his followers, customary material modes were set aside. He faced up to the evil in the world, but he cast it out; to the suffering in the world, but he healed it; to death, but he overcame it. The kingdom of heaven, which he proclaimed, had come not to perpetuate the world's evil either as a direct or indirect instrument of the divine purposes, but to expose and destroy it.

Untouched by sin, complete master over material conditions, Jesus defined God, as fully as possible in terms of a human life, and said: "He that hath seen me hath seen the Father."[19] In his living he exercised without limit the power of Spirit and the power of good; he thus defined God as Spirit and as good. And he commanded his followers to do likewise. He set them the goal, as we see it, of presenting to the world the same definition of an immaculate God that he had himself presented. "Be ye therefore perfect," he said, "even as your Father which is in heaven is perfect."[20] We feel that in this unqualified perfection of God lies humanity's firm assurance of salvation.

A message written by Mrs. Eddy in 1901 offers this counsel: "As Christian Scientists you seek to define God to your own consciousness by feeling and applying the nature and practical possibilities of divine Love."[21] Christian Scientists study daily to gain a closer acquaintanceship with God, as He has revealed Himself in the Bible. And they aim to let this maturing acquaintanceship with divine Love direct in ever growing degree their daily living and their response to the saving and healing power of God.

Men will continue their search to know and define God. But their search can be successful only as they recognize that in a deeper sense God through His Christ is searching for them. Jesus told the Samaritan woman at the well that the Father seeketh true worshipers to worship him.[22] To his disciples he said: "Ye have not chosen me, but I have chosen you."[23] And the Christians at Philippi were counseled: "Work out your own salvation with fear and trembling. For it is God which worketh in you both to will and to do of his good pleasure."[24] In John's words, "We love him, because he first loved us."[25]

As Christians, we can open our hearts and minds to the divine grace by our thoughts and actions, by our prayers and our searching of the Scriptures. But ultimately it is God who discloses to each individual the full definition of Himself. It is the Father, who in individual encounter with each one of His sons and daughters, whether on hilltop or in valley, gives us in saving and in healing the final answer to this question "*Who is God?*" Then it is for us by our living to show how much or how little we have understood Him.

---

1. I Kings, chap. 20.
2. Isa. 57:15.
3. Gen. 14:19.
4. Lev. 24:12.
5. Deut. 30:20.
6. Ps. 103:3.
7. Isa. 33:22.
8. Isa. 65:16.
9. Matt. 3:17.
10. I John 4:16.
11. Mary Baker Eddy, *Science and Health with Key to the Scriptures* (Boston: The First Church of Christ, Scientist, 1906), p. 465.
12. *Ibid.,* p. 587.
13. *Ibid.,* p. 256.
14. F. W. Dillstone, *The Christian Faith* (Philadelphia: J. B. Lippincott Co., 1964), pp. 44, 45.
15. C. S. Lewis, *Miracles: A Preliminary Study* (New York: Macmillan Co., 1947), pp. 93, 94.
16. Robert F. Evans, *Making Sense of the Creeds* (New York: Association Press, 1964), p. 19.
17. Lewis, p. 93.
18. John 1:29.
19. John 14:9.
20. Matt. 5:48.
21. Mary Baker Eddy, *Message to The Mother Church for 1901* (Boston: The First Church of Christ, Scientist, 1901), p. 1.
22. John 4:23.
23. John 15:16.
24. Phil. 2:12, 13.
25. I John 4:19.

# The Resurrection of Jesus

Today the resurrection of Jesus is widely discounted. Many sincere and thoughtful people, including theologians and natural scientists, regard the story as wholly false, as harmful superstition. Others accord it value only as myth or metaphor. Still others accept its truth but explain it as the return of a ghost or spirit or as a subjective experience by Jesus' followers.

Christian Scientists accept the resurrection of Jesus in its most literal meaning, as including resurrection of Jesus' physical body, the same physical body that had been crucified. They regard this to be the plain meaning of the gospel record. They understand the resurrection in this sense to have been historically at the center of the gospel message from earliest times. They regard it as of key importance today.

As a first step, it will be helpful to consider the nature of life. Life, as Christian Scientists understand it, is fundamental. It is not by-product or end-product. Life is substance, original, self-existent, self-sustaining.

So understood, Life is God, Spirit, the divine Principle of existence. Life is not dependent on something other than itself for existence or a medium external to itself and unlike itself for expression.

Life expresses itself in living. Its expression is in individual spiritual identities, in spiritual man and spiritual universe. That

*Ecumenical Papers: Contributions to Interfaith Dialogue* (Boston: Christian Science Committee on Publication, 1969), pp. 8–15. Adapted from the article "Why Should It Be Thought a Thing Incredible?" *The Christian Science Journal,* April 1965.

the universe exists in Life is a more accurate statement than that Life exists in the universe.

Life, as so understood, does not enter existence by birth nor leave it by death. It does not come or go. It is eternal. And the individual living identities, created by Life, God, coexist with Him, indestructible and inviolable.

And Life is complete, perfect. It does not become quantitatively more or less, qualitatively better or worse. Yet Life is always new, always unfolding in fresh ways within the infinitude of its own completeness, its own perfection.

These statements are not philosophical abstractions. As we see them, they are spiritual facts, demonstrable in present human experience to the extent that the individual yields his thinking and living to the Christ. Centuries ago these changeless truths of Life were made flesh in the career of Jesus. Today they are again being made flesh in Christian healing.

We understand Christ Jesus to be a figure in actual history, born in the year of a Roman imperial census, crucified when Pontius Pilate was Roman procurator of Judea. Jesus permitted men to condemn him, crucify him, and lay his body in a sepulcher. Then with this same body he reappeared to companion with his disciples, comforting and giving instructions for the future.

The records in the four Gospels and in the book of Acts may differ in detail; but their tenor is, we feel, clear. The stone was rolled from the tomb's entrance, and the body was gone. The risen Jesus walked and talked and ate, using mouth, hands, feet. He provided the physical evidence of identity asked by Thomas. Between resurrection and ascension he had unique control over this physique, but it was no apparition; it was human flesh and bone. Resurrection may properly be used as a metaphor to designate individual awakening from an earthly material sense of existence to a higher spiritual sense of living. But the resurrection of Jesus was not a metaphor or a myth or a mere psychic experience of his disciples. It was a physical event, concrete in time and place, dated and localized.

It may be hard to fit such an event into today's secular outlook, which bases its hypotheses and reasoning upon measurements by the physical senses or by their instrumental extensions. An increasing number of Christians, influenced perhaps by the intellectual climate of this secular worldview, have concluded that the risen Lord had no human corporeal presence. They correctly recognize the precedence of revelation, or faith, over the evidence of history, yet they may underrate the necessity that understanding faith must manifest itself in history, fully and plainly.

In various fashions the demythologizers regard the resurrection appearances as having occurred solely within the hearts and minds of the disciples; they claim that if the disciples did see an outlined figure, this was a projection of their own inner experience conforming to the current state of thought, prepared to see visions of angels, demons, or spirits. Students of the New Testament who accept this view feel that they find the textual and other Scriptural evidence that proves them right.

The Christian Scientist in his study of the Bible brings to scholarship a very different spiritual experience and insight, and he makes a different assessment of the Biblical record. We gratefully avail ourselves of the useful inventions and technological achievements of the natural sciences. We honor qualities promoted by study of these sciences, dedication, integrity, perseverance, precision. But we challenge the conclusions of natural scientists when these extend into areas outside the competence of natural science or when they discount evidence merely because their limited instrumentation is inadequate to test it. Similarly, we challenge theological conclusions directly or indirectly influenced by such pseudoscientific attitudes in the natural scientist.

Consider now the gospel record. Jesus' resurrection did not occur in isolation. It was the natural climax of what preceded it. The conception of Jesus had not followed accepted human modes, although at the time of the virgin birth only Mary and Joseph knew this. In his ministry Jesus cured mental and emotional disorders, he healed organic and deteriorative diseases, he revived a newly dead child, a young man being carried out to burial, Lazarus four days dead. Only then did he himself, after exhibiting the usual physical evidences of death and being laid in a tomb, emerge on the third day, as the Gospels record, with an active human body. Step by step he had demonstrated the spiritual authority of the Christ over a physical sense of life. His own resurrection was the logical crown to this progressive demonstration.

But did this progressive demonstration of spiritual power, in fact, take place? Those who deny Jesus' physical resurrection usually accept his casting out of devils as comparable to the work of modern psychiatrists, working sometimes with religious counselors. But in general they reject or suspend judgment on healings of organic conditions and restorations of the dead. If they accept them, it is with reservations: they explain them as perhaps on a level with those rare inexplicable cases of spontaneous recovery which now and then puzzle the medical profession.

Christian Scientists, on the other hand, are satisfied that they have good grounds for accepting in full the healing record of Jesus. For us it is an integral part of the founding of basic Christianity. Furthermore, in our own experience we have seen the Christ exercising its authority over physical conditions. We have seen mental and emotional disorders cured; many of us have seen serious organic diseases healed. Some have seen beloved relatives and friends restored to health and vigor after medical opinion has adjudged death to be imminent or even already present. We are not acquainted with this healing work just by hearsay. We bear witness to that "which we have seen with our eyes, which we have looked upon, and our hands have handled, of the Word of life."[1]

Such healings are not just rare inexplicable phenomena. Christian Scientists agree in modesty and humility that they have much to learn and far to go in making their demonstration of spiritual healing uniformly effective. But many individuals and families gladly testify that they have found the power of Christ sufficient to meet their health needs through long lives and successive generations. Such certainly do not find the healing record of Jesus and his physical resurrection hard to accept.

The contemporary world is seeing a notable increase in longevity. Many experts agree that there is no apparent biological necessity for aging and death. Some natural scientists feel there are good grounds for hope that, within a not-too-distant future, healthy physical life will be prolonged indefinitely, accompanied by greatly enhanced intellectual powers and more acute aesthetic sensibilities.

We welcome this increasing longevity and the waning fear of death; but we do not regard indefinite prolongation of physical and temporal life, however enriched, to be humanity's final destiny. This may or may not be a step along the road; but humanity's final destiny is, as we see it, a complete mastery and laying aside of the whole limiting concept of life in matter. It is the demonstration of Life as God and of Life's individual expression as spiritual and eternal, not subject to birth, to passage through time, or to death.

So, for us, the resurrection of Jesus with a physical body provides supreme and unique evidence that the individual manifestation of divine Life, self-recognized and self-identified as such, cannot be driven from the human scene by even the most concentrated and determined physical attack upon it. His subsequent ascension points to humanity's further and final achievement, its rising above the whole space-time continuum.

Paul put this question to King Agrippa: "Why should it be thought a thing incredible with you, that God should raise the dead?"[2] Christian Scientists do not find such a thing incredible. In the light of what they have glimpsed in regard to ever-present divine Life and of their own experiences of Christ-healing, they readily accept the gospel record of Jesus' resurrection in what they understand to be its full and plain meaning. His reappearance was not that of a spirit; nor was it a subjective experience by his disciples; nor is it myth or metaphor. Jesus reappeared with a physical body, the same physical body which the Romans handed over to his friends after they were satisfied he was dead.

Of Jesus' immediate disciples Mrs. Eddy writes: "His resurrection was also their resurrection. It helped them to raise themselves and others from spiritual dulness and blind belief in God into the perception of infinite possibilities."[3] This can be true of his followers today. Unqualified acceptance of the gospel record of Jesus' physical resurrection and the conviction of indestructible divine Life that flows from this acceptance are of incalculable moral and spiritual value. They establish for the Christian the victory of life over death, of spirit over flesh, of love over hate, of good over evil. And they enable him to share in this victory.

----

1. I John 1:1.
2. Acts 26:8.
3. Mary Baker Eddy, *Science and Health with Key to the Scriptures* (Boston: The First Church of Christ, Scientist, 1906), p. 34.

# Sin and Grace

It was unthinkable, Henry Adams wrote after his sister, racked with suffering, had died of tetanus, "that any personal deity could find pleasure or profit in torturing a poor woman, by accident, with a fiendish cruelty known to man only in perverted and insane temperaments."[1] Yet millions of Christians have believed traditionally in just such a God.

Cruelty, waste, indifference, and pain are inherent in the very structure and texture of the natural world. Much of this cannot easily be attributed to human wickedness. It is "natural" evil, in the common phrase, and the Christian apologist has usually explained it as the condition of man's creatureliness. In this explanation the agonies and accidents of material existence are held to be the necessary matrix of its blessings and possibilities.

But why create such a universe in the first place? Could not a perfect God create a perfectly good universe, as in the great vision of Genesis 1, where the flawless creation metaphorically presented for contemplation bears little resemblance to nature as we encounter it through the physical senses, with its ceaseless, savage struggle for existence? From a perfectly good creator would one not expect a world of limitless goodness?

"Ah, but . . . ," says traditional apologetics, "that would be tame, ignoble, leaving man incapable of real development through pitting himself against his environment."

Really? Is God tame and ignoble because He is the very Principle of good? Does supreme goodness, supreme Love, lack the

*Ecumenical Papers: Contributions to Interfaith Dialogue* (Boston: Christian Science Committee on Publication, 1969), pp. 36–44.

power of intelligent self-development? Must God, in Manichaean fashion, have an opposite in order to be really God? Must the joy of pure being rest on a base of blind, appetitive thrust and mutual destruction?

If not, then why must it be assumed that the answer is different in the case of man? "What man is there of you, whom if his son ask bread, will he give him a stone?"[2] Are we then to believe that God has deliberately arranged a natural order which over the centuries has brought into existence countless deformed and imbecile children, children destined to suffer hideous pain, to die of famine and accident, to be slaughtered in war or burned alive in holocaust, to have their lives distorted by inherited criminal tendencies and vicious social systems? Are these the children of a loving heavenly Father?

There is no logical necessity for creating man subject to the gigantic injustice of the natural order and the drag of animal instincts. Faced with this fact, Christian apologists (like pre-Christian Job) have tended to take refuge in the inscrutable mystery of the divine purpose.

Is there, then, a rational explanation of moral evil, or sin?

If God makes men capable of sin, it would seem reasonable that he must take responsibility for their sinning. "Oh, no!" shocked tradition replies. "Free will, and all that." But if He knew from the outset that His hapless creatures would choose to sin, and if He *still* chose to create them, how can He escape ultimate responsibility? "Because," the answer goes, "permissiveness is the necessary precondition of freedom of will. Because without freedom to sin, man would be the mere slave or puppet of God's will."

There is a curious assumption in this: that human dignity demands the right to become the opposite of what one really is. But is God free to sin? Is Truth free to falsify? Is light free to be darkness? Is good free to be evil? If we say no to these questions, do we then pity God and consider Him to be a slave to His own goodness?

True freedom is freedom to fulfill one's highest possibilities. The sinner is the slave, not the man made in God's image who acts spontaneously but inevitably from his God-bestowed nature. The physical organism determined by chancy genes and contingent circumstance is the puppet—though not of God's will (unless one chooses to make God responsible for the worst as well as the best of human behavior). If the man of God's creating is identified with the puppet-mortal evolved from primal matter, free will becomes logically untenable and sin becomes, as in modern scientism, mere sickness and maladjustment, to be healed by social reconditioning rather than by spiritual rebirth.

This leads to the secular point of view that natural and moral evil are essentially one, capable of progressive amelioration through human ingenuity but, in the last analysis, built into the limitations of the material universe. Once again it remains an unfathomable mystery why God, as traditional Christianity maintains, should have created such a universe in the first place. Creation, seen in these terms, may well be considered synonymous with the "fall."

A generation with a distaste for unfathomable mysteries rebels, naturally enough, against being held guilty of the sin of being born estranged and wayward. Is even the proffer of grace through Jesus Christ, as traditionally interpreted, a reasonable recompense for a congenital estrangement so great that millions of people seem incapable of accepting that grace? Or, as some today suggest, is the real message of Jesus: "You're on your own now in a pretty ghastly universe, but here's the way to salvage something noble from it"?

A wholly different answer is possible, an answer which suggests that the drama of redemption is misunderstood if the drama of creation is misread. It identifies the message of Jesus with the vision of Genesis 1: man sinless, guiltless, the crowning glory of a perfectly good creation. This is the man glimpsed through the earthly life of the Saviour, culminating in his resurrection and ascension beyond all the limitations of a mortal and material sense of existence. God's grace, so understood, is not His forgiveness of men's innate sinfulness but His revelation of man's innate goodness. Christ's saving work so understood, is the awakening of humanity from the nightmare of materiality to the present and eternal perfection of God's spiritual creation.

What this basically involves is putting off the old man for the new—the man determined by genes for the man revealed through Christ—not by changing one into the other but by exchanging appearance for reality, the outward for the inward, the humanly plausible for the divinely certain. And what this does is to bring radical healing to the present imperfect sense of existence. As the inner structure of reality comes to light, the illegitimacy of the merciless claims of evil is progressively demonstrated.

Such a process does not "explain" evil, in the sense of justifying it, but step by step wipes it out—as Jesus wiped out sin, sorrow, pain, death, all the limits implied by the word *matter.* Seen in this perspective, ontology relates directly to ethics, including social ethics. "The belief of life in matter sins at every step," writes Mrs. Eddy.[3] Merely to rearrange the material factors in a given situation through social programming—valid and important though this may often be as an expression of intelligent Christian concern—is to leave the basic need untouched. To the dispossessed who need food, housing, opportunity, human dignity, as well as to the privileged who must learn how to relate the ethics of the good Samaritan to the broad social imperatives of today, the primary demand of Jesus still applies: "Ye must be born again."[4]

In I John we read: "If we say that we have no sin, we deceive ourselves, and the truth is not in us."[5]

In the same epistle we read: "Whosoever is born of God doth not commit sin; for his seed remaineth in him: and he cannot sin, because he is born of God."[6]

Here is paradox *par excellence.* Viewed through the dismal lens of unregenerate human experience, man is obviously a sinner; seen with the penetrating vision of spiritual insight, he is found to be the sinless child of God. Santayana has written that love is penetrating but that it penetrates to possibilities rather than to facts. Divine Love, however, penetrates to the possibility as the fact; that is, the good which may appear humanly to be mere possibility is already existent fact in the divine order of being. For God to see is to actualize, and for a man to accept himself as God sees him is to be born again. Then instead of trying to find a legitimate origin for the claims of evil he is in a position to reject them as wholly spurious, fraudulent, and alien to God's purpose for the universe and man.

Jesus made plain that evil is best regarded as a lie, and Paul wrote: "Lie not one to another, seeing that ye have put off the old man with his deeds; and have put on the new man, which is renewed in knowledge after the image of him that created him."[7] What this implies is a different *starting point* for thought and action. Instead of starting with a sinning, fallen mortal subject to all the contingencies of material existence, one starts with the spiritual man made in God's image, reflecting God's purpose and power.

This also means starting with a different universe. The Christian who makes Spirit rather than matter the locus of reality need not flinch from the kind of challenge set forth by Bertrand Russell in a now classic statement:

> That man is the product of causes which had no prevision of the ends they were achieving; that his origin, his growth, his hopes and fears, his loves and his beliefs are but the outcome of accidental collocations of atoms; . . . that all the labours of the ages, all the devotion, all the inspiration, all the noonday brightness of human genius, are destined to extinction in the vast death of the solar system, and that the whole temple of man's achievement must inevitably be buried beneath the debris of a universe in ruins—all these things, if not quite beyond dispute, are . . . nearly certain. . . . Brief and powerless is man's life; on him and all his race the slow, sure doom falls pitiless and dark. Blind to good and evil, reckless of destruction, omnipotent matter rolls on its relentless way. . . .[8]

This picture of cosmic doom suggests a view of reality seen through a distorting lens. The lens in this case is the acceptance of matter as ultimate substance; everything else in the statement follows logically from that premise. Yet the resurrection and ascension of Jesus slash clear across such reasoning—not merely as events in history but as revelations of reality. Even his day-by-day healings constitute evidence of a different *kind* of substance, a different *kind* of power. To classify love, intelligence, joy, courage, humility, inspiration as accidental by-products of fleeting electrochemical impulses and neuromuscular reactions is impossible for one who has experienced in his own body the regenerative power of Spirit.

To the disciples who found his sayings "hard" Jesus declared, "It is the spirit that quickeneth; the flesh profiteth nothing."[9] Certainly the commitment to Spirit and its immortal creation as the sole reality of being is hard for the human mind; but in proportion as we yield to the divine logic of this position and come to grips with its demands on our humanity, we find it life-giving, life-preserving, life-transforming.

This makes for realism about the human scene rather than for wishful thinking. Matter is recognized as a mental outlook which by its nature corrupts our view of man. In *Science and Health,* Mrs. Eddy writes:

> Mortals are not fallen children of God. They never had a perfect state of being, which may subsequently be regained. They were, from the beginning of mortal history, "conceived in sin and brought forth in iniquity.". . . Learn this, O mortal, and earnestly seek the spiritual status of man, which is outside of all material selfhood.[10]

Such a demand calls for regeneration rather than mere re-arrangement, for putting off the old man rather than idealizing him, but at the same time it involves a practical transformation of mortal existence, not a mere retreat into otherworldliness. The fact that God's man is here *now,* for the proving, demands action, healing, change.

"Be ye transformed by the renewing of your mind," wrote Paul, "that ye may prove what is that good, and acceptable, and perfect, will of God."[11] Surely this is the fundamental Christian answer to the problem of evil, an answer leading step by step to the end implicit in our true beginning: "We all, with open face beholding as in a glass the glory of the Lord, are changed into the same image from glory to glory, even as by the Spirit of the Lord."[12]

---

1. Henry Adams, *The Education of Henry Adams* (New York: Book League of America, 1928), p. 289.

2. Matt. 7:9.

3. Mary Baker Eddy, *Science and Health with Key to the Scriptures* (Boston: The First Church of Christ, Scientist, 1906), p. 542.

4. John 3:7.

5. I John 1:8.

6. I John 3:9.

7. Col. 3:9, 10.

8. Bertrand Russell, *Basic Writings of Bertrand Russell,* ed. Robert E. Egner and Lester E. Denonn (New York: Simon & Schuster), pp. 67, 72.

9. John 6:63.

10. Eddy, *Science and Health,* p. 476.

11. Rom. 12:2.

12. II Cor. 3:18.

In a 1988 article in *The Christian Century* on "the crisis in interfaith dialogue," Harvard professor and Baptist clergyman Harvey Cox noted: "For the vast majority of Christians, including those most energetically engaged in dialogue, Jesus is not merely a background figure. He is central. . . ." The article went on to insist that in any meaningful interchange "the question of who Jesus was and is, and what he means today, will inevitably appear."[1]

Cox's observation is borne out in the following excerpt from a 1986 *Christian Century* article, Stephen Gottschalk's "Christian Science Today: Resuming the Dialogue." The centrality of Jesus is unquestionably the most important common ground of faith between Christian Scientists and other Christians—whatever their important differences on "who" he was and "what he means today." As the article also shows, exploring these differences is the best way to understand where Christian Science most sharply diverges from traditional Christian theology.

---

1. Harvey Cox, "Many Mansions or One Way? The Crisis in Interfaith Dialogue," *The Christian Century,* August 17–24, 1988, p. 733.

# Christian Science Today: Resuming the Dialogue

On the crucial theological point of the deity of Jesus, there is a clear and unambiguous difference between Christian Science and traditional Christian doctrine. For example, the fact that Christian Scientists do not believe in the deity of Jesus precludes their church from membership in the World Council of Churches. But their position is seriously misread if it is not understood that in Christian Science, Jesus is regarded as the figure through whom, supremely and uniquely, God's nature was manifested to humanity. In Eddy's theology, Jesus' virgin birth, crucifixion and bodily resurrection were the pivotal events in human history, absolutely indispensable to human salvation.

However distinct the metaphysical context in which she defined the meaning of these events, Eddy saw them as having revelatory meaning precisely because they were historical events. In an age when church leaders can dismiss the virgin birth and question the resurrection without seriously rattling theological teacups, this conviction is bound to seem positively conservative. The first step in grasping Christian Science is to recognize that it not only accepts but builds upon these events, as well as upon the healing stories. As Eddy put it, "The life of Christ is the predicate and postulate of all that I teach."[1]

It might be said that Eddy "demythologized" the healings of Jesus and his resurrection—but in an opposite sense from the way that Bultmann did. She did not deny that these events occurred, but she denied that they should be understood under

---

Stephen Gottschalk, in *The Christian Century,* vol. 103, no. 39 (December 17, 1986), pp. 1146–48.

the category of "miracle." Christian Scientists see these events not as supernatural interruptions of the natural order but as a revelatory appearance of a spiritual reality, shaking the very foundations of human perception.

For Christian Science, this spiritual reality is the Kingdom of God revealed through Jesus' life of obedience and sacrifice. Jesus showed that this spiritual reality is not merely an ethical ideal to be realized, or a future state to be attained; if God is really God, if he is present and supreme, his kingdom must be a present reality. As Eddy wrote, "Our Master said, 'The kingdom of heaven is at hand.' Then God and heaven . . . are now and here; and a change in human consciousness, from sin to holiness, would reveal this wonder of being."[2]

In a sense, the theology of Christian Science takes with radical seriousness the classic Christian doctrine of sin and what the change "from sin to holiness" must include. But it believes that the gospel offers the data of a new reality which, far from being some abstract metaphysical ultimate, can be progressively realized through Christian discipleship. Jesus' emphatic command to heal the sick indicates that this discipleship leads to freedom from disease as well as from sin.

In spiritual healing as Eddy understood it, the human mind does not "do" something to another mind; rather, it witnesses through prayer and self-purification to the presence of the God supremely revealed through Jesus Christ. With the greater apprehension of that presence comes the dawning through "spiritual sense" (a term Eddy adapted from her "New Light" Puritan heritage) of what life in Christ even now can include. The love of God becomes more substantive, more palpable; the distortions and pains which plague human existence less necessary and authoritative. The new reality which broke into human experience in the person of Jesus becomes more distinct not through new conceptions about a transcendent reality, but through the growing experience of the power of that reality to bring transformation and healing in daily life.

A recent editorial in a Christian Science periodical proclaims that "healing, after all, is the name for how God is known and expressed in human experience."[3] But the purpose of this healing is not human improvement so much as it is the renewed God-experience it makes possible. Thus, the complaint that some people use Christian Science in order to attain secular ends of health, wealth or success is a wholly valid one from the point of view of Christian Science itself.

Many involved in Christian healing share the Christian Scientists' belief in spiritual healing as an integral part of a living Christianity, and they share the renewed sense of God's presence that issues from healing. They also share the conviction that God's will is actively ranged against suffering and disease.

What other Christians do not share is Christian Scientists' conviction that God is absolutely not the author of the conditions of finitude—meaning material existence—which give rise to suffering and disease. This may well be the most significant nonnegotiable difference between Christian Science and traditional Christian theology. Christian Scientists understand God as the sovereign creator, absolutely distinct from his creation. However, they see the finitude of God's creation not as his creative will but as the way creation appears within the habitual limits of human perception.

This does not mean that Christian Scientists deny the intensity of the human experience of disease and pain. Eddy herself had far too deep an immersion in the fires of human suffering and spoke too feelingly of its importance in Christian experience to believe that the tribulations of what she once called "the ghastly farce of material existence"[4] could be minimized or ignored. Yet her theology does maintain that sin and finitude are not part of authentic being in Christ, and that a deeper experience of God's presence and our relation to him effectively diminishes and will eventually destroy the conditions of suffering which God does not sanction and never made. We might, therefore, speak of the theology of Christian Science as at once a theology of God's presence and of God's absence. For it holds that all the evils of the human condition are, in the final analysis, traceable to the drastic human failure to acknowledge and experience the reality of His presence.

From this standpoint, the question of whether Christianity is a healing religion is no minor speculative issue. It is a question about the very reality of the God whom the Bible reveals. Christian Scientists see their special role as that of pioneering in the spiritual healing which they see as a natural, though as yet largely unexplored, consequence of Christian discipleship. For them, such healing is the necessary and decisive proof of the revolutionary power of Christianity to transform human experience as a whole.

---

1. Mary Baker Eddy, *No and Yes* (Boston: The First Church of Christ, Scientist, 1891), p. 10.

2. Mary Baker Eddy, *Unity of Good* (Boston: The First Church of Christ, Scientist, 1887), p. 37.

3. Allison W. Phinney, Jr., "What Do You Think about Christian Healing?" *Christian Science Sentinel,* February 4, 1985, p. 195.

4. Mary Baker Eddy, *Science and Health with Key to the Scriptures* (Boston: The First Church of Christ, Scientist, 1906), p. 272.

A presentation at the Ecumenical Institute in Bossey, Switzerland, in 1964 made the point that the insistence of Christian Science on practical healing separates it "not only from all forms of philosophical idealism but also from all forms of gnostic heresy."[1] The mislabeling of Christian Science as a "modern form of gnosticism" has been a particular stumbling block to greater understanding between Christian Scientists and mainline Christians.

Readers familiar with the scholarly literature on historical gnosticism know what a complex subject this is. The recent discovery of important "Gnostic Christian" manuscripts at Nag Hammadi in Egypt has prompted a major reevaluation of previous assumptions about both Gnostic beliefs and early Christianity. While the reevaluation process is far from complete, it has made at least one thing clear—that the term *Gnostic* in traditional Christian polemical literature has frequently been misapplied.

The following letter, reprinted from a 1972 pamphlet entitled *Dialogue with the World,* goes to the theological heart of the issue as it relates to Christian Science. The profound emphasis of Christian Science on Christian new birth, on regeneration from sin, on the human mind's "absolute need of something beyond itself for its redemption and healing,"[2] cuts squarely across Gnostic assertions of a "divinity within" or the Gnostic dualism which denies our need for practical repentance. Similarly, the emphasis of Christian Science on a new understanding of reality grows out of a radical insistence on God's love and sovereignty over His creation, not from a Gnostic belief that the created world is evil.

---

1. Quoted in *The Spirit and Origins of American Protestantism: A Source Book in Its Creeds,* ed. John A. Hardon (Dayton, OH: Pflaum Press, 1968), p. 417.
2. Mary Baker Eddy, *Science and Health with Key to the Scriptures* (Boston: The First Church of Christ, Scientist, 1906), p. 151.

# *From a Letter in*
## *Dialogue with the World*

You{r} firm sense that matter, sin, disease, and death do not "exist" to the Christian Scientist has a misapprehension about it that leads you quite understandably to believe that Christian Science wipes out all that the Christian holds dear in our Saviour's mission. Can we consider this together for a moment? The Christian Science textbook has many pages which show what a danger sin is, and how it must be faced and dealt with; how sickness and disease arise, how real they become to the sufferer, and how they are to be healed; how universal is the belief in death and the fear of its sting, and what benefits come from challenging death as Jesus did. All these factors show that Christian Science neither ignores sin, disease, and death, as if they did not "exist" in human affairs, nor flies over the top of them. The salient point is that in dealing with them, Christian Science challenges them as untrue or unreal *from God's point of view*—the viewpoint that "God saw every thing that he had made, and, behold, it was very good."[1] Christian Science does not therefore deny Jesus' saving mission, or say that there was nothing for him to save people from. On the contrary, it has a wonderful sympathy with every single thought and attitude evident in his healing work, based as it uniformly is on a "Get thee hence" to everything unlike Spirit, God, good.

Then would you not say that healing through the Holy Spirit, as Jesus healed, is the Word made flesh—a lesser sign of the truly wonderful sign of the Word made flesh in the incarnation? Christian Science in no way whatever denies the incarnation—on the

Geith A. Plimmer, in *Dialogue with the World* (Boston: The Christian Science Publishing Society, 1972), pp. 6–8.

contrary, it accepts it as a most wonderful proof of the ability of divine Love to meet humanity's needs.

The view of Christian Science on these basic platforms of the Christian faith really needs much more sympathetic appraisal. When it finally comes, people will see that Christian Science teaching is as close to primitive Christian doctrine as its healing work is to early Christian practice. Indeed, Christian Science goes all along the way of Jesus' saving mission, cross-bearing, crucifixion, resurrection, and ascension with deep appreciation of what he was proving, and the Principle upon which his proofs were based, namely, that sin, disease, and death were not of God, and that he who casts them out by spiritual understanding is doing the will of Him who sent His Son to be the Saviour of the world.

I hope you will pardon the many words needed to put things this way, Mr. ———, but I feel sure that, had you seen them a little more like this, you would have found it easier to look on Christian Science as a reappearance of the Christianity to which your book is devoted, rather than as a strange departure from it.

---

1. Gen. 1:31.

In a letter to her Boston church in 1902, Mary Baker Eddy remarked that within the past decade religion in the United States had passed "from stern Protestantism to doubtful liberalism."[1] Within this century the changes have been even greater and more diverse.

The final selection in this chapter, "Mary Baker Eddy: Her Influence upon Theology," offers a Christian Scientist's perspective on Mrs. Eddy's own place in twentieth-century theology—albeit as a religious thinker and "discoverer" rather than as an academic theologian. Written by Allison W. Phinney, Jr., it was published in the collection *Mary Baker Eddy: A Centennial Appreciation,* one hundred years after the 1866 experience that first opened for Mrs. Eddy what she later called Christian Science.

---

1. Mary Baker Eddy, *Message to The Mother Church for 1902* (Boston: The First Church of Christ, Scientist, 1902), p. 2.

# Mary Baker Eddy:
# Her Influence upon Theology

$M$any years ago a meteor fell into the forests of Siberia, but not until much later, when the region had been completely explored, was the vastness of the impact understood. In a sense, the impact of Christian Science on theology has been made, but its significance has not yet been widely explored or acknowledged.

In the Preface of *Science and Health with Key to the Scriptures,* Mary Baker Eddy, the Discoverer and Founder of Christian Science, writes, "A book introduces new thoughts, but it cannot make them speedily understood." She adds, "Future ages must declare what the pioneer has accomplished."[1]

It is plain from Mrs. Eddy's exchanges with clergymen of her day and from her many references to theology that she knew the magnitude of the challenge Christian Science presents to the mode of thought she sometimes called "scholastic" or "speculative theology." Inspired theology, on the other hand—the clear, healing reasoning on God's allness which flows forth from having that "mind . . . which was also in Christ Jesus"[2]—she recognized as the keystone of the Science of Christianity.

The subject of theology is by definition God. But the theologian has no special access to divinity. Only radical yielding to God can illumine thought and bring forth rightness and healing in human experience. This is as true for the individual who is a professional theologian as for the homemaker, the engineer, or the businessperson.

For centuries Christian theologies have reasoned academically about God. In effect they have dealt with Him as one aspect of a

Allison W. Phinney, Jr., in *Mary Baker Eddy: A Centennial Appreciation* (Boston: The Christian Science Publishing Society, 1966), pp. 89–95.

material cosmos which proceeds otherwise along the lines the material senses suggest. God has been taken as a logical starting point for creation. His influence has been seen primarily in long-range terms. He has been held to be setting His creation gradually right after mankind chose sin and fell from paradise.

God has been considered to be transcendent, unknowable, except in rare mystic experiences. To most Christians, He has been known primarily through a supernatural event in the past, when He supposedly took on flesh in the form of Christ Jesus, sacrificed the Son to cancel the debt of sin, and restored the possibility of salvation to those who would faithfully confess the fact of this event.

One can see that this is a thin outline which those might construct who felt remote from the immense, convincing truths and healing experiences of the Word made flesh. It persists in varying forms today because it is the outcome of thought which begins with matter as the most basic aspect of reality and then reasons toward God.

Mrs. Eddy explains that prior to her discovery of Christian Science the illusion of security in material birth, life, and death had been shattered. In the experience which led directly to her discovery, she turned wholly to God. She writes, "That short experience included a glimpse of the great fact that I have since tried to make plain to others, namely, Life in and of Spirit; this Life being the sole reality of existence."[3] The divine was no longer felt to be waiting above and at the end of human history. It was seen as Immanuel, or "God with us," breaking forth into human experience inevitably in transformation and healing!

In selfless, fearless moments great religious figures had caught sight of the Principle, or Love, at the heart of being. But evil had claimed overpowering immediacy, and the sense of God's presence had seemed to slip away. Through revelation, reason, and demonstration, Mrs. Eddy learned that evil is never real. She saw objectively (as much so as in a natural scientist's study of molecular behavior) that evil exists entirely within mesmerized, fearing, unperceiving thought, or that which St. Paul termed the carnal mind, which is "enmity against God."[4] To the question "What is the cardinal point of the difference in my metaphysical system?"

Mrs. Eddy replies, "This: that *by knowing the unreality of disease, sin, and death,* you demonstrate the allness of God."[5]

The influence of Christian Science was felt first by the pure of heart, who responded openly to the spirit of the Christ and for whom dogma and ecclesiasticism were not authoritative.

As one sits quietly in the Original Edifice of The Mother Church today and sees as through the eyes of those who first attended services the inscriptions on the walls from the Bible and Mrs. Eddy's writings, one can easily experience again the impact of the coming of Christian Science. The healing touch of the Christ was being felt as in the time of the Master. This was no weighing of theological pros and cons but the direct experience of a totally new reality which once seen would not permit one to see the world in the same way as before. It was not mystical, theoretical, nor emotional. As today, it was the breaking of fear and limitations, the bearing onward of spiritual insight, the fading of the dissonance and chaos of material living as unnatural, unreal.

Mrs. Eddy writes, "Jesus established in the Christian era the precedent for all Christianity, theology, and healing."[6] The Gospel of John tells of the meeting of the disciples with a man who had been born blind. They fell into discussion of a theological question, attributing the man's blindness to sin. The question of whether the man or his parents had sinned was taken to the Master. But Jesus, so filled with the compelling reality of man's unity with the Father, moved immediately to restore the man's sight. The irresistible truth of God's presence eliminated any dark supposition of His absence. The mistaken perspective in which the disciples' question arose had ceased to exist.

The coming of Christian Science placed old theological arguments in a clear, intense light. Throughout history theologians as well as natural scientists had taken matter as self-evident. Mrs. Eddy drew the issue with the point of a sword. She writes thus of the dilemma of matter: "To seize the first horn of this dilemma and consider matter as a power in and of itself, is to leave the creator out of His own universe; while to grasp the other horn of the dilemma and regard God as the creator of matter, is not only to make Him responsible for all disasters, physical and moral, but to announce Him as their source, thereby making Him guilty of maintaining perpetual misrule in the form and under the name of natural law."[7]

Academic theologians and philosophers had considered this issue before. But in men's experience in the twentieth century it was to be sharpened to a cutting edge.

From the time of the Renaissance, academic theology was progressively forced to give up its comfortable province of discussing a supernatural and highly imaginary cosmogony. Then in the mid–nineteenth century the pressure of natural science suddenly increased. Work in the fields of anthropology, psychology, astronomy, physics, and genetics steadily pushed back the claims of religion to describe the workings of even the visible material world as God-directed. With the twentieth century came more universal concepts of love and justice, together with such an overwhelming knowledge of the extent of mankind's suffering that few could link it any longer with a coherent divine plan.

Religious thinking was heavily influenced by the apparent darkness of the human situation. Existential philosophy probed the anxiety and absurdity of mortal life. The dominant theology of these years, known as neoorthodoxy or "crisis" theology, emphasized men's hopelessly sinful plight. Man, it is said, could only throw himself on the mercy of the distant historical event of God's coming to earth in Christ Jesus.

Other theologians currently stress the suffering of Jesus and his love for others, suggesting that it is God's purpose to make man live a supremely unselfed life in the world without resting on any hope of intervention by God. The "absence of God" or the "death of God" so far as modern men are concerned is widely discussed. Long-established concepts of a supernatural God have been shaken for many religious thinkers.

Mrs. Eddy writes, "As the finite sense of Deity, based on material conceptions of spiritual being, yields its grosser elements, we shall learn what God is, and what God does."[8] At present the spiritually awakening thought of humanity wrestles desperately with the supposition of a tragically imperfect material universe in which there seems so little evidence of an infinitely good and omnipotent God. But great changes in theology in only a century's time foreshadow the outcome of this long conflict.

Today increasing numbers of religious men readily conceive of God as Love and are reluctant to attribute anthropomorphic attitudes to Him. The concept of the atonement has moved from that of satisfying a wrathful God's justice toward that of reconciling man to God, to his true relationship with the Father. Heaven and hell are now widely understood as states of thought, not as distant localities in which reward and punishment are to be administered. Prayer is more frequently recognized as the awakening of men to God's healing ever-presence, rather than as obtaining His change of heart toward a human situation.

There is greater readiness to accept the possibility and the necessity of apprehending the meaning of Jesus' teachings through the illumination of the Christ in one's own life. Profession of a creed is seen as a less and less adequate expression of Christianity. There are constant demands for demonstration of the spirit of the Christ in some way in the midst of the human experience.

Perhaps most significant is the breakdown of the ancient artificial line between the so-called sacred and the secular. Two of the theologians in modern times who have received the greatest response to their writings—Paul Tillich and Martin Buber—have stressed the divine as a dimension of reality which is always present in every human activity and in which "all things are become new."[9] To a limited extent, they have turned from the external world and a supernatural imposition upon it and looked within to their own deepest intuition of Love and of Spirit.

As Mrs. Eddy discerned would be the case in the twentieth century, Christian Science has led to the recovery of healing through spiritual means in the Christian churches. Calvinism had considered the New Testament healings the evidence of "miraculous powers" of "temporary duration." Clergymen turning anew to the gospel accounts are becoming convinced of something far different.

One recent denominational report, "The Relation of Christian

Faith to Health," observes: "He [Jesus] regarded the healings which took place as so many signs of God's power breaking in upon the kingdom of evil. . . . He [Jesus Christ] regarded illness as something to be overcome. He did not acquiesce to it. He did not ignore it. . . . He coped with illness, and he conquered it. It was his teaching that God wills healing." Similar reports specifically mention the part Christian Science has played in a reawakening to the "New Testament teaching about God's will for us to be healed and to be whole."

Healing services are carried on regularly in hundreds of Episcopal and Methodist churches in the United States. Other denominations have established commissions to investigate the possibility of spiritual healing. Extreme differences remain between the theology and practice of Christian Science and that of other denominations. But for any awareness of the healing presence of "God with us," Christian Scientists feel the most earnest gratitude.

Mrs. Eddy points out, "The confidence inspired by Science lies in the fact that Truth is real and error is unreal."[10] The impact of the Science of Christianity will be continuously explored in our time and in centuries to come. The lesson of its unequivocal statement of the allness of God, Spirit, the nothingness of matter, and the perfect or new man as the present scientific fact will be learned. The deep Christianity of its insight into the hypnotic, illusory nature of evil will be gained. The joy and good which men have thought fragile and fleeting will be found again and again the essence, the structure, the entire substance of real being.

1. Mary Baker Eddy, *Science and Health with Key to the Scriptures* (Boston: The First Church of Christ, Scientist, 1906), p. vii.

2. Phil. 2:5.

3. Mary Baker Eddy, *Miscellaneous Writings* (Boston: The First Church of Christ, Scientist, 1896), p. 24.

4. Rom. 8:7.

5. Mary Baker Eddy, *Unity of Good* (Boston: The First Church of Christ, Scientist, 1887), pp. 9–10.

6. Eddy, *Science and Health,* p. 138.

7. *Ibid.,* p. 119.

8. Mary Baker Eddy, *The People's Idea of God* (Boston: The First Church of Christ, Scientist, 1886), p. 2.

9. II Cor. 5:17.

10. Eddy, *Science and Health,* p. 368.

# Further Exchanges

*Some people say that Christian Science isn't really Christian because it holds a philosophic and abstract view of God as a cold, impersonal principle whom one cannot really love, trust, or turn to for comfort.*

Could there be a *less* cold or abstract concept of God than that expressed in Mrs. Eddy's communion address to The Mother Church in 1896: "For 'who is so great a God as our God!' unchangeable, all-wise, all-just, all-merciful; the ever-loving, ever-living Life, Truth, Love: comforting such as mourn, opening the prison doors to the captive, marking the unwinged bird, pitying with more than a father's pity; healing the sick, cleansing the leper, raising the dead, saving sinners."[1]

Yes, Christian Science *does* break sharply with the old anthropomorphic view of God as a changeable being who loves, hates, and inflicts terrible suffering on His creatures. And Christian Scientists feel nothing but gratitude for being liberated from such a circumscribed view of Him as less than wholly good—a view that neither comforts, heals, nor redeems. They do indeed see Him as the infinite, divine Principle, Love, and at the same time as the Father and Mother of the universe of whom James could write: "Every good gift and every perfect gift is from above, and cometh down from the Father of lights, with whom is no variableness, neither shadow of turning."[2]

This is truly the God of Abraham, Isaac, and Jacob, not the "God of the philosophers." It is the God whom we can love in the full spirit of the Biblical command, "Thou shalt love the Lord thy God with all thy heart, and with all thy soul, and with all thy mind."[3] And when Christian Scientists speak of God as

Love or Spirit or Truth, it's in precisely the same sense that the Scriptures themselves use these terms for Him.

. . .

*Christian Scientists speak of God as All-in-all. Doesn't this support the claim that Christian Science is really a form of pantheism akin to Hinduism?*

Not for anyone who has given careful attention to what it really teaches on this point. Christian Science maintains a clear and consistent distinction between God as creator, or Father, and man and the universe as His creation. Speaking of God as All signifies His all-embracing infinitude and underscores the essential point in Christian Science that there can be no real entity or power opposed to Him. But it does not eliminate the essential point summed up in the words of *Science and Health with Key to the Scriptures:* "Man is not God, and God is not man."[4] Nor does it support the contention that Christian Science is akin to Hinduism. Readers of the King James Version of the New Testament will recognize a source much closer to home in St. Paul's recognition that "in him [God] we live, and move, and have our being."[5] Neither in the New Testament nor in Christian Science is there any suggestion that individual being is absorbed in "the fulness of him that filleth all in all."[6] Instead, both point to the variety of ways in which individuality is expressed, "but it is the same God which worketh all in all."[7]

. . .

*Isn't it true that Christian Scientists separate Jesus from Christ and hold that Jesus was just a good man?*

Typical of the many passages in Mrs. Eddy's writings that are seldom if ever quoted by her evangelical critics are such statements as "The divinity of the Christ was made manifest in the humanity of Jesus" and "This Christ, or divinity of the man Jesus, was his divine nature, the godliness which animated him."[8] Christian Science draws a distinction between the Saviour's divine title of Christ and his human history as Jesus. But it by no means separates the two, for it fully accepts Jesus as the incarnation or embodiment of the Christ.

Often critics who claim to be former Christian Scientists complain that they never learned about Jesus in Christian Science. One wonders how they could have missed one of the most deeply moving discourses on his life ever written, the chapter "Atonement and Eucharist" in *Science and Health*.

There is a legitimate theological difference, to be sure, between Christian Scientists and those denominations which believe Jesus to be God. But Christian Scientists do believe that he demonstrated fully and uniquely man's spiritual sonship with God. Further, they see this spiritual sonship as defining the true Godlike nature of man. They therefore love and revere him not only as their Lord and Master, but also as the Exemplar for all mankind. Paul writes, "Let this mind be in you, which was also in Christ Jesus,"[9] and "this mind" or motivation they understand to be divine.

In sum, they gratefully acknowledge the Messiahship of Christ Jesus, his human and divine role in history as the mediator between God and men, the "only immaculate,"[10] the "highest earthly representative of God," [11] "Jesus the God-crowned or the divinely royal man."[12]

. . .

### Do you believe in the Trinity?

If you would ask most Christian Scientists if they "subscribe" to the doctrine of the Trinity, meaning belief in God as three distinct "persons"—really a post-Biblical concept—I'd have to say no.

Actually, Christian Scientists are more likely to think of religious beliefs in terms of how we understand and experience God's reality, rather than in terms of doctrinal formulations.

I like the way a Methodist theologian put it recently when he spoke of God as Creator, Redeemer, and Sustainer. Christian Scientists' sense of the Trinity is very close to this. They stress a radical monotheism and speak of God as the infinite Person, rather than three persons in one. But Christian Scientists do believe that God reveals Himself to humanity, and can be experienced, in a threefold or triune way.

In Mrs. Eddy's words, "Life, Truth, and Love constitute the triune Person called God,—that is, the triply divine Principle, Love. They represent a trinity in unity, three in one,—the same in essence, though multiform in office: God the Father-Mother; Christ the spiritual idea of sonship; divine Science or the Holy Comforter."[13]

I should add that it's as natural for a Christian Scientist to speak of God in this triune sense as it is for a traditional Christian to speak of the Trinity.

·  ·  ·

### Do you believe in the virgin birth?

Yes, we believe that Jesus was born of a virgin. As we understand it, Mary's pure concept of God as the Father of man was the avenue or means by which the Christ, Truth, found expression in the human Jesus.

·  ·  ·

### Do you pray to Jesus?

No. The basis for that is that Jesus prayed to God—not to himself, nor to the prophets or saints. The Saviour prayed to God—fervently. He taught his followers to pray to "our Father which art in heaven." We do not pray to or through Mary Baker Eddy (in case that is another question you might have). She followed Jesus' example and prayed to God. Students of Christian Science do the same. We see Jesus just as he said—as "the way, the truth, and the life."[14] His marvelous example is the very core of our efforts to live his Sermon on the Mount and work out our salvation. We recognize him as Jesus the Christ, or as Christ Jesus.

·  ·  ·

*What about Jesus' suffering and being sent by God to suffer and to die for our sins? Do you believe that God sent Jesus to suffer and to die?*

Do you mean, Do I think of God like Abraham, laying His Son on an altar as a sacrifice? No, I don't think of God, the Father, that way. I do understand that Jesus suffered because of the sins of others and showed us how to overcome sin through self-sacrifice.

The Founder of our Church, Mary Baker Eddy, had a lot to say about the crucifixion. She saw Jesus as bearing the cross of "the world's hatred of Truth and Love," and she wrote, "The distrust of mortal minds, disbelieving the purpose of his mission, was a million times sharper than the thorns which pierced his flesh."[15] One can't help feeling unspeakable gratitude for all that Jesus endured for us. But when you stop to think about it, it wasn't the suffering itself which brought the disciples back from their nets and gave life to Christianity. It was his triumph over the suffering—and over death—which had such tremendous power.

. . .

*Don't Christian Scientists really deny the atoning work of Jesus Christ on man's behalf?*

Christian Scientists feel that the understanding of the atonement in Mrs. Eddy's writings makes it more, not less, meaningful. They see Jesus' sacrifice in undergoing the crucifixion as the supreme exemplification of divine Love, which human hate could not vanquish or death destroy. They agree that he "hath abolished death, and hath brought life and immortality to light through the gospel"[16]—through the "good news" of his triumph over the grave. They see in this central event of history not only the revelation of the Saviour's unity with God, eternal Life, but the promise of all men's at-one-ment with the Father as they learn what it means to be "heirs of God, and joint-heirs with Christ."[17]

Mrs. Eddy writes, "His goodness and grace purchased the means of mortals' redemption from sin. . . ."[18] But she further explains,

> While we adore Jesus, and the heart overflows with gratitude for what he did for mortals,—treading alone his loving pathway up to the throne of glory, in speechless agony exploring the way for us,—yet Jesus spares us not one individual experience, if we follow his commands faithfully; and all have the cup of sorrowful effort to drink in proportion to their demonstration of his love, till all are redeemed through divine Love.[19]

· · ·

*Aren't all our sins already forgiven through Jesus' atonement for us?*

We believe that Jesus' atonement is absolutely vital to the destruction of sin in our lives. But his atonement doesn't provide us with automatic forgiveness. Instead it gives us the spiritual means for grappling with and overcoming sin. When sin is destroyed through repentance and regeneration and through taking part in Christ's atonement, we experience forgiveness. And we begin to see that sin never really was a part of our actual nature.

In other words, we're forgiven, not in the middle of indulging sin but when we're freed from living sin in our own lives. The Bible teaches us to love good and hate evil. This doesn't mean that we hate sinners or treat them self-righteously. We hate *sin*—with a "perfect hatred"[20]—but we love and forgive the victims of sin and help them to reform if they'll let us.

· · ·

*If I were more of a sinner than you, would you get eternal life sooner than I would?*

We both already have eternal life, since God is our real Life, but I would be more ready to see that fact and be blessed by it then you would under those conditions.

· · ·

*Can you be saved without personally accepting Christ?*

Using the words "I accept Christ" may not mean as much as actually following Christ. Someone may be touched by the Christ and not realize it, whereas a devout churchgoer may be rigid and unloving. The one who's living what the words imply may be farther along the road to salvation than the one who's saying them.

. . .

*How do you view evil?*

We do not ignore it, but we do believe in a very profound and practical way that sin, sickness, and other evils are not created by God and that only what He creates has the reality of power and life. Therefore, in confronting evil in daily life, we can stand fearlessly upon the rock of the All-power and ever-presence of a God who is entirely and eternally good. Evil is not merely something to be "explained away" on this basis. It must be conscientiously faced and overcome through a life of Christian discipleship in which faith and works are both seen as of vital importance. We find this to be a very demanding Christian discipline.

. . .

*What do Christian Scientists mean by the term "animal magnetism"?*

The answer is neither mysterious nor complex but involves a little background. Mrs. Eddy believed that the true meaning of the gospel—the real "good news" that Jesus brought and lived— is that man is wholly spiritual and, as the beloved child of God, is inseparable from Him and His love. What *appears* to separate us from God—whether it is sin, cruelty, betrayal, a chronic moral problem, a tormented relationship, anxiety, feelings of personal inadequacy, or disease—is not brought into being by God. Rather, it is the result of an ignorance of God, a blindness to His presence. It is what Mrs. Eddy called "error," and the activity or operation of this error is what she termed "animal magnetism."

In Mrs. Eddy's time this term was associated with mesmerism and hypnotism. She used it to convey the fact that what Paul called "the carnal mind . . . enmity against God"[21] *always* operates hypnotically, or through what's commonly called "suggestion." Fear, anxiety, confusion, all that leads us in a false direction, blinding us to God, comes initially through mental suggestion. It's at this point that the Christian can meet and defeat them, as Paul puts it, by "bringing into captivity every thought to the obedience of Christ."[22] And as we do that through dropping our most cherished beliefs and yielding to God's will, not only is our thought transformed, but so is our body or the troubling situation.

. . .

### *How do you explain the suffering in the world?*

Let's start with a very simple analogy. A shuttered room may be in utter darkness, but throw open the shutters and the room is flooded with light. A person could spend weary hours sitting there in the dark, trying to understand and explain the nature of darkness, but his real need is to let in the light. So with the anguish, the loss and pain and waste of human life, all the crippling and imprisoning conditions that can seem to have such nightmare reality. Our need is never for an explanation that legitimizes these aspects of mortal existence. Our need is for the clear understanding of God's omnipresence that dispels the claims of evil as light dissipates the terrors of the dark. Then we begin to understand Isaiah's words: "The people that walked in darkness have seen a great light: they that dwell in the land of the shadow of death, upon them hath the light shined."[23]

. . .

### *What does Mary Baker Eddy mean by "mortal mind"?*

It's a term used by Mrs. Eddy to describe unregenerated human thought in distinction to what the New Testament calls that "mind . . . which was also in Christ Jesus."[24] It's really the equivalent of Paul's terms *carnal mind* or *fleshly mind*. *Mortal mind* refers to the mass of things summed up in such words as *hatred, prejudice, selfishness, greed, envy, disease*—all things that Christ comes to save or redeem us from. (You'll find the word described even more fully in the denominational textbook, *Science and Health with Key to the Scriptures* by Mrs. Eddy, p. 114.)

.   .   .

*What do Christian Scientists mean by the word "real"?*

The word *real* is used in Christian Science in a somewhat unusual way, but in a way that is exact and logical.

Paul the Apostle writes eloquently of his conviction that nothing in the universe "shall be able to separate us from the love of God, which is in Christ Jesus our Lord."[25] To the Christian Scientist the ever-presence of God's tender, all-encompassing love is fact, is "real." Therefore from this standpoint, any evidence suggesting an absence of God's love or a separation of man from God is false—regardless of its impression on our physical senses—and needs correction.

Such an approach does not put a rosy tint on everything but does present a clear standpoint from which to view God and man's relationship to Him. It is the spiritual understanding of God's love and of our relationship to Him that brings healing.

.   .   .

*Mrs. Eddy's definition of death as "an illusion, the lie of life in matter . . ."[26] seems absurd. How can you say death is an illusion?*

Christians over the centuries have maintained that death is not the end of a person's identity or being, as much as that may seem to be the case. This is not to deny the human phenomenon of death. Nor is it to say that Christian Scientists don't fight death for all they're worth, in what they see as the most effective way. But rather it's to say that death is something other than what it seems to be, that ultimately it's deceptive, even as the seeming solidity of matter has been called into question from the standpoint of twentieth-century quantum physics. Such convictions, as difficult as they may be for someone with your beliefs to agree with, are at the heart of a ministry that has helped many Christian Scientists, even under such horrific conditions as the German concentration camps, to be more, *not* less, engaged with human life. They don't claim to have fully conquered death, but through their healing ministry many human lives have been spared and extended that otherwise would have been cut short. And thus, many lives have been given new joy, new purpose, new usefulness.

. . .

*How can you say that matter is unreal?*

Although Mrs. Eddy came to the conclusion that matter has no ultimate reality—and no spiritual authority—no Christian Scientist claims to have understood or proved this completely for himself. What we feel called upon to do is to prove it by degrees through a commitment to healing—healing of bodily ills and all other appearances of man's alienation from God. Jesus must have known something about matter that other people didn't when he walked on the water, fed the five thousand, stilled a storm, and healed multitudes. Who would be willing to say that at our present limited point of development, we are really beholding the fullness of God's creation?

It's only through healing that a Christian Scientist feels he begins to understand more about matter's insubstantiality and what God's creation really includes. He is usually modest in his claims. But he continually seeks to understand more about life, good, reality, Spirit.

. . .

*Most Christians believe that Jesus' advent in the flesh and his crucifixion and resurrection were the crucial events in human history. When Christian Scientists speak of matter as unreal, don't they deny the very meaning of these events—indeed, that they even took place?*

No other Christian could possibly take the gospel record of Christ Jesus' life, including his virgin birth, crucifixion, and bodily resurrection, more literally and more seriously than the

Christian Scientist. These are historical events in the fullest sense of the term.

Mrs. Eddy writes in regard to the "dangerous skepticism" on this subject that "Christians and Christian Scientists know that if the Old Testament and gospel narratives had never been written, the nature of Christianity, as depicted in the life of our Lord, and the truth in the Scriptures, are sufficient to authenticate Christ's Christianity as the perfect ideal."[27]

The foregoing helps explain a statement of Mrs. Eddy's which is invariably plucked from context by religious critics: "If there had never existed such a person as the Galilean Prophet, it would make no difference to me."[28] Although her writings are characterized by constant references to the supreme importance of Jesus' life and example, detractors look instead to isolated passages which they can twist to their own meaning. In this case Mrs. Eddy was describing what she said to an agnostic detractor who had challenged her on the proof of Jesus' existence. She followed the words quoted with, "I should still know that God's spiritual ideal is the only real man in His image and likeness." In not wholly dissimilar terms the evangelist Billy Graham has stated that even if "there were no historical record of Jesus' life and ministry, He would still be real to me because I know Him by personal and daily experience."[29]

Christian Scientists joyfully emphasize the importance of Jesus' actual resurrection from the grave while some in other churches question its truth but remain nominally within the Christian fold. The truth of the resurrection sustains Christian Scientists' faith in the supremacy of spiritual over physical power. And it is basic to the healing practice through which they seek to prove, step by step, that matter and its limitations are no part of God-established reality.

· · ·

*Christian Scientists use Christian language, but some say they do so deceptively to attract people into accepting ideas which are not really Christian at all.*

Anyone who has really studied Christian Science knows that its use of key Christian terms is perfectly comprehensible and familiar. When Mrs. Eddy speaks of God she does not mean "an abstract principle" or "an impersonal force," as some of her critics claim. Like Thomas Aquinas in the thirteenth century and Jonathan Edwards in the eighteenth century, she uses the term *Principle* to denote God as the source of all spiritual law and order, but He is also to be known as the "infinite *Person*"[30] to whom we turn as the tender Shepherd and loving Redeemer of each individual. Where her writings do give new meanings to terms which over the centuries had been narrowed to arbitrary doctrinal definitions, she is careful to explain the difference. On the doctrine of atonement for instance, she writes:

> The real atonement—so infinitely beyond the heathen conception that God requires human blood to propitiate His justice and bring His mercy—needs to be understood. The real blood or Life of Spirit is not yet discerned. Love bruised and bleeding, yet mounting to the throne of glory in purity and peace, over the steps of uplifted humanity,—this is the deep significance of the blood of Christ. Nameless woe, everlasting victories, are the blood, the vital currents of Christ Jesus' life, purchasing the freedom of mortals from sin and death.[31]

1. Mary Baker Eddy, *Miscellaneous Writings* (Boston: The First Church of Christ, Scientist, 1896), p. 124.

2. James 1:17.

3. Matt. 22:37.

4. Mary Baker Eddy, *Science and Health with Key to the Scriptures* (Boston: The First Church of Christ, Scientist, 1906), p. 480.

5. Acts 17:28.

6. Eph. 1:23.

7. I Cor. 12:6.

8. Eddy, *Science and Health,* pp. 25, 26.

9. Phil. 2:5.

10. Mary Baker Eddy, *Message to The Mother Church for 1901* (Boston: The First Church of Christ, Scientist, 1901), p. 8.

11. Eddy, *Science and Health,* p. 52.

12. *Ibid.,* p. 313.

13. *Ibid.,* p. 331.

14. John 14:6.

15. Eddy, *Science and Health,* p. 50.

16. II Tim. 1:10.

17. Rom. 8:17.

18. Eddy, *Miscellaneous Writings,* p. 165.

19. Eddy, *Science and Health,* p. 26.

20. Ps. 139:22.

21. Rom 8:7.

22. II Cor. 10:5.

23. Isa. 9:2.

24. Phil. 2:5.

25. Rom. 8:39.

26. Eddy, *Science and Health,* p. 584.

27. Mary Baker Eddy, *The First Church of Christ, Scientist, and Miscellany* (Boston: The First Church of Christ, Scientist, 1913), p. 179.

28. *Ibid.,* pp. 318–319.

29. Quoted in Robert Peel, *Christian Science: Its Encounter with American Culture* (New York: Holt, 1958), p. 193.

30. Eddy, *Science and Health,* p. 116.

31. Mary Baker Eddy, *No and Yes* (Boston: The First Church of Christ, Scientist, 1891), p. 34.

# 4

# Healing as Christian

# Experience

Has ecumenical dialogue had any practical impact on the direction of contemporary Christianity, or has it served merely as a salve for the collective religious conscience? There's an answer to be found, at least in part, in the emergence of healing ministries over the last century.

The seeds of ecumenism—specifically a willingness to observe and learn from one another—have had a significant role in the increased commitment to practice New Testament healing today. For instance, it has been noted by more than several spokespersons of healing that mainstream Christianity took its initial cue on the subject from Christian Science—although disagreeing with basic elements of its theology of healing. And charismatics from numerous mainstream denominations have drawn on healing practices and inspiration from Pentecostal churches, while maintaining their own essential theologies. As for more formalized ecumenism, periods of ecumenical strength tend to be times of growing expectancy of God's power to heal.

The mutuality of these two trends—ecumenism and healing—has by no means resulted in a monolithic view, as the variety of healing practices, services, and theologies bears out. In fact, a clear understanding of the different positions held by churches in the healing community is essential to the prosperity of ecumenism.

"Prayer and Spiritual Healing," a talk aired on a Christian Science radio series during the 1960s, began by pointing out some of the common ground shared by Christian Scientists and other Christians involved in healing. It went on to examine the unique perspective that Christian Science brings to Jesus' expectation that his followers should do the works that he did. Later this talk was published as a pamphlet.

# Prayer and Spiritual Healing

In recent years there has been a notable revival of interest in spiritual healing in the Christian Church. A number of churches are holding healing services, and a good deal of attention is being given to the early Christian ministry to the sick as well as to the sinning.

In fact, many writers on the subject have pointed out that the very word *salvation* is derived from the Latin word *salvus,* which means hale and whole. The Saviour was a healer, and he repeatedly said that his followers should do the same works that he did. We know that his disciples healed all manner of sickness and that healing continued to be a prominent feature of Christianity for several centuries. It was only as Christians increasingly compromised with the materialism around them that healing largely disappeared from their religious practice.

Of course, there have been occasional examples of Christian healing right down through the ages. Instances have been recorded in connection with Luther and Wesley and George Fox, for example. But the modern revival of systematic spiritual healing is something new. One of its landmarks is an event which occurred in 1866.

In that year a New England woman, Mary Baker Eddy, was healed of severe injuries she had received from an accident. The healing occurred while she was reading in Matthew 9 of Jesus' raising of the palsied man. As she read, her thought was flooded with the presence and power of God and she, too, rose from her bed healed.

---

*Prayer and Spiritual Healing* (Boston: The Christian Science Publishing Society, 1967).

Now, the outward experience itself may not have been unique. What was unique was Mrs. Eddy's determination to understand the power that had healed her. Later she described the experience as a spiritual discovery, and she wrote about it in these words:

> For three years after my discovery, I sought the solution of this problem of Mind-healing, searched the Scriptures and read little else, kept aloof from society, and devoted time and energies to discovering a positive rule. The search was sweet, calm, and buoyant with hope, not selfish nor depressing. I knew the Principle of all harmonious Mind-action to be God, and that cures were produced in primitive Christian healing by holy, uplifting faith; but I must know the Science of this healing, and I won my way to absolute conclusions through divine revelation, reason, and demonstration.[1]

That quotation is from Mrs. Eddy's book *Science and Health with Key to the Scriptures,* published nine years later, in 1875. The opening chapter of the book, in the final, revised form she gave it, is "Prayer," and prayer is the basis of all true spiritual healing. There are many differences of belief among Christians of various denominations who practice spiritual healing, but probably all who have thought about it very much would agree that it's turning to God with a deep desire to let His will be done that opens the way for His healing and saving power to be experienced.

### More than Blind Faith

In the first sentence of the chapter "Prayer" in *Science and Health,* Mrs. Eddy writes: "The prayer that reforms the sinner and heals the sick is an absolute faith that all things are possible to God,— a spiritual understanding of Him, an unselfed love."[2]

Here is mentioned absolute faith, defined as spiritual understanding and unselfed love. Many people think of spiritual healing as simply faith healing. But a good deal more than a blind faith in God is required for the systematic, reliable practice of the healing power of Christianity. An absolute, continuing faith must be rooted in understanding. Jesus himself declared: "If ye continue in my word, then are ye my disciples indeed; and ye shall know the truth, and the truth shall make you free."[3]

For an engineer to build a bridge, it is not enough for him to have faith in engineering principles; he must understand them. If he does understand them properly, then he will obviously have faith in them; but his faith cannot be absolute until his understanding is complete.

In a somewhat similar way the Christian's faith becomes absolute as he comes to understand God as the very Principle of perfection, as the loving Father of all that is good and true. In the Epistle of James we read: "Every good gift and every perfect gift is from above, and cometh down from the Father of lights, with whom is no variableness, neither shadow of turning."[4]

Here is a picture of God who is universal, undeviating Love. Such a God could not play favorites. He could not act out of sudden, arbitrary whims. He could not send healing just because someone implored Him to—as though our all-wise Father were a hard-hearted and indifferent parent who would be good to his children only if they kept after him, pleading with him to be kind to them. Yet isn't that what we often do with God—implore Him to be good to us, to save us and heal us?

Now, a humble prayer of that sort is not without its value. It may make us search our own hearts to see how much of God's mercy we deserve. It may bring us to the recognition that God's power far surpasses that of men. It may make us receptive to the infinite good He is always pouring out. But a blind petition of that sort assumes that we can persuade God to do something He might not otherwise do. It assumes that He doesn't know what is good for us until and unless we tell Him.

## Jesus and Prayer

When Jesus prayed at the tomb of Lazarus—before demonstrating the power of God to raise Lazarus from the dream of death—he said, "Father, I thank thee that thou hast heard me. And I knew that thou hearest me always."[5] How could he know this? How could he be so sure that he knew his Father's will? How could he know, before the fact was evident, that his Father's will for man was health, not sickness; life, not death; victory, not defeat? Surely it was because he knew God so intimately as the divine Principle of good, as all-embracing Love, as the very Life of man. And because the Saviour's understanding of God was so profound, he could say with authority to the sick, the suffering, the sorrowful: "Be whole."[6] Be *healed*.

"But," you may say, "that's all very well for our Lord. But that was different. He was the Son of God." True enough. Jesus was constantly aware that all power came to him through his divine sonship, his unity with God the Father. But surely he did everything he could to lift us into an awareness of *our* sonship with God, *our* unity with "the Father of lights, with whom is no variableness, neither shadow of turning."[7]

Toward the end of his earthly career he said to his disciples, "I ascend unto my Father, and your Father; and to my God, and your God."[8] On another occasion he told them, "He that believeth on me, the works that I do shall he do also; and greater works than these shall he do; because I go unto my Father."[9] Jesus always claimed that it was the Father who did the works, not he himself. He even went so far as to say, "I can of mine own self do nothing."[10]

Certainly this is the point from which the present-day disciple must start in his practice of spiritual healing. He must recognize that it is always God who is the real healer, not he. He must acknowledge all power as vested in an infinitely good God. He must bring his thinking and living into accord with God's law, not expect the divine Principle of being to accommodate itself to his own personal tastes and wishes.

### Truth the Healer

If we blindly pray to God to work a special miracle for us, we cannot be very sure of an answer to our prayer. But if we turn understandingly to the God whose nature has been revealed to us through Christ Jesus—to the God who is Truth itself—then we can claim with assurance the promise that Jesus has given us: "Ye shall know the truth, and the truth shall make you free."[11] Truth is like the light, which frees us from darkness. To know

God as Truth is to look beyond material appearances to spiritual reality—to find a new basis for our thinking. To know God as Truth is to glimpse the true man of His creating.

When Jesus looked at a crippled man, a blind man, a leper, a sinner, he didn't see a man condemned by God to hopeless suffering or deprivation. He saw man as the child of God, the object of God's loving care, created by God to manifest His glory—and the Master's very seeing of the cripple or leper in this way brought healing. The suffering and deprivation were shown to be products of the fleshly or carnal mind, which St. Paul later described as "enmity against God."[12]

Paul has a great deal to say on this subject that is of help to the present-day practitioner of Christian healing. The apostle makes it clear that we must increasingly exchange the carnal mind or material-mindedness which is the source of sin and suffering for what he calls "the mind of Christ."[13] In one place he writes, "Let this mind be in you, which was also in Christ Jesus."[14] As we learn to understand God as Mind and to see man as Jesus did, we are able to follow his example and obey his command to heal the sick.

Christian Scientists draw a sharp distinction between the divine Mind, or God, and the carnal, or mortal, mind which is "enmity against God." To them, human will or suggestion has no place in divine healing. Learning to know and do God's will, accepting the true view of man as God sees him—it is this that corrects the distortions of a limited, mortal sense of things. In other words, Christian healing on these terms is simply the result of a change from material-mindedness to spiritual-mindedness, from self-centered to God-centered thinking.

## *Unselfed Love*

This brings us to another element in the sentence quoted earlier from *Science and Health*: "The prayer that reforms the sinner and heals the sick is an absolute faith that all things are possible to God,—a spiritual understanding of Him, an unselfed love." The love of God, the love of Truth for its own sake, the love of good, the love of our fellow men—that is the sort of love which conquers the most stubborn physical disabilities. Sometimes it brings healing in an instantaneous flash of inspiration, sometimes through a slow process of character regeneration. In every case the love that opens the way for such results is a reflection of divine Love, the Love that is God.

This is not just theory. In Christian Science alone hundreds of thousands of people have experienced healing of chronic disease during the past hundred years through the power of divine Love. Today increasing numbers of people in other Christian churches bear witness also to the vitality of spiritual healing.

An example drawn from the book *A Century of Christian Science Healing* illustrates the importance of unselfed love. A man writes of being healed of inoperable, quick-growing cancer after he turned to Christian Science for help and began to learn that God is actually Love—loving him and loving the universe. His testimony continues:

> I pondered these things over a period of months, and I grew continually stronger. When finally after some weeks I walked into a Christian Science church I heard them singing as I walked in—"His arm encircles me, and mine, and all." I actually felt that it was God's arm, divine Love's arm, that was holding me. Not only did the cancer disappear, but one by one headaches, stomach trouble, and a long list of other ailments left me.

Continuing his explanation of the transformation of his thought, the man writes:

> I started to reverse every unloving thought I had about people and things. I was pressed to the understanding that to be the image of Love, I had to love. I had to see through the eyes of God. I had to change my thought. I had to see that the other fellow was also the image of Love. I had to reject the suggestion that any evil can be done in a universe filled with Love, filled with infinite good. One friend in particular I had to see as in the presence of Love. And suddenly, after two or three months, this man whom I had most hated came in with his wife and offered to help me to go in business.[15]

Most people in the Christian churches who have had any experience with spiritual healing would probably agree on the importance of such love as an element in the practice of healing. Christian Science stresses love not merely as a human sentiment but as the divine, creative Principle of being. It uses the term *Principle* to make God more understandable as Love acting through law to form, sustain, and govern man.

## What God Is

To know God as Love is to open one's life to a purifying, regenerating, inexhaustible flood of divine power. It is to let the heart as well as the mind be in you which was also in Christ Jesus. Many a person has found healing of his own difficulty when his heart has been moved by a deep desire to help his brother. Such desire is in itself a prayer.

In one of her shorter works, called *No and Yes,* Mrs. Eddy writes:

> True prayer is not asking God for love; it is learning to love, and to include all mankind in one affection. Prayer is the utilization of the love wherewith He loves us. Prayer begets an awakened desire to be and do good. It makes new and scientific discoveries of God, of His goodness and power. It shows us more clearly than we saw before, what we already have and are; and most of all, it shows us what God is.[16]

What God is! This is the substance of all religion. Healing can never be more than incidental to the larger purpose of coming to know God, our divine source and sustainer. Healing is a by-product rather than the ultimate aim of the Christian's search for God.

Many of the Christians who have become involved in the current revival of spiritual healing see it as one of the signs of the appearing of God's kingdom, as in the first century of the Christian era. They see it as one of the added things of which Jesus spoke when he said, "Seek ye first the kingdom of God, and his righteousness; and all these things shall be added unto you."[17]

If the kingdom of God is understood as the consciousness of

divine Truth—of the infinite, divine Principle, Love—then healing is indeed an evidence of the appearing of this consciousness
in human experience. It is an evidence that the deceitful suggestions of the carnal mind are being exchanged for the life-giving
ideas of the divine Mind. It shows, too, that we are learning
what it means to be the children of God.

There is much besides sickness that needs healing in human
experience. Sin, poverty, hunger, selfishness, greed, pride, hatred, prejudice, ignorance, fear, stupidity—all these and a thousand other things need to be washed away by opening our lives
to the flood tides of divine Love. We cannot separate one sort of
healing from the other. Every genuine spiritual healing leaves
the individual a better human being than he was before, that is,
more conscious of his true nature as the son of God.

As individuals, we all still have a great deal to learn as to how
to demonstrate more effectively the infinite power of good, or
God. But the way has been made clear, and we can rejoice for
the progress already made as well as the boundless possibilities
ahead.

---

1. Mary Baker Eddy, *Science and Health with Key to the Scriptures* (Boston: The First Church of Christ, Scientist, 1906), p. 109.

2. *Ibid.,* p. 1.

3. John 8:31, 32.

4. James 1:17.

5. John 11:41, 42.

6. Mark 5:34.

7. James 1:17.

8. John 20:17.

9. John 14:12.

10. John 5:30.

11. John 8:32.

12. Rom. 8:7.

13. I Cor. 2:16.

14. Phil. 2:5.

15. *A Century of Christian Science Healing* (Boston: The Christian Science Publishing Society, 1966), pp. 151–154.

16. Mary Baker Eddy, *No and Yes* (Boston: The First Church of Christ,
Scientist, 1891), p. 39.

17. Matt. 6:33.

The preceding talk was deliv-
ered during a period in which the renewed interest in spiritual healing was developing across a broad denominational
spectrum. To date, there has been little serious study of the
influence of Christian Science on this development. As one
writer puts it, "The impression one gains from scattered comments on Christian Science in the literature on Christian healing is one of a certain embarrassment in acknowledging a
debt which is probably real."[1]

The following interview with the Reverend Paul Higgins, a
United Methodist minister who has been actively committed
to spiritual healing over many years, has a useful bearing on
the relation of Christian Science to healing in mainstream
Christian churches.

---

1. Stephen Gottschalk, "Update on Christian Science," *Theology Today,* vol.
44, no. 1 (April 1987), p. 113.

# Christian Science and Spiritual Healing Today: A Conversation

*We might start just by asking you how you first became interested in Christian healing.*

It goes way back to my early childhood. My mother taught me how to pray. She taught me especially that God is Love and that I am to take all matters to Him and to count on help from the Divine for a good and healthful life. And then I had two aunts who were Christian Scientists. I personally was very, very fond of them. They were wonderful to me, and their thought and ideas had a lot of influence on me—not so much by telling me about Christian Science but by the way they lived and practiced. There was a consistency about the two of them that appealed to me and that had an important influence on me.

That was a part of my heritage. There were other people too: a remarkable family doctor and my Bible class teacher. They made great impressions upon me; they had a breadth of viewpoint that's so different than you often meet today.

Also, from the study of the New Testament, I began to realize Jesus' commission to us to preach the gospel and heal the sick.[1] We'd done the first to some extent, but we hadn't done enough on the healing of the sick. That was my strong feeling; and then when I was studying John Wesley's life, I found that he held the same view. I felt the Methodists had not done enough along that line—that we needed to recover the commission of Christ in the Protestant churches of today.

---

"Christian Science and Spiritual Healing Today: A Conversation with the Reverend Paul Higgins," *Christian Science Sentinel,* October 6, 1986, pp. 1857–64.

*When you think about it, it's hard to separate truly experiential faith from healing. They tend to join, don't they?*

They do, they do, absolutely. Wonderful Christians through the ages have felt that real unity of faith and practice. They have had an experience of God's presence in their lives that was so linked with their everyday practice—in their everyday thought and prayer—they were able to commune with the Divine. They were able to feel the presence of God wherever they were and whatever they were doing.

*That reminds me of something Mrs. Eddy said about some of the ministers who had a great influence on her in her youth: ". . . their piety was the all-important consideration of their being, the original beauty of holiness that to-day seems to be fading so sensibly from our sight."[2] Undoubtedly this sense of holiness helped to lead her to Christian healing. But what is it that has kept Christianity generally from becoming more involved in healing? Why have we been so slow really to practice the healing that Jesus and his disciples did?*

As you go back to the New Testament, you read about Paul and John and Peter and how they and the other apostles practiced healing. Many church fathers in both the East and West wrote about this and practiced healing themselves. Many of the saints of the early Church performed what were called miracles, and most of these related to some form of healing. During the Protestant Reformation, Luther practiced healing. So did George Fox (the Quaker) and Wesley too, along with some of the German Pietists in the Mennonite movement.

I think sometimes the Church has lost that. People become satisfied with just what they're doing in the Church, and they don't look beyond that. They don't see what other things they need to be doing. That's just where Christian Science, as I see it, has made such a big contribution.

*Aren't a growing number of Christians beginning to appreciate that God does not send sickness and pain? Doesn't there need to be a shift away from the view of sickness and pain as something you need to accept?*

That's right, and it's so very important. I think that's a theological principle that we have had to break away from because it is a mistaken, confused idea. It prevents a lot of people from getting well. And when we break through it, that is a great step forward. It's really getting beyond a narrow, little concept of God and gaining a larger concept of God as Love.

*You place the emphasis on intercessory prayer and symbolic acts such as laying on of hands. Christian Scientists see healing as a matter of the conscientious, heartfelt practice of spiritual law, which they feel Mrs. Eddy conclusively discovered and stated. Is that a fair way to put it?*

I think it's a very fair way; yet these acts that you mention here are for me a way of reconciling, coming home again, really. They are ways that symbolically help us come back home and be reconciled with God.

*It's interesting to see how Christian Science entered into your background, but it would be interesting to explore too, for a minute, where you might differ from it.*

I agree in basic principle that there are spiritual laws. If we abide by them, we will find ourselves in harmony with the divine plan. It's important to find our way into this plan and to abide by these spiritual principles that God provides for us. But I would be hesitant as to how much we know about them. Perhaps that's why we sometimes fail, because sometimes we don't know them all.

*Christian Scientists might be more likely to say that we fail when we don't practice or understand what is already here to be known of the reality of God and of man as His spiritual expression. We have to bring our lives—or at least be striving to bring our lives—into accord with the paramount spiritual fact of God's allness and the nothingness before Him of anything that denies His nature and goodness. Even so, it is tremendously encouraging to find such agreement with others who, like yourself, put such emphasis on the entire goodness of*

*God and on spiritual healing as the evidence that we're understanding more of our relation to Him.*

I like to think of healing as the opening up of the individual to one's real nature—reclaiming one's real nature, which is intended by God in terms of goodness and truth and health.

And that means a whole affirmative approach, as St. Paul put it so beautifully when he said, "Whatsoever things are true, whatsoever things are honest, whatsoever things are just, whatsoever things are pure, whatsoever things are lovely, whatsoever things are of good report; . . . think on these things. . . . And the God of peace shall be with you."[3] That, I think, is one of the most important approaches that we need.

---

1. Mark 16:15–18.

2. Mary Baker Eddy, *Message to The Mother Church for 1901* (Boston: The First Church of Christ, Scientist, 1901), pp. 32–33.

3. Phil. 4:8, 9.

As the preceding interview with the Reverend Paul Higgins noted, it is important to pay careful attention to the differences between Christian Science and other forms of spiritual healing, however much one may appreciate the similarities.

One of the distinct elements in Christian Science healing is its view that the ultimate cause and nature of disease lie beyond the detection of stethoscopes, CAT scans, and medical technology's most advanced instruments. The spiritual perspective on health and disease that's central to Christian Science healing is explained in the following excerpt from "The Position of the Christian Science Church," a statement by Nathan A. Talbot, Manager for the Church's Committee on Publication, that was requested by and published in *The New England Journal of Medicine*.

# The Position of the Christian Science Church

Actually, a basic conviction underlying the healing practice of Christian Science is one that some readers of the *Journal* may share: that disease and physical suffering are in no sense caused or permitted by God, and that since they are profoundly alien to His creative purpose, it is wrong to resign oneself to them and right to challenge them. To the Christian Scientist this conviction is rooted in both the Old and New Testaments. In its fullest implications, such a conviction furnishes the basis on which illness, seen as an aspect of human alienation from God, can be actively confronted and overcome.

Obviously, Christian Scientists are normal people who feel just as bad as others when they are ill and want just as much to get well. The common misconception that they try to ignore sickness as an "illusion" is based on a confusion of theological and commonsense usages. They certainly do not close their eyes to human pain and suffering, but neither do they accept disease as part of humanity's genuine, God-given being. They believe that human beings are vastly more than biochemical mechanisms, that because they have a direct relationship to God who is Spirit, their true nature—life and health included—must ultimately be found in a day-by-day spiritual discovery of this relationship. The function of the full-time practitioner of Christian Science is not intended to be equivalent to that of a medical doctor, since it consists entirely of heartfelt yet disciplined prayer that brings to a case needing healing a deeper understand-

Nathan A. Talbot, in *The New England Journal of Medicine*, vol. 309 (December 29, 1983), pp. 1641–44.

ing of a person's actual spiritual being as the child of God. This understanding is held to be the crucial factor in dissolving the mental attitude from which all disease ultimately stems.

This does not deny that within a strictly physical framework of causation, certain conclusions are warranted—for example, that many infections have a bacterial origin. And a Christian Scientist would not presume to question the accuracy from a medical standpoint of a competent diagnosis. What a Christian Scientist does question is the physical framework of causation itself. The basic Christian Science "diagnosis" of disease involves the conviction that whatever apparent forms the disease assumes, it is in the last analysis produced by a radically limited and distorted view of the true spiritual nature and capacities of men and women. To take a medical analogy, a Christian Scientist regards all forms of disease as symptomatic of an underlying condition that needs to be healed. This is the healing, or spiritual wholeness, that he or she seeks to effect through prayer.

Perhaps nothing throws light on basic convictions about healing quite as directly as the way a church's healing ministry actually functions. What is the experience that, according to Christian Science, brings forth Christian healing? A lucid answer can be found in a description of Mary Baker Eddy's pivotal healing in 1866 as reported by a student with whom she had discussed the experience:

> At that time it was not clear to Mrs. Eddy by what process she had been instantaneously healed, but she knew that her thought had turned away from all else in contemplation of God, His omnipotence and everpresence, His infinite love and power. It eventually dawned upon her that this overwhelming consciousness of the divine presence had destroyed her fear and consciousness of disease exactly as the light dispels the darkness. She afterwards "noticed that when she had entertained similar thoughts in connection with the ills of her neighbors they too were benefited and it was in this manner that she discovered how to give a mental treatment."[1]

The term *mental treatment* applies to the specific form of prayer in Christian Science in which the redemption of one's own mentality opens the way for God's healing light and power to pour into one's life as well as the lives of others.

"The Christian Science Practitioner," an article by Robert Peel that appeared in the *Journal of Pastoral Counseling,* describes the work of those who are involved in the full-time healing ministry of Christian Science. It is followed by "Spiritual Healing as the Cutting Edge of the Future," informal comments by practitioners from a film prepared for a 1985 conference of Christian Scientists enrolled in colleges and universities.

---

1. Quoted in Robert Peel, *Mary Baker Eddy: The Years of Discovery* (New York: Holt, Rinehart and Winston, 1966), p. 212.

# The Christian Science Practitioner

In the ministry of healing, as in the worship of God, it is evident that the Father's house has many rooms.

Within the Christian tradition the pastoral counselor, the charismatic faith healer, the Christian Science practitioner, and the priest anointing the sick with oil have at least three things in common. They have the inspiration of a common Lord and Master, a common conviction that the ministry of healing and the worship of God are profoundly related, and a common purpose to bring to the sufferer not merely bodily well-being but genuine spiritual health.

In considering the distinctive role of the Christian Science practitioner, a few preliminary facts may be useful.

Christian Science, although best known for its healing work, is also a way of life, a religious discipline, a metaphysical study, a denominational structure. In one sense, every Christian Scientist is expected to be a practitioner of his religion—that is, to prove his faith and understanding by his works. Like the moral and spiritual regeneration to which it is closely allied, healing is regarded as the natural fruit of drawing closer to God.

Yet it is obvious that those who encounter apparently insuperable obstacles in their endeavor to do this need expert help. In such cases they may turn to an experienced Christian Scientist who, on a professional basis, devotes his full time to the ministry of healing in its broadest sense. This is the Christian Science practitioner properly so called, and his is a religious

Robert Peel, in *Journal of Pastoral Counseling,* vol. 4, no. 1 (Spring 1969), pp. 39–43.

vocation to which any committed and qualified Christian Scientist may aspire.

Since the Church of Christ, Scientist, has no clergy, the practitioner is a lay member like any other. His ministry is not an office in the church structure, although he may on occasion be elected to church office in the same way as other members. He has no special part in church services, no special administrative duties. His ministrations are for anyone who seeks them—members of the general public as well as Christian Scientists.

The role of pastor and practitioner have some slight similarity in that each includes prayer and spiritual counseling with individuals. However, the practitioner is exclusively concerned with this, is not restricted to a local congregation in his ministry, and is self-supported in the way that a general practitioner of medicine is—by his patients' payments.

The training for this task begins with the individual's first commitment to the study of Christian Science. Basically this is a self-conducted study, centering on the Bible and the Christian Science textbook, *Science and Health with Key to the Scriptures* by Mary Baker Eddy. From the outset it imposes a strict discipline on the serious student. The Word was made flesh, he is emphatically reminded; the abstract must become concrete, understanding be tested in healing, ontological concepts be related to life situations, if he is to make any real progress.

At some point he must complete a short course of intensive instruction from an authorized teacher of Christian Science, but the chief and continuing emphasis is on his daily practice of a discipline which includes the demand for practical results as well as for prayer, study, application, and spiritual growth. There is no resting satisfied with the advancement made at any given point, since nothing less than the New Testament record of instantaneous healing is the standard of achievement held before him.

The pragmatic component in Christian Science has sometimes led onlookers to suppose that bodily healing is the *end* at which the practitioner aims. It is certainly the end result for which many patients are looking, but the practitioner sees it as the by-product of some degree of spiritual awakening, and in this connection he is likely to remind the avid health-seeker of the verse from Matthew 6, "Seek ye first the kingdom of God, and his righteousness; and all these things shall be added unto you."[1]

It is impossible to say what part of a practitioner's time is devoted to the healing of physical disease and what part to the dealing with emotional disturbances, family problems, questions of employment, schooling, professional advancement, environmental adjustment, theological confusion, existential anxiety, and so forth. The proportion differs with individuals, and in any case, the two classes of problems are too closely interrelated to be logically separable. The important thing is that the word *healing* be understood to apply to the whole spectrum of human sins, fears, griefs, wants, and ills.

At the core of every dilemma, as Christian Scientists see it, is the individual's sense of alienation from this divine source, from a God who is in very fact Life, Spirit, Love. The particular problem is regarded always as a phase of the belief that man is material and mortal—a chance configuration of electrochemical impulses or interacting behavior patterns—and the challenge is to bring to light the patient's true spiritual status as the child of God.

The pattern for Christian Science treatment is set forth in a key passage in *Science and Health:* "Jesus beheld in Science the perfect man, who appeared to him where sinning mortal man appears to mortals. In this perfect man the Saviour saw God's own likeness, and this correct view of man healed the sick."[2]

Healing on these terms is understood to be a seeing into the structure of reality rather than a manipulation of epiphenomena. At its clearest and best it may be instantaneous; in other cases hours, days, weeks, or months of treatment may be necessary in order to uncover and destroy the hidden phase of thought which, as Christian Science explains it, is obscuring the patient's God-given identity.

One experiential pattern which many practitioners have encountered is that of working long and fruitlessly over a difficult case, then in a flash of insight one day seeing clearly the needed "truth" in regard to the patient, only to have this followed by an immediate healing. The same experience has been recorded by Christian Scientists who are not practitioners, in connection with their own working out of a problem, and some of them have added expressions of gratitude for the delay that has caused them to study, pray, and search their hearts more persistently to discover the offending "error."

This points to the fact that the practitioner's diagnosis is neither medical nor psychological, in the accepted sense of that word, but spiritual. The same thing is true of his treatment. Essentially it is prayer, as the word is understood in Christian Science, and such discussion or counseling as he may carry on with the patient is distinctly subservient to his silent prayer, or metaphysical treatment.

Whenever possible, however, the patient's help is likely to be enlisted by encouraging him to take a firm mental stand himself. Sometimes he may be given specific study to do, at other times guidance as to how he can best spiritualize his thinking, purify his motives, and strengthen his resolve, but a wise practitioner seldom gives advice as to what decisions he should make in running his affairs. The basic aim is to turn the patient to the divine Mind for guidance rather than attempting to steer him into a given course of action.

In the practitioner's work there is no substitute for compassion—the genuine Christian concern and love which make prayer inspiration rather than technique. In this connection a brief anecdote illustrates Christian Science treatment in its most simplified form.

A friend of mine, a Christian Scientist, had been struggling for some time with what seemed an unyielding problem. One day as he silently drove his car with his five-year-old son sitting beside him, the small boy—who knew nothing of his father's problem—reached out, touched his arm, and said simply, "Daddy, God loves you." Instantly he was healed.

Why? A Christian Scientist might point out several things. The little chap had enough love to feel his father's need, enough love to want to do something about it, and—most important of all—an intuitive perception that the love he felt was evidence of the infinite, divine Love at the heart of existence. If he had said only, "Daddy, *I* love you," the remark would undoubtedly have been comforting, but it would hardly have had the radical healing thrust of his simple statement.

As *Science and Health* puts it, "If the Scientist reaches his patient through divine Love, the healing work will be accomplished in one visit, and the disease will vanish into its native nothingness like dew before the morning sunshine."[3] This is the desideratum of all Christian Science treatment. The mental argument—the subjective interplay of affirmation and denial which generally characterizes such treatment—is no more than the scaffolding by which the practitioner attempts to raise his thinking to the level at which it becomes a transparency for the divine Love.

---

1. Matt. 6:33.

2. Mary Baker Eddy, *Science and Health with Key to the Scriptures* (Boston: The First Church of Christ, Scientist, 1906), p. 476.

3. *Ibid.*, p. 365.

# Spiritual Healing as the Cutting Edge of the Future

*Scott Preller:* Healing isn't just a matter of problem fixing; it's a matter of our lives being animated by the reality of God's allness.

*Phil Davis:* The practice of Christian Science is God-centered. Its very thrust is learning about God and who we are because of God. So we want to bring our hearts and minds into a simple trust, into an enlightened understanding of what God is doing—to be God-directed, God-oriented, God-governed.

*Dorothea Luther:* To really yearn for redemption, to yearn to be made clean—I mean that is really what Christian Science is about. This is opening the way to the new birth.

*Sondra Elkins:* That's what I have found very often: when a situation doesn't yield with the patient, the need may be for a deeper cleansing in my own heart. It's an experience I had recently. I felt the need was for a healing of the patient's human will, and I ended up really reducing a great, strong argument of human will in my own life. I actually spent the whole day, sometimes in tears, recognizing the error in my own thought. And then it was so clear by evening what was needed that the patient called back later that night and said that there had been a healing, and that she realized what it was—it was a release of human will in her life. There's only healing in proportion as we're a transparency.

*Scott Preller:* Opening our lives to God's power. Being reborn. Feeling spiritually alive. This is what Christian Science is all

---

"Spiritual Healing as the Cutting Edge of the Future," *The Christian Science Journal,* October 1987, pp. 14–19.

about. When we begin to think seriously about this kind of living Christianity—about being a part of a revolution, about being on a cutting edge—it's easy to feel pretty inadequate. But remember Moses saying, "Who am I, that I should go unto Pharaoh . . . ?"[1] Or when Jeremiah said, "I am a child."[2]

This recognition that the human mind is utterly inadequate to bring about healing—this yearning and humility as in the story of the woman known as Mary Magdalene—this is what opened them up to the divine grace that empowered them to do God's work. It still does!

*Robert Mitchell:* Something that I learned from [being healed of deafness] is that we need to listen, but to listen on a different level, to get self out of the way and really listen spiritually. And that to me is the basis of the practice—to let God speak to us, let God reveal Himself to us in any situation.

*Jill Gooding:* There are times when I've gone down on my knees mentally and physically and said, "Father, show me how we can see more of Your presence in this situation." The practitioner has to pray to be a prophet, to be a spiritual seer, to see what God is seeing in that situation—not to be overwhelmed by what the material senses are shouting. It does require humility to put aside a sense of self that would say a person can heal. It's always God.

*Dorothea Luther:* To listen to what God says. To be quiet. To "be still, and know that I am God,"[3] as it says in the Bible. If one is ready to do that, then surely one will get an answer.

*Scott Preller:* It's so clear that real spirituality isn't soft, vague, and ephemeral. It's tough. Really loving and serving God ally us to the spiritual power that cuts through the most difficult human circumstances.

---

1. Ex. 3:11.
2. Jer. 1:6.
3. Ps. 46:10.

A broad-ranging summary of Christian Science healing—its nature, its relation to Scripture, the way it is practiced—is provided in the following abridgment of "The Horizon of Healing," the final chapter of *A Century of Christian Science Healing*. The book was published in 1966 to commemorate the one-hundredth anniversary of the discovery of Christian Science.

# The Horizon of Healing

## Healing and Salvation

"And as ye go, preach, saying, The kingdom of heaven is at hand."[1]

In the New Testament narratives, the first impact of the good news of the kingdom is repeatedly felt as physical healing in the life of a particular person—a cripple waiting hopelessly at the pool of Bethesda or sitting at the gate of the temple day after day. The man healed of blindness by Jesus, pressed by his neighbors for a "proper" explanation, fell back on the tangible evidence, on what he himself had experienced. "One thing I know," he said, "that, whereas I was blind, now I see."[2]

To a Christian Scientist the real importance of a healing is the light it lets through. The change in physical condition or personal circumstance is only the outward and visible evidence of an inward and spiritual grace—a hint of a perceived spiritual fact. In looking back on a healing, the Christian Scientist is likely to think, not "That was the time I was healed of pneumonia" but "That was the time I learned what real humility is" or "That was the time I saw so clearly that all power belongs to God."

It is within individual consciousness that all Christian Science healing takes place. The outward results are regarded as among the added things of which Jesus spoke in Matthew 6:33. The real meaning of even the most remarkable bodily healing is not in the observed physical change but in what it indicates about the unseen structure of reality. Again Christian Scientists find this implied in Jesus' words: "The kingdom of God cometh not with

A Century of Christian Science Healing (Boston: The Christian Science Publishing Society, 1966).

observation: Neither shall they say, Lo here! or, lo there! for, behold, the kingdom of God is within you."[3]

The real change, as Christian Scientists understand it, is from material-mindedness to spiritual-mindedness, from self-centered to God-centered thinking. This is illustrated by many of the testimonies in this book and by thousands more like them. A single comment by a woman healed of arthritis of the spine may stand as a typical example:

> My healing was not immediate. But "man's extremity is God's opportunity," and this was my opportunity for spiritual growth. I studied with a thirst I can hardly describe, month after month. At first I looked daily for a physical healing, but it didn't come. Finally I realized that, healing or not, Christian Science was the Science of all Being, and the most important thing in my life. And I studied for the joy of unfoldment and the quenching of that great thirst. I no longer anxiously looked for a physical healing, for I had forgotten the material self in my joy and discovery of my real self.
>
> I really don't know exactly when during those weeks the complete healing came. But I know that the pain began to fade as I searched avidly for Truth, forgetting to search for physical healing.[4]

Today there is a growing recognition of the identity of healing (in its broadest sense) and salvation, an identity made clear by the root meaning of the two words. The phrase in Luke 1:77 which is translated "knowledge of salvation" in the King James or Authorized Version of the Bible was rendered by Wycliffe in the fourteenth century as "science of health" (or in some printings as "science and health"). This is sound etymology and sound metaphysics, for salvation necessarily means the rescue of men from all that would separate them from the fullness of being.

## Practical Aspects

The purpose of spiritual healing is never simply to produce physical ease. It is rather to put off the limited, physical concept of man which binds thought to matter, and thus bring to light Paul's "new" man. This is the man whom Christian Scientists understand to be the "real" man, created by God in His own image, spiritual and whole.

Here is the reason Christian Scientists do not turn to a doctor if they are not quickly healed through their own or a practitioner's prayers. Bodily conditions they view as effect rather than cause—the outward expression of conscious and unconscious thoughts. On this premise what needs to be healed is always a false concept of being, not a material condition. The purpose of turning to God for healing is therefore not merely to change the evidence before the physical senses but to heal the deeper alienation of human thought from God.

This is a purpose which, as Christian Scientists view it, deserves the most rigorous effort. Their very persistence in holding to what they call the truth of being in the face of alarming physical evidence to the contrary may be what is needed to bring about a healing. Testifiers sometimes express special gratitude for a long-delayed healing which has forced them to search their hearts, discipline their thoughts, and spiritualize their motives more thoroughly.

When a Christian Scientist fails to demonstrate the healing power of God in a given situation, he does not question the goodness of God. Instead he asks himself where he needs to bring his own thinking and living into closer conformity with God's law. Like the student of mathematics who may fail to solve a difficult problem through improper application of the relevant mathematical principle, the Christian Scientist does not blame the perfect Principle of being for the faulty result but seeks through the experience to grow in understanding and obedience to divine law.

The willingness to yield to the demands of Principle in a given situation—or even to recognize them—may sometimes come only after bitter experience. In some cases a relatively minor physical ailment may require a longer struggle with ingrained traits of character than does an acute need which turns the individual more wholeheartedly to God. The newcomer to Christian Science who has experienced a remarkable healing discovers, as he progresses in his study, that the blessings are inseparable from the demands.

Christian Science healing is in fact one way of worshiping God. It is an integral part of a deeply felt and closely reasoned view of ultimate reality. This very fact sometimes causes its use of the words *real* and *unreal* to be misunderstood. For when Christian Scientists speak of sickness as unreal, they do not mean that humanly it is to be ignored. They mean rather that it is no part of man's true, essential being but comes from a mortal misconception of being, without validity, necessity, or legitimacy. Like a mathematical error which has no substance and no principle to support it, sickness is not to be ignored but to be conscientiously wiped out by a correct understanding of the divine Principle of being. Prayer reaches out to God as the very Life of man, the eternal Truth transcending and embracing every human circumstance, the Father-Mother of a flawless spiritual universe. This is the vision of reality involved in metaphysical healing.

Christian Scientists, like all Christians, have a long way to go humanly to reach the standard set by their Master: "Be ye therefore perfect, even as your Father which is in heaven is perfect."[5] Like practitioners of other systems of healing, they learn from their mistakes and failures as well as from their achievements and victories. They learn, too, that Christian discipleship never permits them to settle down complacently on past proofs of God's care. But they have reason for immense gratitude in what they have already proved of the omnipotence of good, and they are challenged to higher proofs in the future.

## The Whole Man

Traditionally salvation has been thought of in connection with sin, and healing in connection with sickness. The "soul" has therefore been assigned to the clergyman and the "body" to the physician.

Today, with the growth of psychosomatic medicine, chemical-controlled behavior, and a pastoral counseling movement which has been conditioned to a large extent by psychological and medical disciplines, the distinction is breaking down. The "miserable sinner" of yesterday is the "sick" man of today. It is often a question whether he will turn to the doctor, the psychiatrist, or the minister for help in his trouble.

The common element in many diverse and even contradictory trends in medicine and theology is a sense of the interrelatedness of physical, mental, and spiritual health. Christian Science is posited on such an interrelation, though it maintains a common-sense distinction between sickness and sin. These are seen as variant manifestations of the belief that man has a finite, material existence apart from God. Both are to be healed by understanding man's true unity with his divine source.

The concept of wholeness plays an increasing role in modern thinking, which has been so fragmented by specialization that it now seeks anxiously a unifying principle to bring the pieces together again. To the Christian Scientist the "whole" man is St. Paul's "new" man, the man who is wholly united through Christ with God. Since reality is centered in Spirit, healing becomes a matter not of manipulating the human mind or body but of turning unreservedly to the divine Mind, in which man has his true, essential being.

In one place Paul writes of the new man "which after God is created in righteousness and true holiness."[6] Wholeness and holiness are etymologically related, and in Christian Science they are understood as synonymous. A contemporary theologian, Paul Tillich, recognized the same point when he wrote: "The word salvation is derived from the Latin word *salvus,* which means heal and whole. . . . But saving also means delivering, liberating, setting free. . . . Saving is healing from sickness and saving is delivering from servitude; and the two are the same."[7]

To many people this implies a closer cooperation between the doctor and the minister. For instance, a leaflet of the American Medical Association which stresses the need to treat the whole and not the part recognizes that "the faith of the individual patient is a vital factor in total health," but it interprets this aim in terms of better communication between physician and clergyman.[8] This is the explicit objective of the association's recently established Department of Medicine and Religion.

By contrast, Christian Science emphasizes entire reliance on spiritual means for the healing of both sickness and sin. It sees these as products of the "carnal mind" which Paul describes as "enmity against God"[9] and the answer to both as being found within the divine Mind, or God. The healing of bodily conditions and of human behavior follows as the natural result of exchanging the false suggestions of the carnal or mortal mind for the true facts of being as they are known to the divine Mind.

This radical position rules out the possibility of dividing faith between prayer and drugs, or between spiritual discipline and psychiatric techniques. In much pastoral counseling today the answer to disease-producing hates and fears is sought chiefly through the human mind's gaining insight into itself. By contrast, Mrs. Eddy writes in *Science and Health:* "The human mind is opposed to God and must be put off, as St. Paul declares. All that really exists is the divine Mind and its idea, and in this Mind the entire being is found harmonious and eternal."[10]

Physical healing experienced on this basis never leaves the individual mentally and morally just where it found him. Even if, as sometimes happens, he starts out with a blind faith in the practitioner who is helping him, he learns in time that it is always God who does the healing, not man. What is involved is a yielding of human character to divine influence, never a yielding of one human mind to another.

While a practitioner may help a patient to progress step by step, giving him friendly encouragement, counsel, and inspiration to meet the different phases of a particular problem, thousands of testimonies show that healing can take place when patient and practitioner are far apart. They may never even have met or communicated, beyond the initial request for help. While this phenomenon is unknown in psychological counseling, it was familiar to Jesus, as when he healed the centurion's servant at a distance (Luke 7:6–10), and it is natural enough if the divine Mind is not localized. Genuine Christian healing is never projected from person to person through space but flows freely to all who understand that infinite Mind is no respecter of persons.

This rules out the concept of "suggestion," which plays a key role in much psychological counseling. The word is reserved in Christian Science to describe the kind of thinking that seems to shut one off from the presence and power of God. A Christian Science practitioner does not "suggest" health to his patient any more than he would try to make the sun shine. His task, as he sees it, is simply to rise into that altitude of thought in which the unobstructed light of Truth shows him man as he really is. This is not a matter of mystical transport or the result of repeating esoteric formulas; it is a humble and rational turning to Mind for light.

When the skeptics of Jesus' day insisted that he healed—"cast out devils"—by Beelzebub, the prince of the devils, his reply indicated that this might indeed be the method used by some of his critics. "But," he added, "if I cast out devils by the Spirit of God, then the kingdom of God is come unto you."[11]

Instead of rejecting this as a reference to an obsolete demonology, the Christian Scientist sees in it a figurative description of two ways of handling the evils that bedevil human existence. One way would use the powers of the human mind to control the evils arising from the human mind's own shortcomings. The other way endeavors simply to "let this mind be in you, which was also in Christ Jesus"[12]—and understands this to be the eternal Mind or Spirit called God.

On this latter basis the healing of sickness and the healing of sin are closely related, as Jesus showed when he healed the palsied man.[13] Christian Scientists do not, however, imply that all sickness is the result of sin, in the narrow sense of that word. Perhaps the most common cause is fear, and behind that they see ignorance of the true nature of being. Yet in the root sense in which sin is defined as a missing of the mark, all belief in a life apart from God is ignorantly sinful. Christian Science insists that such belief is a slander on the pure and sinless man of God's creating.

Sin may have disappeared from the vocabulary of modern psychology but it remains an essential term in the Christian Scientist's spiritual arsenal. The higher mission of the Christ-power, writes Mrs. Eddy, is "to take away the sins of the world."[14]

ORIGINAL SIN ?

## Healing in the Churches

The revival of Christian healing in this century has been quietly gathering momentum. A considerable body of lay and clerical literature bears witness to the steadily growing interest in the subject. In recent years one denomination after another has taken official cognizance of the challenge offered religion by the ministry to the sick.[15]

More than seventy years ago Mary Baker Eddy wrote in *Pulpit and Press:* "If the lives of Christian Scientists attest their fidelity to Truth, I predict that in the twentieth century every Christian church in our land, and a few in far-off lands, will approximate the understanding of Christian Science sufficiently to heal the sick in his name."[16] Though there are wide divergences in doctrine, method, and scope among those who are now endeavoring to practice spiritual healing, their common aim is to heal the sick in Christ's name. To that extent at least, Mrs. Eddy's prediction is already being realized.

Yet both Christian Scientists and Christians of other denominations would be quick to point out the distance which still separates their methods. The revival of the Protestant ministry of healing is taking place within the organizational patterns and historic doctrines of the respective churches. Thus priests or pastors of denominations with a strong emphasis on ritual conduct services featuring laying-on-of-hands and anointing with oil. Others, with less of a liturgical heritage, have maintained that such ministrations are better carried on in private or after appropriate psychological counseling. Still others contend that healing is a special gift, a charisma, and seek to exercise it in the tent-meeting atmosphere of the evangelical crusader.[17]

What is common to all these methods as well as to Christian Science treatment is a deep conviction that disease is contrary to God's will. There is a general repudiation of the older disposition to believe that God sends pain and disability to man as a necessary discipline—in which case it would seem illogical and even impious to seek to contravene His will by means of a pill or serum.

That God in His inscrutable wisdom should torture a small

child, for instance, in order to punish its parents is repugnant to moral sense and unthinkable of the loving Father revealed through Christ. While Jesus himself prayed for submission to his Father's will, Christianity rests on the conviction that God's will for him was to triumph over the agony and death imposed on him by men—to triumph spiritually, morally, and physically. His whole ministry of healing involved intelligent conformity to God's will.

As the Christian Scientist understands it, such conformity includes the overcoming of faith in matter and of reliance on material means of healing. For the Christian traditionalist who believes that God works through matter it may be possible to combine some measure of reliance on prayer with some measure of reliance on medical skills. Generally it has been accepted that God creates both germs to cause disease and drugs to cure it, and many Christians are not troubled by this appearance of a house divided against itself. But the more uncompromising position of Christian Science reflects the radicalism of Jesus' words: "It is the spirit that quickeneth; the flesh profiteth nothing."[18]

Thus the differences of method between various types of religiously oriented healing reflect more profound differences of religious conviction. Christian Science in particular rests on metaphysical postulates which rule out any sense of healing as miraculous, in the sense that a miracle is a supposed violation of law. Christian transformation from sin to grace in daily living might appear a miracle from the standpoint of the psychiatrist. But orthodox Christianity does not usually put repentance and rebirth into the category of miracle. In the same way, physical changes following a changed relationship to God do not seem mysterious to the Christian Scientist, for whom matter is an expression of thought.

Despite all the differences which mark the various forms of religious healing, a common core of Christian faith—a shared spirit of service—unites them at their best.

The writer of a popular survey of present-day healing developments in the churches comes to the conclusion that they all have in common an outreaching love and the recognition of a power or force beyond oneself, to which one can turn in total humility and trust.[19] This is essentially the Christianity of the Sermon on the Mount, with its faith in God's love overflowing in love for one's fellow man. This is at the heart of Christian Science, as of all genuine Christianity.

The opening sentence of the first chapter of *Science and Health* reads: "The prayer that reforms the sinner and heals the sick is an absolute faith that all things are possible to God,—a spiritual understanding of Him, an unselfed love."[20] Christian faith and Christian love are both essential to Christian healing. And if Christian Science also demands an *understanding* of Spirit which shows healing to be logically consistent with universal law, this does not make faith unnecessary, it merely makes it absolute.

---

1. Matt. 10:7.

2. John 9:25.

3. Luke 17:20, 21.

4. Mary M. Terryberry, Grand Rapids, Michigan, in the radio/TV series *How Christian Science Heals,* 1962. The complete healing occurred seventeen years before the testimony was given.

5. Matt. 5:48.

6. Eph. 4:24.

7. Paul Tillich, *The Eternal Now* (New York: Charles Scribner's Sons, 1963), pp. 113, 114.

8. *The Physician, the Clergy, and the Whole Man* (American Medical Association, 1964).

9. Rom. 8:7.

10. Mary Baker Eddy, *Science and Health with Key to the Scriptures* (Boston: The First Church of Christ, Scientist, 1906), p. 151.

11. Matt. 12:28.

12. Phil. 2:5.

13. Matt. 9:1–8.

14. Eddy, *Science and Health,* p. 150.

15. See, for instance, the report of the Archbishop's Commission of the Church of England (1958) "The Church's Ministry of Healing"; report adopted May 1960 by the 172nd General Assembly of the United Presbyterian Church in the U.S.A. "The Relation of Christian Faith to Health"; report of the Committee on Anointing and Healing, United Lutheran Church in America (1962); and report of the Commission on Church and Ministry, United Church of Christ, Evangelical and Reformed (1960).

16. Mary Baker Eddy, *Pulpit and Press* (Boston: The First Church of Christ, Scientist, 1895), p. 22.

17. The differences in the history and methodology of the pastoral counseling movement, the liturgical healing movement, and the metaphysical movement represented by Christian Science are explored in an unpublished doctoral dissertation, B. Crandell Epps, "Religious Healing in the United States: 1940–1960" (Boston University, 1961). Epps, who has served as a Protestant chaplain in the United States Army, is himself a Christian Scientist.

18. John 6:63.

19. Will Oursler, *The Healing Power of Faith* (New York: Hawthorn Books, 1957), p. 330.

20. Eddy, *Science and Health,* p. 1.

# Further Exchanges

*It just seems incredible to me that anyone can talk seriously about spiritual healing.*

First of all, Christian Scientists don't believe that they're the only people to have healed through prayer. It's not an unknown experience in Christian history. And throughout the Bible there are examples of spiritual healing. The early Christian community accepted healing as a natural part of their faith. Christ Jesus healed all kinds of both sickness and sin. And he taught his disciples and many other followers to heal as he did. Didn't he say, "He that believeth on me, the works that I do shall he do also"?[1]

A question that every Christian faces is, Can we take Jesus at his word? Can we literally accept that promise and begin to practice what he preached and lived? Has God changed since Jesus' time? Why should the Christian of today consider radical spiritual healing—the same type of healing as Jesus performed—impossible or weird or undesirable? Are we really believing the Bible fully if we have no faith in Jesus' approach to healing?

Christian Science teaches that the Biblical promise "The prayer of faith shall save the sick, and the Lord shall raise him up"[2] must be as true now as it was then. And my experience in healing in Christian Science has convinced me that there is no greater Physician than God.

. . .

*Why do you put so much emphasis on healing?*

Actually, we don't put any more emphasis on it than the New Testament does. Christian Scientists are not obsessed with a desire for physical well-being; indeed, they think and talk less about their bodies than most people. In one sense a healing is only a by-product of drawing closer to God through coming to know the lovingkindness of His divine laws and the perfection of His spiritual creation. Healing, as we see it, is an important proof of God's care for man, but it is only one element in the full salvation at which Christianity aims.

. . .

### How do you go about healing?

Through prayer. Through turning completely to God for the answer to one's problem—whether the problem seems to be a disease in the body or a discord in the family. Now, this isn't just a matter of blind faith, and it certainly isn't a matter of will-power or mental suggestion or merely taking a cheerful attitude of positive thinking. It calls for an understanding of God and His laws; it calls for systematic study of the Bible and of the Christian Science textbook; it calls for opening one's heart and mind to the love and the law of God. In the old Christian phrase, it means being born again.

. . .

### What would you say that prayer is in Christian Science?

It's many things. But for me it includes profound spiritual reasoning in terms of what the Bible teaches about God's goodness, His love for His creation, and His willingness and ability to help everyone in time of need. It's understanding that because the Bible says God made man in His image, this means that man really is spiritual—"made of" spiritual qualities such as purity and love and integrity and joy. It's the expression of these spiritual qualities, rather than the flesh, that determines our health. As Jesus said: "It is the spirit that quickeneth; the flesh profiteth nothing; the words that I speak unto you, they are spirit, and they are life."[3]

This prayer involves faith, but a faith that is rooted in spiritual understanding. Faith in God is vital, indeed essential, to us in our work, but the understanding of what God is and of our relationship to Him is what makes prayer in Christian Science so unique—and so practical. And for me it's this spiritual understanding of God that undergirds and develops Christian faith.

· · ·

*I understand that your healers study the Scriptures, pray a lot, and are pretty faithful. Well, does the person they heal have to know as much or be as faithful?*

Not necessarily. Many people have been healed simply because the clear, pure thought of a Christian Science healer, or practitioner, enabled them to feel the love of God more deeply and fully.

If you take a bright light into a room, what happens? You can see everything clearly—how it really is. It's the same thing with practitioners—what they understand about themselves and others, as children of God made in His spiritual likeness, radiates God's light. When you are with someone who radiates or imparts God's light, you find—at least if you are willing to open your eyes—that you begin to glimpse yourself in that light, and that opens the way for healing. You may never have heard about God and yet could be healed by His tender love. I think an important ingredient is not how much you know about God but your yearning to know, your desire to live more faithfully, your own willingness to be transformed and reborn—that's what makes one receptive to healing. Actually, the most experienced practitioner also needs that same humble yearning and striving to know God better if he or she is going to do any healing work!

· · ·

*How do you know you were really healed and a problem didn't just go away by itself?*

When you're in pain, for example, and the pain has gone on for a while and after asking a Christian Science practitioner for help through prayer you're suddenly free, you fairly readily note the connection. Such "connections" may also come of course through your own praying, and there is just no question that the prayer, or the recognition of spiritual truth, is intimately related to the healing.

Someone asked me once, "Doesn't that take a lot of faith?" I had to stop and think because I'd honestly never thought of it in those terms. Reliance on God for healing feels perfectly normal because it is part of a whole way of life in which you turn to God for guidance, find spiritual fulfillment in drawing close to Him, and learn the necessity for obeying God—not just when you're sick or need something but all the time.

It isn't a matter of asking God to fix something and then blindly having faith that He will. It's that you feel you've gained at least some understanding of His great goodness and so you want to open up your thought through prayer to see and feel more of this divine, all-inclusive reality. God is the Principle of healing, and to feel His presence is to find healing and help coming into your life.

·   ·   ·

*Must a person have faith in Christian Science in order to be healed by it?*

Not necessarily. Some people have been healed when they turned to Christian Science as a last resort, though with very little hope that it could help them. But faith is a valuable asset—faith not so much in Christian Science as in God's willingness and power to save humanity from evil of every kind. The Bible tells us that he who comes to God must believe that God is and that He is a rewarder of those who diligently seek Him.[4] But Christian Science teaches that faith, to be really firm and effective, must rest not on blind belief but on an understanding of the present perfection of God's spiritual creation. This is the crucial difference that separates Christian Science from "faith healing."

·   ·   ·

*How does Christian Science healing differ from faith cure, suggestion, or psychotherapy?*

It does not rest on a blind faith in the unknown but on an enlightened understanding of God as infinite, divine Mind, Spirit, Soul, Principle, Life, Truth, and Love. It recognizes God as acting through universal, immutable, spiritual law, an understanding of which constitutes the Science of Christianity.

This Science draws an absolute distinction between the divine Mind, God, and the false mentality of which Paul declared, "The carnal mind is enmity against God."[5] On the basis of this distinction it repudiates the use of suggestion, willpower, hypnotism, and all those forms of psychotherapy which employ the human mind as a curative agent. Instead Christian Science turns human thought to the enlightening and saving power of divine Truth.

Christ Jesus said, "Ye shall know the truth, and the truth shall make you free."[6] *Science and Health* declares, "It is our ignorance of God, the divine Principle, which produces apparent discord, and the right understanding of Him restores harmony."[7]

. . .

*What does your view of matter have to do with healing?*

A lot. In fact, I think the best way to understand how we view matter is within the context of healing. People tend to think of themselves as the flesh they see and touch, as a bunch of nerve endings, and basically a physiological being with electromagnetic impulses, and so forth. And when we have a physical problem we tend to see that as a part of the same being—it's just as material and tangible, and just as permanent unless some other material means is used to change it.

Yet when you look in the Bible at the woman with an issue of blood for twelve years or the man with the withered hand, or a physical problem that we might have today, and then look at what happened when they turned to Christ for healing, you begin to see that what they had thought of as so tangible and substantial was shown through Jesus' healing them to be something very different. Jesus' healing proved that the real substance of their life was spiritual—and that this spiritual substance was every bit as tangible as what they'd thought of as so concretely material.

When you're faced with a physical challenge and you turn to God and then find yourself healed, during those moments you suddenly get powerful views of life as essentially spiritual—and that isn't in any abstract kind of way. In fact, it's really a very moving discovery to see that the substance of life isn't subject to all of the pains and threats of the flesh, but really is literally subject to God alone. We feel that the spiritual facts of man's identity that we affirm to be true in prayer must be manifested in our lives. As it says in the Lord's Prayer, "Thy will be done *on earth* as it is in heaven." The spiritual reality of man is tangible and powerful, and often best understood in healing.

. . .

*So you don't just deny that man has a body?*

No, we don't. But we understand the substance of that body to be spiritual. When we speak of man as spiritual it's important to understand that that is not understood as some kind of abstract ideal to us. It's very concrete and real and experiencable. The fact is, the five physical senses have absolutely no way of perceiving God. God simply doesn't exist if all we're going by are the five senses. Yet every one of us here knows that isn't so. We know it because of the spirit within us that cries, "Abba, Father." To take a very simple little example, When you and I first meet, all we may know of each other is what we see—I know you've got brown eyes and hair and so on. But as we get to know one another we see that there's much more to us than that. Well as we really get to know each other as God knows us then we see that the real substance of man is indeed spiritual.

. . .

*What about suffering? Can't it be a means for drawing closer to God?*

Basically, a Christian Scientist understands that suffering in and of itself is no guarantee of anything—except pain. Theologically, we do believe suffering can lead one to a deeper understanding of God. Mrs. Eddy speaks in many places of how suffering can have the effect of turning us more earnestly to the arms of God. But, of course, suffering simply is not the only way in which we learn more about our relation to God. This can also come through a deep Christian desire to put off the old man and to discover who we are in Christ, to discover more of our capacities to live that discovery—all of which describe the "provable" nature of Christianity, which is why we use the word *Science*.

This overcoming of the old man and discovering our own spiritual sonship can come, according to Mrs. Eddy, by "suffering or Science."[8] But in that suffering we're faced with a choice. We can either accept it as "part of life" or we can—through faith—understand that suffering is not ordained by God, that it can therefore be challenged and the burden of suffering lifted from humanity. And in that challenging process we most certainly do feel closer to God.

---

1. John 14:12.
2. James 5:15.
3. John 6:63.
4. Heb. 11:6.
5. Rom. 8:7.
6. John 8:32.
7. Mary Baker Eddy, *Science and Health with Key to the Scriptures* (Boston: The First Church of Christ, Scientist, 1906), p. 390.
8. *Ibid.*, p. 296.

## 5

# Christian Healing in the Modern World

Christian healing begins with the heart and mind and spirit being transformed by God. In other words, it involves the inner man and is a relatively private matter. At the same time, it can't be denied that healing takes place within a social context, as the blind man whom Jesus sent to wash in the pool of Siloam discovered when he returned seeing. "How were thine eyes opened?" the Pharisees immediately asked. "Where is he [that healed you]?" They even questioned the man's parents: "Is this your son, who ye say was born blind? How then doth he now see?"[1]

It is not the purpose of this sourcebook to address such questions—that is, to provide a substantial collection of Christian Science healings—although individual healings are referred to from time to time, primarily as a means of illustrating various theological points. A large body of such reports already exists and is easily accessible in works such as *Spiritual Healing in a Scientific Age* by Robert Peel.

Published by Harper & Row in 1987, this book provides affidavits of numerous healings in which the disease had been medically diagnosed and the healing medically confirmed. These affidavits include healings of disorders such as spinal meningitis, breast cancer, cancer of the uterus, double club-feet, compound pelvic fracture, broken vertebra, third-degree burns, acute rheumatic fever, polio, eczema, epilepsy, appendicitis, rheumatoid arthritis, tuberculosis, blood poisoning, diphtheria, and glaucoma, among others.

A further sampling of healings, in this case from the early days of the Church to more recent times, is contained in *A*

*Century of Christian Science Healing,* the final chapter of which is reprinted in part in chapter 4 as "Horizon of Healing." Undoubtedly the most comprehensive source is Church periodicals, each issue of which includes accounts of healing—more than fifty thousand since the turn of the century. And Christian Scientists have experienced countless healings that have not been submitted for publication.

This chapter offers a window on some of the interchange that has occurred on issues of healing between Christian Scientists and contemporary society as a whole. It begins with an excerpt from "Christian Scientists and the Medical Profession: A Historical Perspective," a historical article by Thomas C. Johnsen on the Church's interaction with both the medical community and the legal system during the early days of the Christian Science movement.

---

1. John 9:19.

# Christian Scientists and the Medical Profession: A Historical Perspective

The immediate question for the medical community in 1910 was how to respond to the nearly one hundred thousand followers of Christian Science. Public policy was unclear. Some favored allowing Christian Scientists freedom of practice while others felt they should be unqualifiedly restricted. Opinions differed inside as well as outside the medical profession on the proper dividing line between individual choice and state authority.

The battles over the legal standing of spiritual healing extended from the courts to state legislatures. In some states as in Rhode Island following the Mylod case medical boards lobbied for legislation expressly banning the practice of Christian Science. Others wanted state statutes revised to expand the definition of the "practice of medicine" to include all forms of non-medical healing. This approach had the tactical advantage of appearing less discriminatory toward a particular religious group, though such measures could, in actuality, be almost as restrictive in their ultimate effect as a specific legal injunction. Mark Twain—no friend of Christian Science—noted ironically in 1903 that "if the Second Advent should happen now," Jesus himself "could not heal the sick in the state of New York" under the medical practice acts then being proposed.[1]

Medical societies in virtually every state worked vigorously to mobilize support for these enactments. The *Albany Morning Express* reported in 1899 that Philadelphia physicians planned "to commence a national war against the Christian Scientists,"

Thomas C. Johnsen, in *Medical Heritage,* vol. 2, no. 1 (January–February 1986), pp. 70–78.

with its ultimate goal of persuading Congress to act against the group.[2] In New York several hundred physicians and a number of interested lawyers met at the Waldorf-Astoria hotel in the summer of 1899 to form a "Medical and Legal Relief Society." Their purpose was to lobby in the state legislature against Christian Scientists. The AMA [American Medical Association] went on record endorsing a Detroit physician's suggestion that candidates for the legislature be supported or opposed according to their position on the "legal toleration or recognition" of Christian Science—surely one of the more unusual political litmus tests in American history.[3]

These efforts met with surprisingly little success, considering that the Christian Scientists were hardly a serious political force. Their membership in some states included moderately influential civic leaders, but they had neither the political clout nor the legislative connections of organized medicine. Their chief asset was probably the strength of their convictions about the efficacy of spiritual healing—convictions they defended vigorously.

The American tradition of tolerance worked in the denomination's behalf—and continues to do so—because of what a New York newspaper called the "cumulative" experience of the movement in its healing practice.[4] Many non-adherents who had witnessed healings of Christian Scientists in their own communities spoke out strongly against restrictive measures—in 1903 in Eddy's native New Hampshire, a bill outlawing the practice of Christian Science by name was voted down overwhelmingly even "before the Christian Scientists of the state had time to oppose it."[5]

The issue was rarely settled so quickly in states where Christian Science was less familiar. Nevertheless, nearly every state legislature in the country had specifically rejected proscriptive proposals, sometimes on three or four occasions, by the decade after Eddy's death in 1910. In the few states where such measures were initially passed, governors actually vetoed them or they were revised in subsequent legislative sessions. In the wake of the court cases brought against Christian Science under medical licensing laws, many states incorporated explicit "saving" clauses into their codes affirming the legality of the practice of spiritual healing.

From the Christian Scientists' standpoint, such recognition

was a matter of equitable treatment under the law, not of preferential legislation. As former Iowa Judge Clifford Smith explained in 1914, in *Christian Science: Its Legal Status,* they did not seek any "special privilege" or legal establishment of religion, but solely to preserve rights threatened by efforts to prohibit their system of healing.[6] The Smith book, probably the denomination's most thorough articulation of its position, was subtitled *A Defense of Human Rights;* the fact that the subtitle did not include the term *religious rights* was significant, since Christian Scientists saw the issue under consideration as far more than a narrow Constitutional question, or even than merely one of religious freedom. Judge Smith acknowledged, in any case, that such freedom is not absolute, and that it involves not only rights but also responsibilities—what Christian Scientists could properly expect from society and what society could reasonably demand from them.

Christian Scientists saw due regard for public health as a responsibility. In 1901 Eddy herself issued a statement instructing church members to diligently obey legal requirements on vaccination and reporting of suspected contagious conditions—citing Jesus' injunction to "render to Caesar the things that are Caesar's."[7] While the *JAMA* [*Journal of the American Medical Association*] pronounced this statement an implicit "confession" of the failure of Christian Science, her student Alfred Farlow pointed out that it was consistent with the broad emphasis of her teaching of respect for the rights of others: "I readily concede that Christian Scientists must not attempt to set aside the laws which stand for the general good of any community." Farlow admitted that "there may be unwise and careless Christian Scientists, who do and say unwise things," but insisted that "such people would be unwise and careless" whatever church they belonged to and could not be taken as representative.[8] In practice, the group's record of cooperation with public health authorities over many years has borne out the latter assertion.[9]

The most difficult issues of responsibility then, as now, involved the care of children. Christian Scientists could understand the "honest opinion" of doctors on the necessity for medical treatment—most having earlier shared this opinion themselves.[10] They did not believe, a church official told the *New York Evening Telegram* in 1903, that a parent simply has the right to "sacrifice" a child "to his own belief. . . . I would state without reservation that he has no such right."[11] But neither did they feel that conscientious reliance on spiritual instead of medical means for healing should automatically be defined by the law as neglect. Their position, which sought a balance between parental and state responsibilities, received considerable support in the press, and eventually in the law. The newspaper publisher William Randolph Hearst, a non-adherent, wrote about one "miracle" in which his own infant son, in critical condition because of a closed pylorus but considered too frail to survive an operation, was healed overnight after a Christian Science practitioner was called in as a last resort.[12] Similar experiences led other parents to feel the same kind of gratitude. Rightly or wrongly, Christian Scientists maintained that their overall record in the care of children was comparable to care rendered by others. They held that decisions on treatment of their own children should be left to the children's "natural guardians, who are at the bedside and to whom the little one's life means more than it does to all other persons."[13]

When the distinguished medically trained philosopher William James broke with his peers to testify against a medical bill targeted at Christian Science in Massachusetts, he confided to a friend that he "never did anything that required as much moral effort" in his life. "Bah! I'm sick of the whole business," he wrote in 1898, "and I well know how all my colleagues at the Medical School, who go only by the label, will view me and my efforts." James found the prevailing "medical materialism" in the orthodox practice of the profession inadequate. He was neither versed in nor drawn to the theories of the Christian Scientists, but as an exponent of pragmatism in medicine as well as philosophy he saw their "facts" as "startling" and did not wish to see closed a potential avenue of healing: "Why this mania for more laws? Why seek to stop the really extremely important experiences which these peculiar creatures are rolling up?"[14]

Few critics charged that testimonies published in the church's periodicals were dishonest, but from a medical perspective they were hardly written with laboratory exactitude. By their nature they involved life situations rather than clinical case studies. Traditional doctors produced a veritable subgenre of popular articles "debunking" these testimonies and attributing the phenomena of healing to a standard litany of causal factors: time, suggestion, *vis medicatrix naturae,* the placebo effect, misdiagnosis, the power of will. The challenge to the profession, Dr. John Chadwick Oliver told colleagues in 1899, was to have charity for the Christian Scientists' superstitions and "educate and enlighten" them as to the "real foundation" of their experiences.[15]

The question would not be resolved so easily. Christian Scientists maintained that their practice was often dismissed by the medical profession irrespective of results because it challenged conventional methods. As Clifford Smith remarked, it was often simply assumed "that the drug system is scientific in its practice and certain in its results; that Christian Science does not heal anybody, or if it did, they were not sick; that Christian Scientists are actuated by religious fanaticism and not by reason and convincing experience. . . ."[16] The situation was complicated both by the dramatic publicity given individual failures and the frequent misattribution to Christian Science of cases in which it was involved marginally if at all—as in the death of the American novelist Harold Frederic in 1898, which became something of a medical *cause célèbre.* On the other hand, it was undeniable that a large number of those who testified to healings in Christian Science had turned to it in what were to all appearances circumstances in which attending physicians had given up.

Medical practitioners themselves faced an ethical challenge in maintaining objectivity when evaluating a massive body of testimony that ran contrary to their predilections. In 1907, the *Journal of the American Medical Association* published a detailed medical history of an unexplained case believed to be the "first instance recorded of recovery from generalized blastomycosis,"[17] but refused to print a letter from the husband of the patient pointing out that the recovery took place only when a Christian Science practitioner was called.[18]

Alfred Farlow noted sensibly enough that "the recitation of Christian Science healings" even with scientific diagnosis does not answer the question of their medical significance, though it points to the breadth of the experience on which Christian Scientists' convictions—and their claim to legal toleration—have been based.[19] People might differ as to the explanation for these results, Farlow acknowledged, but that there were results not easily explained away he saw as more than a matter of purely subjective faith. As the early controversy over the movement abated, the practice of spiritual healing became less a topic of headlines, but it continued as a quiet way of life in many thousands of Christian Science families—a collective "test" of spiritual healing on an unprecedented scale.

The transformation of medical practice in this century has changed markedly the terrain in which Christian Scientists pursue such healing, but not the nature of their commitment. This commitment runs strikingly counter to the pervasive influence of secular medicine in Western culture—a contrast which clearly places great demands on the Christian Scientists for actual healing results if their claim to toleration is to remain viable. At the same time, the "materialism" that William James saw as underlying conventional medicine has produced its own excesses as well as successes. The dilemmas arising from purely mechanistic approaches have prompted new and serious consideration of the spiritual dimensions of health care—the role of patients in their own recovery, the distinction between healing in the fullest sense and medical engineering, the whole range of concerns deemed "the nonscientific side of medicine."[20]

If any point of consensus can be found, it may come from this direction. The influence of spiritual factors in well-being is a truism in medical as in religious circles, but in practical terms "most of us," as one Quaker commentator on healing has written, consciously or unconsciously "assume the supremacy of mechanical determination and the helplessness of love."[21] In no respect was Eddy's teaching more radical than in its insistence that mankind has barely begun to understand the full therapeutic power of love (or as she would have it, of the Love which is God). Eddy saw such understanding as a discipline quite as rigorous, in its own way, as the quest of modern medicine for scientific legitimacy. The challenge growing out of the experience of Christian Scientists lies in recognizing that the deepest spiritual realities in human life are not peripheral to, but at the center of, any truly scientific mode of healing.

1. Mark Twain, *Christian Science* (1907; reprint, New York: Prometheus Books, 1986), p. 80.

2. *Albany Morning Express* excerpt from "Persecuting a Cult" reprinted in *Christian Science Sentinel,* July 13, 1899.

3. "A Test for 'Christian Scientists,' "*JAMA,* vol. 34 (1900), p. 759.

4. Excerpt from *New York Morning Telegraph* reprinted in *Christian Science and Legislation* (Boston: The Christian Science Publishing Society, 1909), p. 128.

5. *Christian Science and Legislation,* p. 128.

6. *Ibid.,* p. 35.

7. Mary Baker Eddy, *The First Church of Christ, Scientist, and Miscellany* (Boston: The First Church of Christ, Scientist, 1913), pp. 219–222.

8. Excerpt from *Boston Post* reprinted in *Christian Science Sentinel,* March 15, 1900, p. 453.

9. Cf. Massachusetts Department of Public Health, "Christian Science and Community Medicine," *New England Journal of Medicine,* vol. 290, no. 7 (February 14, 1974), pp. 401–402.

10. Alfred Farlow, "Plea for Toleration of Their Honest Beliefs," *Christian Science Sentinel,* March 22, 1900, p. 469.

11. William D. McCrackan, Excerpt from "Freedom of Choice" in *New York Evening Telegram* reprinted in *Christian Science Sentinel,* April 11, 1903, p. 506.

12. William R. Hearst, *Faith* pamphlet (San Simeon, CA, Privately printed, 1941).

13. Clifford P. Smith, *Faith* pamphlet.

14. William James, *The Letters of William James,* ed. Henry James (Boston: Atlantic Monthly Press, 1920), pp. 66–72.

15. John Chadwick Oliver, " 'Christian Science' and Allied Fads," *JAMA,* vol. 32 (1899), pp. 1363–65.

16. Clifford P. Smith, " 'Christian Science' and Allied Fads," *JAMA,* vol. 32 (1899), p. 51.

17. J. B. Herrick, "Generalized Blastomycosis: Report of a Case with Recovery," *JAMA,* vol. 49 (1907), p. 328.

18. B. O. Flower, *Christian Science as a Religious Belief and a Therapeutic Agent* (Boston: Twentieth Century, 1909), pp. 105–115.

19. Alfred Farlow, Reply to "Review of Rev. Lyman Powell's Book," *Boston Times,* January 11, 1908.

20. D. Bok, "Needed: A New Way to Train Doctors," *Harvard Magazine,* May–June 1984, p. 35.

21. C. Murphy, "The Image That Heals," *Pastoral Psychology,* vol. 22 (February 1971), p. 41.

The climate of legal toleration that finally emerged through the process described in the preceding selection has prevailed for a good part of this century. Christian Scientists have been allowed to practice their spiritual method of healing, for the most part accommodated specifically by the law. During the last decade, however, currents have been shifting. In a handful of cases parents are facing legal prosecution for their reliance on Christian Science healing for their children.

Obviously no system of healing, Christian Science included, can claim a perfect record. The death of a child is always tragic. Since deaths under medical care are not routinely prosecuted, however, many have questioned the justice of the cases brought against Christian Scientists. As Eugene D. Robin, a professor at the Stanford University Medical School, commented in an article on this issue: "And suppose every physician whose errors led to the death of a patient was sent to jail. There would be no room to imprison all of us doctors."[1]

In the course of this public controversy, Christian Scientists have spoken out about their personal experience of spiritual healing and the continued need for evenhandedness and toleration in approaching these matters. Several examples of such statements are provided here. The first, "Prayer's Not a Gamble," is an essay by a Christian Scientist, a former university teacher, that appeared in *U.S. News & World Report.* It is followed by an excerpt from a "Dialogue on Healing in *Update,*" a reply by a Church spokesman in Denmark in a Lutheran publication that had carried an article on the issue of

Christian Science care for children. The reply refers to some of the deep convictions about God and the practical nature of His love that underlie Christian Scientists' commitment to healing.

---

1. Eugene D. Robin, "It Wasn't a Crime but an Error of Judgment," *The Press-Enterprise* [Riverside, CA], June 13, 1988.

# Prayer's Not a Gamble

I'm a concerned grandmother—concerned about the way the media cover criminal prosecutions in my state, California.

Several parents, who are Christian Scientists, have been charged with murder and manslaughter for turning to spiritual healing instead of seeking medical aid for a child who died.

I can't speak for the parents, but as a Christian Scientist I know how much they loved these children. And I know they are not criminals any more than the many equally loving parents who have had a child die under medical care.

My own family has relied on Christian Science healing for four generations. I have never considered prayer a gamble. Please understand: I'm not speaking of some crude kind of "faith healing" that implores God to heal and says it was His will if nothing happens. I'm speaking of responsible spiritual healing practiced now over a century by many perfectly normal citizens and caring parents.

I'm concerned about not being taken seriously—that nobody in the media (and this includes *U.S. News & World Report*) is really taking into account that these healings have been happening over many years. Not just in my family, not just my friends. I'm speaking of the massive, long-term experience in a whole denomination.

These healings just don't seem to register. Again and again, articles are written as if they had never occurred. It seems as if a portion of our society just can't stand to have its "enlightened" secular assumptions questioned by seriously considering the evidence of Christian healing in our time.

Lois O'Brien, in *U.S. News & World Report,* April 28, 1986, p. 81.

Christians in many denominations are taking spiritual healing more and more seriously. Why then should it be dismissed in the media and in the framing of public policy?

In a country founded on a quest for religious freedom, there needs to be room for differences—even major ones. This is *not* to say that religious freedom gives anyone the right to neglect or mistreat their children. Or that Christian Scientists any more than others should be given a blank ticket. But where there is a caring home environment and a track record of healing in many thousands of families, the law should not take away the choices of those who love these precious children most. Nor should the media ignore the overwhelming record of good care they have been given.

# A Dialogue on Healing
# in Update

The death of even a single child is as agonizing for Christian Scientists as it is for any others who cherish children and hold every human life sacred.

If such incidents were typical of Christian Scientists' past experience, few would remain Christian Scientists. We do not turn to spiritual healing in order to be loyal to a religious doctrine. The human situation cannot be reduced to the scenario of "benighted believers" versus "enlightened proponents of medicine."

In fact, both sides in this exchange do agree on one crucial point. They both see *compassion* as the essential issue. But is this compassion merely a valuable "extra" in an otherwise mechanistic or biophysical process of restoring sick bodies to health? Or is the selfless love to which the New Testament bears witness actually rooted in divine love, and therefore the most powerful source of healing in human experience?

This latter contention may not seem very remarkable until one begins to take it seriously.

On what they believe to be this thoroughly biblical basis, Christian Scientists hold that the pain and suffering of the mortal condition are consequences of human blindness to the power and reality of love as revealed in the life and works of Jesus Christ. To believe less, they feel, would be virtually to lay all

Stig K. Christiansen, in *Update: A Quarterly Journal on New Religious Movements,* vol. 9, no. 3 (September 1985), pp. 61–62.

human tragedy at the feet of God. But fulfilling Jesus' commission to all his followers to heal the sick affirms the power of the gospel in the most practical terms.

The prayer that brings about such healing is spoken of by Christian Scientists as treatment, because they see it as a spiritual discipline which effectively eradicates the mental elements of fear, ignorance, and sin to which all human beings are subject and which lie at the root of disease.

Obviously, Christian Scientists recognize the distance they have to go in realizing the full potential of spiritual healing. But would even the most conscientious doctor claim a perfect record for the medical profession? The key point is that, for the Christian Scientist, treatment through prayer is an active process which long-term experience has shown secures remarkably consistent results. In the words of the Founder of Christian Science, it is "the utilization of the love wherewith God loves us."[1]

To deny that this power can be utilized is tantamount to denying that it exists. The debate over Christian Science healing for children, therefore, involves far more than the specifics of Christian Science theology or the evaluation of its very substantial healing record and impact on Christian healing in general. It involves the whole question of what the gospel itself means to the world if the spiritual healing it teaches is a sham and if the love supremely exemplified by Jesus cannot make a healing difference in present experience.

As thoughtful Christians have always known, living consistently in the light of this love is not easy. Christian Scientists certainly recognize how much further they have to go in this respect. In one sense it would be much easier not to make the effort. But the many who have seen or experienced the effects of such love in actual healing understandably feel it to be, in the Psalmist's words, "a very present help"[2] more basic and dependable than any other in caring for people's needs.

Christian Scientists see this insight as one which, far from being outmoded, is only just beginning to be explored.

---

1. Mary Baker Eddy, *No and Yes* (Boston: The First Church of Christ, Scientist, 1891), p. 39.
2. Ps. 46:1.

Christian Scientists' practice of spiritual healing for the care of children has also raised significant constitutional and legal issues for contemporary American society. An article by David N. Williams, the Church's representative on federal questions in Washington, DC, provides an overview on these issues. The article was written for the magazine *Church and State,* published by Americans United for Separation of Church and State.

# Christian Science and the Care of Children: The Constitutional Issues

Children's health care has become a major issue on the national agenda in recent years.

For those who care about the First Amendment as well as families, one particular aspect of this issue has presented something of a moral dilemma: the care of children whose parents rely on healing prayer in time of sickness. Six cases now in the courts have focused attention on this issue as it relates to Christian Scientists, a group long known both for the practice of spiritual healing and for a strong tradition of family life.

Should spiritual healing as Christian Scientists practice it be accommodated in state law, or should that practice be restricted by state statute and parents who have lost children under spiritual treatment be subject to criminal prosecution? Americans should consider the following points as they seek to answer that question.

The formation of public policy should not begin with the premise that such healing is irrelevant or imaginary—which would pit the state against religious life—but should broadly and fairly reflect actual experience. Yet behind the current prosecutions of Christian Science parents is the assumption that reliance on healing through prayer is the equivalent of "martyring" children. Prosecutors in these cases have often cited the legal principle that parents can "martyr themselves for religious reasons, but have no right to martyr their children."

That is a well-founded principle as it applies to religious practices that *are* harmful or irresponsible. What has not been considered is the possibility that serious spiritual healing might not

David N. Williams, in *Church and State,* September 1989, pp. 19–20.

belong in that category—that the benefits for turning consistently to this way of healing might be real and significant.

As both an ethical and constitutional principle, Christian Scientists agree that the responsibility of parents to maintain the health and welfare of children is primary. The question is whether a religious mode of healing and caring for children should be ruled out essentially because it *is* religious. The constitutional issue in the current debate over spiritual healing for children revolves around the free exercise and establishment clauses of the First Amendment: "Congress shall make no law respecting an establishment of religion or prohibiting the free exercise thereof." But *no one*—Christian Scientists included—is saying that parents' religious freedom supervenes children's right to live, or that the First Amendment, or any legal or religious principle, entitles them or others to "martyr" children on the altar of their religious beliefs.

Those who maintain that the state should prohibit the practice of spiritual healing for children frequently cite the Supreme Court decision in *Reynolds v. United States* (1879) to the effect that while the right of religious belief is absolute and unrestricted, the right to act on religious belief is not. While limitations on religious practice are sometimes warranted, high court decisions since *Reynolds* have included repeated reminders that it is the clear intent of the Constitution to protect the "free *exercise* of religious belief" and not just belief itself. And as established in *Sherbert v. Verner* (1963) and subsequent cases, the state must prove a truly compelling interest in restricting any religious practice, showing that no less restrictive means "are available to achieve" that interest.

In other words, First Amendment rights are so basic to society that free exercise must be guarded up to the very point at which overriding state interest compels us to place these limits. In view of the fundamental role in our tradition of the right of free exercise, the burden of proof that the state has a compelling interest to restrict Christian Science healing for children must lie on the opponents of that practice who wish their view written into law.

Granting that the state's duty to protect the health of children is sufficiently basic to override free exercise of religious belief, does that duty in the case of Christian Scientists' children warrant restriction of the practice of spiritual healing on their behalf?

Any defensible answer to this question must be based on more than mere assumptions plucked from the air of the current views within a segment of our society. Even taking into account recent medical advances, insofar as the law is concerned, a method of treatment must be judged by its results rather than by the a priori assumption that one method is inherently superior to another.

Over the twenty-year period from 1969 to 1988, for example, *The Christian Science Journal* and the *Christian Science Sentinel* published over 7,100 testimonies of physical healings. While these accounts are definitely religious documents rather than clinical histories, some 2,338 of the healings described involved medically diagnosed conditions. In many more cases the testimonies implied that there had been diagnosis but did not specifically state it. Many—literally hundreds—of the diagnoses involved x-rays or were confirmed by second opinions by specialists or other physicians.

The range of conditions healed included congenital, degenerative, infectious, neurological, and other disorders, some considered terminal or incurable. These testimonies included over 2,400 healings of children. More than 600 of these involved medically diagnosed conditions, life-threatening as well as less serious, including spinal meningitis (in several cases after antibiotics failed to help), pneumonia and double pneumonia, diabetes, food poisoning, heart disorders, loss of eyesight from chemical burns, pleurisy, stomach obstruction, epilepsy, goiter, leukemia, malaria, mastoiditis, polio, rheumatic fever, and ruptured appendix.

Obviously, these healings represent a body of individual cases rather than controlled experimental results. By its sheer volume and variety, however, this body of cases underscores the fact that healing in Christian Science has been regular and tangible— not the exception—and that it cannot be dismissed as merely "doing nothing" or waiting on natural processes.

Christian Scientists acknowledge that failures have occurred under their form of treatment just as they have under medical care, in pediatric as in other kinds of cases. Physicians argue, understandably, that some who have died might have been saved under their care. Yet there is no evidence that disproportionate numbers of Christian Scientists' children have been lost. In fact, such figures as are available would indicate that the very opposite is the case.

Christian Scientists feel that a greater number of children would, in effect, have been "martyred" to medical technology if their parents hadn't had the freedom to turn in a wholly different, spiritual direction for healing. The small number of deaths of children in Christian Science families are clearly *exceptions*— no less tragic than similar occurrences under medical care, but also no more common proportionately and no more criminal.

Taking account of the positive evidence for spiritual healing and other available indications of its relative healing record in comparison to medical treatment, it cannot plausibly be maintained that there is a compelling state interest in restricting Christian Science practice for children. Laws in most states have traditionally sought a balance between accommodation of responsible spiritual healing and the power of the courts to order medical treatment in extreme individual cases. This balance preserves the state's authority under the doctrine of *parens patriae,* while recognizing that there has not been a demonstrable compelling interest which would warrant drastically restricting spiritual healing for children across the board.

Still, Christian Scientists would by no means wish a general legal accommodation to furnish an umbrella for the protection of nonmedical healing that the state may well have a compelling reason to restrain. There are fundamental differences among the various groups that practice some form of nonmedical healing. A growing consensus, including Christian Scientists, holds that God's will is *always* for life and healing and approaches the healing ministry on the basis of this conviction. But some who practice what is conventionally known as "faith healing" accept disease and death as God's will when a healing does not occur.

Many, however, ask how our laws functioning under the First

Amendment can implement state accommodation of responsible spiritual healing, without at the same time protecting any and every kind of religious healing, regardless of whether it can provide the kind of creditable record that justifies such protection. There is a well-established tradition, based on such Supreme Court decisions as *Wisconsin v. Yoder,* for legal accommodation of special needs of such diverse religious groups as the Amish, the Seventh-day Adventists, Jews, and Roman Catholics. But can the state implement the free exercise clause of the First Amendment without violating the nonestablishment clause that directly precedes it?

If the issue were simply a matter of choosing between the merits of different *faiths,* the answer in constitutional terms must be clear and unequivocal: There is no constitutional basis for such discrimination, which would clearly violate the establishment clause of the First Amendment. If, however, grounds for accommodation were strictly *secular*—i.e., that all who sought it must give reasonable evidence of providing children with a responsible system of health care—the criteria for recognition would be secular and not religious, and no violation of the establishment clause would be involved.

These criteria constitute an ethic of responsibility for all who practice spiritual healing for children. On this basis, the hard-won legal right to practice spiritual healing does not provide unlimited license nor does it reflect state bias in anyone's favor. Rather, it reflects the warranted acknowledgment that parents can provide spiritual care for children in a context that fulfills the commonly acknowledged secular standard of responsibility.

Those who are uncomfortable with provisions recognizing responsible spiritual healing for children might wish to consider the alternative: If the state discriminated against such healing— not because it was ineffectual but only because it was not medical (at least in the conventional sense)—the result would be significant growth in the already discernible tendency for the state to become not only the prisoner but the *agent* of the secular assumptions of a portion of our society. As a May 1, [1989], editorial in the *Cincinnati Enquirer* noted, one of the current prosecutions of Christian Science parents "deserves watching for what it may signal about society's ability to substitute its precepts for religion's."

For this reason, all citizens, not just Christian Scientists or other advocates of spiritual healing, have a compelling interest in ensuring that our laws do not needlessly discriminate against religion and translate the secular assumptions of some into laws that all are compelled to obey.

In this "golden age" of technology, why invest so much prayer and effort in a spiritual approach to healing? Christian Scientists are likely to answer by pointing to family members or friends who have been healed, often after conventional medical treatment could do no more for them. They might go on to talk about changes that spiritual healing has brought to their character, providing a whole new outlook on life. They might say there simply isn't anything deeper.

In fact, Christian Scientists believe that the future of Christianity is tied directly to the act of bearing witness to God's power to heal—just as Jesus' mission was inseparable from his ministry of healing.

"The Spirituality of Mankind," by Allison W. Phinney, Jr., published as a lead editorial in the weekly *Christian Science Sentinel,* relates the right to practice Christian Science healing to the broad issue of religious freedom. It is followed by "Christian Healing—'Indispensable,' " an interview with Lee Z. Johnson, Archivist of The Mother Church, showing why Christian Scientists continue to see spiritual healing as indispensable even in today's technological world.

# The Spirituality of Mankind

In the early years of this century, a concerted attempt was made in the United States to suppress Christian Science and render its practice illegal. Society consciously rejected the attempt on grounds that it interfered with religious rights under the Constitution of the United States.

Thinking people—including legislators, newspaper editors, state governors—recognized the threat of class legislation. They also saw that the campaign represented a form of persecution and intolerance at odds with the very spirit of a country which has its roots deep in the principle of religious liberty.

As one paper editorialized: "In this country a man has the right to worship God as he pleases. The Christian Scientist is certainly religious. His belief is a religion, and the fact that it inculcates healing without medicine, as taught by Jesus Christ, should not debar him from the protection of law, nor make him an object of tyrannical legislation."[1]

But in 1984 two mothers who are Christian Scientists have been charged in the courts of California with reliance on Christian Science instead of medical care for their children. In one instance the father of the child and a Christian Science practitioner have also been charged. Counts include involuntary manslaughter, second-degree murder, and felony child endangerment.

Parents who customarily rely on medical care have had children pass on, but neither these parents nor the medical doctors

Allison W. Phinney, Jr., in *Christian Science Sentinel,* September 3, 1984, pp. 1529–33.

who treated the children have been charged by the state with any crime. The assumption obviously is that the proper practice of medicine cannot be faulted when it fails to heal but that a Christian Scientist who fails in some instances to fulfill the Biblical promise of Christian healing may be "guilty" of a crime.

To bring the issues into sharper focus, one needs to understand what has been happening over the past seventy or eighty years. At the time of early efforts to pass restrictive legislation, an editorial in a New Jersey newspaper commented: ". . . the fundamental principle involved is the right of the person who is sick or in pain to seek relief where he thinks he can get it. This is an affair of personal liberty."[2] It is in fact *no longer* considered a matter of personal liberty by many government officials, though this is not comprehended as yet by the general public.

Unlike the situation eighty years ago, medicine now shapes society's thought much more extensively than do considerations of religion and constitutional law. Thus medical treatment is increasingly mandated by law and government for adults as well as children. It is a trend that has foreboding parallels. In most countries where centralized authoritarian government has gained a foothold, and wherever totalitarian government has control, religious life has been shrewdly regulated and subtly diminished.

Yet at the same time there are heartening signs of currents of thought in the world that point in a very different direction. To mention only a few, there is continuing interest in Christian healing on the part of some reputable and theologically responsible Christian groups (not fringe-group faith healers). There is a growing understanding that mental factors underlie illness and health. And questions are being raised even from within the medical profession as to whether prevailing medical theory actually offers sufficient explanation of an individual's whole being to be taken as the infallible law for living that it has become.

In addition, for the first time in perhaps thirty years a new assurance that religious thought can be considered intellectually viable has begun to surface. And a hunger for spirituality, especially among young people, is rapidly increasing.

Christian Scientists are called to realize the breadth and significance of the issues that are being tested late in this twentieth century. It is not simply their own religious freedom that is in question, but the continuing development of mankind's spirituality and the survival of faith in God as something more than impractical emotion.

Christian Scientists' awakened prayer and their willingness to work are vital to the outcome. Their fidelity will determine the future of their Cause and have significant bearing on Christianity as a whole for centuries to come.

Mary Baker Eddy, who discovered and founded Christian Science, foresaw an unavoidable conflict between materialistic hypotheses and the advancing spiritual comprehension of mankind. But she also had deep trust in God's impulsion and His disposal of events. She writes in her *Message to The Mother Church for 1900:* "All that worketh good is some manifestation of God asserting and developing good. . . . Conflict and persecution are the truest signs that can be given of the greatness of a cause or of an individual, provided this warfare is honest and a world-imposed struggle. Such conflict never ends till unconquerable right is begun anew, and hath gained fresh energy and final victory."[3]

Until now, hatred, prejudice, or sheer unfamiliarity has attempted to paint a largely absurd picture of Christian Science. But this need not continue as public thought more intelligently and calmly understands the issues. Mrs. Eddy once remarked at a high point of public criticism: "The combined efforts of the materialistic portion of the pulpit and press in 1885, to retard by misrepresentation the stately goings of Christian Science, are giving it new impetus and energy; calling forth the *vox populi* and directing more critical observation to its uplifting influence upon the health, morals, and spirituality of mankind."[4] And this certainly proved to be the case in the years immediately following.

The facts will come into sharper focus today also, as they did one hundred years ago. Christian Science, contrary to recent public misrepresentation, is not positive thinking, mind cure, or an alternative health care system. It is a profoundly Christian denomination, with its priority on the worship of God and the living of a Christian life.

Christian Science is not naively unaware of the human condition. It doesn't, contrary to deliberately misleading depiction, inculcate blind optimism but fosters independent thought, understanding, and reasonable caring for human needs. Since this really is the case, it must finally be found to be the fact. An individual member of the Church of Christ, Scientist, is of course left wholly free to make what must ultimately be an individual choice in regard to Christian Science healing or medicine; he or she is not under righteous judgment or pressure from peers. It is simply not that kind of church.

But those who choose to rely on Christian Science are not in their view sanguinely choosing nothing. They are choosing the tangible somethingness of divine law—the healing power of God—that has been effectively demonstrated in the lives of some families for four and five generations. In a ten-year span from 1971 to 1981, for example, well over 4,000 testimonies of healing and regeneration appeared in *The Christian Science Journal* and the *Christian Science Sentinel*.

Slightly over 1,400 of these referred to the healing of a specific physical problem. Among diseases and disorders named as having been healed were multiple sclerosis, epilepsy, curvature of the spine, cancer, cataract, glaucoma, diabetes, spinal meningitis, blindness, and more.

Out of 1,430 cases specifying a physical problem, 655 or 46 percent had been medically diagnosed, either prior to the individual's choice to rely on Christian Science or because of other circumstances beyond his control. Some 102 or 7 percent had been X-rayed, and 141 or 10 percent of the healings were later confirmed by a follow-up diagnosis. From a total of 269 children's healings, 138 or 51 percent had been medically diagnosed.*

There is little likelihood that even physical evidence will convince the adamantly skeptical thought. It did not do so in Jesus' time. But because God Himself, divine Principle, is the attraction behind mankind's gravitation toward spirituality, the ultimate victory is assured. It will be hastened, however, by prayer and strong demonstration of the spiritual facts which dissolve con-

---

*For an update on these figures, see "Christian Science and the Care of Children: The Constitutional Issues," page 181 of this book.

fusion and cut through mesmeric misconceptions to reveal the naturalness of justice, truth, and spirituality.

It is a time that makes new demands on serious Christians and Christian Scientists precisely because the potential for the spiritual progress of mankind is so great. This latter part of the twentieth century requires less complacency, more continuous watching and praying, more of the spirit of the living Christ. As the Master promised on the eve of his greatest demonstration: "These things I have spoken unto you, that in me ye might have peace. In the world ye shall have tribulation: but be of good cheer; I have overcome the world."[5]

1. *Christian Science and Legislation* (Boston: The Christian Science Publishing Society, 1909), p. 109.

2. *Ibid.,* p. 113.

3. Mary Baker Eddy, *Message to The Mother Church for 1900* (Boston: The First Church of Christ, Scientist, 1900), p. 10.

4. Mary Baker Eddy, *Miscellaneous Writings* (Boston: The First Church of Christ, Scientist, 1896), p. 245.

5. John 16:33.

# Christian Healing—"Indispensable"

*Interviewer:* Could you say that Mary Baker Eddy saw healing as the thrust, the cutting edge, of Christian Science?

*Mr. Johnson:* Most definitely! We, of course, share immensely in the fundamentals held by true Christians of all denominations. Mrs. Eddy writes, "As the ages advance in spirituality, Christian Science will be seen to depart from the trend of other Christian denominations in no wise except by increase of spirituality."[1]

But she also speaks of the absolute necessity for our Church to sustain healing as "the principal characteristic of its denomination."[2] Elsewhere she writes: "In different ages the divine idea assumes different forms, according to humanity's needs. In this age it assumes, more intelligently than ever before, the form of Christian healing. This is the babe we are to cherish."[3]

*Interviewer:* But why? Was the emphasis on healing just a matter of what appealed to the public or what would bring Christian Science to public attention?

*Mr. Johnson:* Neither, as I read it. Her call for healing went far, far deeper than that—even to, as just mentioned, the "increase of spirituality." Healing is essential to achieve the ends of Christian Science, which are, of course, moral and spiritual growth. Healing demonstrates—that is, illustrates for the student—the availability of spiritual power through Christian Science. Mrs. Eddy states, "Demonstration is indispensable to the understanding of this Science."[4] "Indispensable," not a by-product, not a luxury.

---

Lee Zeunert Johnson, Interview, in *Christian Science Sentinel,* February 3, 1986, pp. 191–196.

*Interviewer:* In other words, the student of Christian Science learns from the healing work as he can in no other way?

*Mr. Johnson:* Can you imagine a chemistry student who never held a beaker in his hand or an astronomy student who never looked through a telescope? Healing is the means by which we attain that goal stated by Christ Jesus: "Ye shall know the truth, and the truth shall make you free."[5]

Mrs. Eddy writes, "The question, What is Truth, is answered by demonstration,—by healing both disease and sin; and this demonstration shows that Christian healing confers the most health and makes the best men."[6]

*Interviewer:* Is Christian healing, as she saw it, a way of improving the world, another technology, so to speak?

*Mr. Johnson:* No, in the sense that Mrs. Eddy was devoted overwhelmingly to the purpose of a reformation that would change humanity radically, not just make it more comfortable with things the way they are, with the materialism of our time. Yes, in the sense that she looked forward to the deliverance of mankind from all of the tragedy, ugliness, and craziness of the world. But she saw this deliverance not as a human method but as salvation in the deepest religious sense. She says of her Church, "From first to last The Mother Church seemed type and shadow of the warfare between the flesh and Spirit, even that shadow whose substance is the divine Spirit, imperatively propelling the greatest moral, physical, civil, and religious reform ever known on earth."[7]

But she started from the premise that mankind on its own is actually powerless to reform itself. She saw that God, divine Mind, works through the Christ in human thought to heal hearts, minds, and lives, but that the carnal mind or matter "profiteth nothing." A favorite passage of mine is from *Unity of Good* where she says, "Is not our comforter always from outside and above ourselves?"[8]

Mrs. Eddy differed from other reformers in her understanding that the power required for reform derives from a science to be demonstrated! In Christian Science, Science and spirituality

meet; Christian Science is the Science of spirituality, of the relation of God and man. Setting forth this Science to be demonstrated in healing, she was totally serious about the availability
here and now of spiritual power—not electrical, chemical, or
nuclear power. She saw that mankind is absolutely dependent
upon this divine energy. Spiritual power to her was more tangible than the chairs we are sitting on.

Indeed, this reform has for its purpose the breaking *up* of
materialism, of the conventional materialistic ways by which
mankind does things, and the breaking *through* of reality, of the
spiritual, God-given facts of man and the universe.

*Interviewer:* And such healing by purely spiritual means is what
was to take the movement forward?

*Mr. Johnson:* Without question! Church members were, as was
said in her time, recruited from the graveyards.[9] Consider the
healing of a young man from Connecticut—Joseph Mann—
accidentally shot by a family member. His affidavit on the healing is published in the book *We Knew Mary Baker Eddy.*[10]

After no less than four doctors concluded that the bullet from
the .32 caliber revolver had touched his heart and nothing could
be done to save him, a Christian Science practitioner who was
in the vicinity took up the case. According to Mann: "Within
about fifteen minutes after Christian Science had been admitted
into our house I began suddenly to grow warm again under its
treatment. My breath was again revived and normal. I became
conscious, opened my eyes and knew I should not die, but
would live." And he did live, eventually serving Mrs. Eddy in
her household and becoming a Christian Science teacher.

Through the courtesy of a descendant of the Mann family, The
Mother Church recently received material dating back to the
early weeks of the accident. May I quote from letters, which,
though homespun, bear tribute to the grateful exuberance of
family members and neighbors who had seen a loved one return
from the brink?

First, from a letter written by Mann himself: "In three days I
was out of bed and playing my violin and dancing, a happier
family you never saw than we were. All the week nothing but

singing and dancing—everybody happy. We have just found God, and how to live free from sin, sickness, and death. . . . I shall devote the rest of my life to teaching people to find God and healing the sick. . . ."

A family member wrote, "Well, Joe is glad it happened; he said it [has] made such a change in us all. Especially Father; he needed a change; he was getting terrible lately. He doesn't drink any more gin. It was time for him to stop."[11]

*Interviewer:* Yet isn't it true that at the same time Christian Science roused interest it also attracted persecution?

*Mr. Johnson:* Unfortunately yes!

But whatever the challenge our neighbors and communities find in Christian Science, the challenge to you and me is even greater. The healing he (Jesus) expected his followers to do is the cutting edge not only of Christianity but also of the effort to save humanity from oblivion.

---

1. Mary Baker Eddy, *Miscellaneous Writings* (Boston: The First Church of Christ, Scientist, 1896), p. 21.

2. Mary Baker Eddy, n.d., Archives & Library, L09887.

3. Eddy, *Miscellaneous Writings,* p. 370.

4. Mrs. Eddy to E. J. Smith, January 2, 1884, Archives & Library, Z02064.

5. John 8:32.

6. Mary Baker Eddy, *Science and Health with Key to the Scriptures* (Boston: The First Church of Christ, Scientist, 1906), p. viii.

7. Mary Baker Eddy, *Pulpit and Press* (Boston: The First Church of Christ, Scientist, 1895), p. 20.

8. Mary Baker Eddy, *Unity of Good* (Boston: The First Church of Christ, Scientist, 1887), p. 18.

9. See Edward A. Kimball, *Answers to Questions* (Boston: The Christian Science Publishing Society, 1909), p. 19.

10. *We Knew Mary Baker Eddy* (Boston: The Christian Science Publishing Society, 1979), pp. 167–170.

11. Joseph Mann to his brothers and sisters, November 17, 1886, and letter from a family member, November 26, 1886, Archives & Library; text corrected.

$A$ final article, "The Future of Christian Healing: Fresh Convictions and Spiritual Realism," from another Church publication, the monthly *Christian Science Journal,* raises the question of whether Christian healing could be lost again, "just as it was in any cohesive sense" from early Christianity, unless some important issues are faced.

# The Future of Christian Healing:
## Fresh Convictions and
## Spiritual Realism

Fresh convictions concerning prayer, healing, and, most important, God, are cutting across years of entrenched public thought. The way is opening for people throughout Christian denominations to begin to experience more of the Bible's promise, specifically with regard to healing. The following are just a few of the signs of progress:

- "Taste and see how good our God can be" is often sung as a refrain in charismatic healing services. It's a direct challenge to the image of an angry, formidable God that has long dominated Christianity.

- Christians are increasingly rejecting the age-old notion that God causes or wants man to suffer. A letter to *The Lutheran* concludes: "It is just not scriptural to say that 'all suffering (or death) is God's will.' God's will in Christ is for wholeness and health."[1]

- In a well-publicized account, a young Protestant woman tells how she was able to do less and less physically and so began to do more and more spiritually while suffering from multiple sclerosis. Her minister said he often found her carrying on conversations with God when he visited her in the hospital. Although her condition had worsened for years and the medical prognosis at one point was that she would die shortly, probably in several weeks, she was instantaneously and completely restored as the result of prayer. Examining her after the healing, her doctor said it was as if she had never had the disease.[2]

---

David Brooks Andrews, in *The Christian Science Journal,* June 1988, pp. 30–33.

In many respects, it is as if stale air, built up over centuries, were being washed away by a cool breeze. In this changing mental climate, it shouldn't be surprising to hear of people from various Christian churches who have been cured of suffering and disabilities as the result of turning to God in prayer—even with a great deal more to learn about His nature.

A few basic convictions—such as those concerning God's goodness and His desire for our wholeness—are held in common by almost all who are engaged in the various ministries of healing. But beyond these convictions there's little real agreement. Practices range from prayer groups quietly meeting in individual homes to the drama of television evangelism, and from intercessory prayers to speaking in tongues. Readers may find some of these practices (and the convictions which underlie them) unfamiliar and at odds with their own approach to healing.

Looking at the sweep and development of Christianity, one might naturally ask: "Where does Christian Science come into the picture?" "What role do Christian Scientists have in the progress of Christian healing?"

The remarks of one of the more prominent figures in the history of contemporary Christian healing, Agnes Sanford, help to provide an answer. She said in a newspaper interview: "I think Christianity should be very grateful to Christian Scientists for reviving belief in spiritual healing. . . . The Christian Scientists have reawakened the world to the power of faith."[3] Her observation is based on the fact that Mary Baker Eddy, the Founder of Christian Science, practiced and taught Christian healing well before the revival of interest at the beginning of this century. This point was echoed recently by a United Methodist minister, J. Ellsworth Kalas, who said in a sermon: ". . . the general body of Christendom was forced to ponder the emergence of the Christian Science movement, and thus to ask itself if perhaps God was raising up this new body to fill a gap which basic Protestantism had neglected."[4]

But many who have acknowledged the historic role of Christian Science in awakening Christian churches to New Testament healing have gone on to proclaim, in no uncertain terms, that Christian Science is now obsolete, since many Protestant churches have started up ministries of healing. This line of reasoning is usually offered with unquestioned assurance as if it were wholly reasonable and natural.

But has Christian Science completed its service to Christianity? Should Christian Scientists now yield to less demanding and more widely accepted forms of healing? Would the ministry of healing within other Christian churches really be better off without the existence and commitment of the Church that was established wholly to restore primitive Christianity and its healing? There is immense evidence for a strong and well-reasoned "No" on all counts!

When I talked not long ago with a United Church of Christ minister, she argued against rejecting Christian Science outright, saying that it "has been there all the way through, doing its own thing in a quiet unobtrusive manner, which over the long haul tends to give it credence as something to be dialogued with *at the very least.*" Whether others agree fully with it or not, Christian Science offers a unique and fresh perspective on many widely held assumptions.

For instance, Mrs. Eddy took a strikingly realistic position on what's involved in establishing and preserving pure Christian healing today. Realism is not necessarily a popular view, particularly in the midst of the enthusiasm, self-promotion, and promises generated by many healing ministries today. Nevertheless, Christian Science warns that genuine spiritual healing could easily be lost, just as it was, in any cohesive sense, not many centuries after Christ Jesus' ministry, unless important issues are faced squarely and honestly, by individuals and churches.

The key factors on which the progress and survival of pure Christian healing hinge are related to an unavoidable and primary issue: do we, Christian Scientists included, attempt to use the human mind—with its familiar habits and what may appear to be insignificant weaknesses—to practice healing? Or is our healing ministry built upon the very act of yielding any personal sense of mind to God as the only Mind, the source of all true thought and being?

The answer to these questions may seem obvious. Christian Science teaches that the first approach is to build on sand, wholly incapable of supporting healing in any permanent sense. The latter is to build on the rock. While it may be easy to respond to these questions in theory, it's a different matter to bring their penetrating light directly to bear on one's own practice of healing.

Merely being a church member—regularly attending Christian Science services, reading the Bible Lesson-Sermon,[5] saying the Lord's Prayer—does not guarantee an answer or the assurance that one is actually contributing to the permanency of Christian healing. This issue calls for deep self-examination.

Facing it, we may wonder just what it means to use the human mind to practice healing. Isn't everything in this life accomplished through the human mind anyway? It may seem impossible to conceive of any alternative to human reason, emotions, opinions, reactions. After all, they claim to be the only perspective, the only basis for understanding or action, the only self we know.

Through a deep search of the Bible, testing its promise in her everyday life, Mrs. Eddy found a different self altogether, an identity that was wholly given to her, and to each one of us, directly by God. It's an identity that is spiritual and good and discoverable here and now. To turn consistently to God instead of material evidence for one's bearings and life is to find this identity and to build scientifically on the foundation of Christianity. Mrs. Eddy found this approach to Christianity (which she called Christian Science) to challenge the entire premise of mortal selfhood. With characteristic bluntness, she wrote in the denominational textbook, *Science and Health,* "The human mind is opposed to God and must be put off, as St. Paul declares."[6] In this light, the human or mortal mind can be identified as all thought that opposes God. And to the degree that this mind is put off, one's real, beautiful, complete identity appears, bearing healing.

The most serious threat to the progress of healing in our lives may occur when the very mentality which ultimately opposes God is not put off and instead is permitted to go through the motions of worshiping and serving Him, even praying for healing. Although this counterfeit approach may at first bring a change of symptoms, it offers no solid foundation for the development of Christian healing in our experience and for "working out your own salvation," as Paul admonishes us.

Adopting the mere appearance of prayer without substantial changes in one's human nature is not only a threat to healing in our individual lives but is precisely what led to the eventual demise of healing within the Christian Church as a whole. It's often pointed out by church historians that the sharpest blow to primitive Christian healing was not the severe persecution of Christians—the persecutions, in fact, caused them to deepen their faith and rally together. Far more damaging was the fact that countless Romans assumed the mere appearance of Christians once the emperor's stroke of a pen had "converted" the empire to Christianity, making it politically advantageous to put on such appearances. The genuine and vital Christianity that had naturally resulted in healing soon became outnumbered and largely replaced by its counterfeit.

Few people argue that one can expect physical healing while parading as a Christian and indulging in sinful actions and thought. But Christian Science teaches that the unregenerate human mind is much more insidious and far-reaching in its nature than has been commonly recognized. Should this be surprising when Jesus constantly challenged the thought of those around him, often before they had even opened their mouths? Or when he warned against committing adultery simply within one's heart? No! In fact, what should be surprising is that in the age of Freud and Jung, of mental manipulation and hypnosis, Christians don't take more seriously in their own way the reach of the human mind, its effect on our lives and bodies, and, most important, its tendency to oppose God.

In her writings Mrs. Eddy time after time exposes the mentality that wears the mask of piety while attempting to defy Christ and God's supremacy. She urges us to take Jesus' view of this mentality when she writes: "The great Nazarene, as meek as he was mighty, rebuked the hypocrisy, which offered long petitions for blessings upon material methods, but cloaked the crime, latent in thought, which was ready to spring into action and crucify God's anointed."[7] She uses a variety of carefully chosen words to describe the carnal mind's ability to justify itself and argue for its own existence. A term she adopts for the effort to imitate divine healing, for instance, is *faith-cure*.

Many Christians who have ministries of healing reject the label "faith healing." It's becoming apparent that *blind* faith doesn't stand up to the scrutiny of an increasingly sophisticated and technological society.

Christian Science welcomes any move away from faith healing and toward healing based on a deep, scientific understanding of God, but it insists this involves far more than merely making a disclaimer or changing the style of worship. It isn't a matter of abdicating our role in the process of healing. Rather it's a matter of understanding more precisely what that role is.

The following statement by Mrs. Eddy helps to point out the individual's role in healing and to illumine the stark difference between faith healing and pure Christian healing: "It demands less cross-bearing, self-renunciation, and divine Science to admit the claims of the corporeal senses and appeal to God for relief through a humanized conception of His power, than to deny these claims and learn the divine way—drinking Jesus' cup, being baptized with his baptism, gaining the end through persecution and purity."[8]

Christian Science calls on us constantly to examine our approach to healing to see if we are being tempted merely "to admit the claims of the corporeal senses and appeal to God for relief through a humanized conception of His power" rather than following faithfully in Jesus' footsteps. The very act of dropping elements of faith-cure from one's practice and allowing one's thought to come more directly from God brings healing to what may seem impossibly stubborn conditions and situations. It enables us to love others and see them more as Jesus would have.

From this spiritual perspective, Mrs. Eddy was able to gain a new view of the universe—not based on matter but on the truths of the Bible. She saw that matter was something entirely different to Jesus than it is to unredeemed humanity. It didn't prevent him from feeding five thousand people with a few loaves and fishes. Or from actually walking *on* water. It didn't determine a person's health. And it wasn't the source of Lazarus's life or the life of Jairus's daughter. His disciples, too, must have experienced freedom from the limitations of matter as they healed others.

This new view opens to us as we leave behind merely human conceptions for what God is revealing. Prayer becomes no longer a process of pleading with God to intercede in a material universe but of gaining a larger sense of Him and His creation. From this new perspective we discover that matter is not immovable or causative substance, as we had once assumed, but ultimately an objectification of the human mind. To begin to sacrifice sinful, unregenerate human thought for the joy of finding God as the only Mind is increasingly to be freed of the limitations of matter. It's to begin to enter into the kingdom of God here and now.

Christian Science may go further than other churches in its estimate of the depths of unredeemed thought as well as the spiritual heights that are to be achieved by yielding that thought to God. But it's this very realism that provides Christian healing with a foundation for the future and makes Christian Science a friend of humanity.

---

1. *The Lutheran*, February 2, 1987, p. 33.

2. See Rodney Clapp, "One Who Took Up Her Bed and Walked," *Christianity Today*, December 16, 1983, pp. 16–17.

3. Quoted in *Dallas Times Herald*, March 6, 1969.

4. J. Ellsworth Kalas, "The Ultimate and Complete Physician," October 11, 1987.

5. Found in the *Christian Science Quarterly*.

6. Mary Baker Eddy, *Science and Health with Key to the Scriptures* (Boston: The First Church of Christ, Scientist, 1906), p. 151.

7. *Ibid.*, p. 597.

8. Mary Baker Eddy, *Retrospection and Introspection* (Boston: The First Church of Christ, Scientist, 1891), p. 54.

# Further Exchanges

*In this age of medical technology, why do you still put such emphasis on spiritual healing?*

Actually, we have a real appreciation for the dedication of the members of the medical profession in their efforts to alleviate disease, and we have no quarrel with those who choose medical care. But we do view the healing accomplished by Christ Jesus as having been brought about by the operation of divine law, and we choose to live by that law as best we can. After all, didn't Jesus tell his disciples, "Verily, verily, I say unto you, He that believeth on me, the works that I do shall he do also"?[1]

Many people who become adherents of Christian Science are attracted to it in the first place by their need for healing, but if they stay with it after they are healed, it becomes a new way of life to them. They've felt the healing touch of Christ and have caught glimpses of what the Bible means when it speaks of knowing ourselves as the sons and daughters of God. Selfishness, prejudice, loneliness, and fear begin to fade in this new light of Truth, and the frustrations and tragedies that often mar human relationships are replaced by joy and more expectation of good. The Bible makes clear that God's purpose for man is wholly good. Claiming and understanding that heritage of spiritual good are what Christian Science is all about.

. . .

*Why isn't the Christian Science Church growing rapidly in numbers like other churches that are involved in healing?*

Actually we have quite a different approach to healing from the Pentecostal or charismatic churches that have been growing so rapidly.

I can't speak for the religious practice of others. But in Christian Science, spiritual healing involves deep inner regeneration, reformation, and character transformation. It often means parting with the world's ways of living and approaching experience. It's a matter of deep, consistent Christian discipleship. None of this may be particularly popular in a society that can often appear to be driven by ever-changing trends and commercial materialism.

Another aspect of Christian Science healing that may not make it an "attention grabber" is its quiet nature. In Christian Science the process of healing is not dramatic—it does not involve the "laying on of hands," praying in tongues, being "slain in the Spirit," or other phenomena. It's not a public event. Praying for healing in Christian Science takes place quietly within one's thought, feelings, and actions, and so there may be little that's visible to the human eye until the physical conditions change. Christian Scientists avoid ritual and emotionalism in an effort to give themselves fully to their spiritual relationship to God. They find that healing comes as they yield to and better understand this sacred relationship, which they find exemplified in Christ Jesus' sonship.

When you get right down to it, Christian Science healing may be less popular because it asks more of those who choose to practice it. It's one thing to believe that God occasionally intervenes supernaturally with a miraculous healing. ·It's another to see healing as a way of life—to believe, as Christian Scientists do, that healing is not a matter of miracles but of learning about and acting upon God's spiritual laws.

All of this may lead one to ask, "Why doesn't the Church of Christ, Scientist, take a more popular approach to healing, an approach that would draw Pentecostal-size crowds?" Perhaps it comes down to the fact that we don't believe that simply attracting large numbers is a reliable measure of what makes a church effective or meaningful today. It can be said that we don't view our church's mission in terms of numbers any more than early

Christians viewed their purpose that way. Now, as then, it is the Christ and healing that attract and build up a church. Nothing else lasts.

. . .

*How has new medical technology affected Christian Scientists' view of healing?*

Christian Scientists on the whole are as aware of technical developments in medicine as anyone who reads a newspaper or watches the nightly news. They appreciate the sincerity and compassion that many medical professionals bring to their efforts to relieve the suffering of others. But like many people in our society, Christian Scientists don't believe that technical achievements can ever truly result in some utopia of perfect health.

There is a growing recognition—even among a number of doctors—that one's approach to life is inextricably related to one's health. Even so the mental and emotional needs of the patient, not to mention the spiritual hunger, so often seem left behind in the pursuit of increasingly refined technology.

Christian Scientists obviously take the tradition of Christian healing and the reliability of prayer far more seriously than most. Their conviction is that genuine health lies in learning to know God better—not in developing an ever more sophisticated technology.

. . .

*Is it true that Christian Scientists are against doctors?*

The way that's put sounds like a political position! Obviously, doctors are not something one is "against." No one can be against humanitarian and selfless motives. I couldn't be against the doctor who took care of a neighbor's child when his mother was away, and we took him to the hospital, realizing that would be the wish of his parents. This guideline for Christian Scientists is found in Mary Baker Eddy's writings: "A genuine Christian Scientist loves Protestant and Catholic, D.D. and

M.D.,—loves all who love God, good; and he loves his ene-
mies."[2] It's true, of course, that Christian Scientists believe that
healing through prayer and spiritual means is a very real part of
the Christian Church. They choose healing through spiritual
means for themselves, but they are not "against" doctors or
medicine for those who want to rely on this type of healing.

. . .

*So is Christian Scientists' reliance on spiritual treatment solely a
matter of free choice?*

This needs a little perspective. Some people set up either/or
alternatives that don't have anything to do with the way things
actually happen. They may think that Christian Scientists go
back and forth between spiritual treatment and medicine (and
that this is acceptable and normal in Christian Science) or that
the church rigidly controls its members and dictates their choice
of health care.

No, the church doesn't tell its members what to do in these
matters. But it would be hypocritical to call going back and
forth between medicine and Christian Science "normal" for
Christian Scientists. This is because full reliance on spiritual
means for healing is really the only kind of practice within the
parameters of legitimate Christian Science.

When church members, as sometimes happens, opt for medical treatment, they're not put out of the church. But they
certainly are, in that instance, departing from the practice of
Christian Science—they are not violating a church rule but are
relying upon a form of treatment that is based on a completely
different premise. This doesn't necessarily mean that people need
resign from the church in such instances, although some have
chosen to, when medical reliance becomes normal for them.

No one is *forced* to join a church that includes spiritual healing
as part of its way of life. People do so voluntarily, out of the
conviction that spiritual power heals and that this healing means
something for the spiritual life of humanity. This conviction is
not peripheral to Christian Science. It is central to it. But no one

can tell you or me that this is how we should feel. And our church does not claim to.

The church's purpose is not to make and enforce edicts, but to nurture and support members in their commitment to practicing what they feel Mrs. Eddy discovered—how to follow Christ Jesus in daily life.

. . .

*Why can't Christian Science treatment be mixed with medical care?*

The Christian Science practitioner is helping the patient away from dependence on matter toward a fuller dependence on Spirit. The effect of a patient's thought being drawn in two directions is unhelpful to him. As Jesus put it, you can't serve two masters— we've found in our healing ministry that it simply doesn't work.

. . .

*Does a practitioner give up on a patient who has turned to medical care?*

He leaves the case, yes, but he certainly doesn't stop loving the patient! The reason practitioners help patients in the first place is their deep love for others. That love is not given up because the patient selects another method of care. I remember a case I had where the patient turned to medicine and I went to the hospital to visit him and to be supportive of him. We respect the individual and his choice, and we care very much about people regardless of their choice of treatment.

. . .

*What do you do about broken bones?*

Some Christian Scientists have a broken bone set by a surgeon, others prefer to rely wholly on God's power. The setting of a bone, of course, doesn't involve drug therapy; it's a kind of mechanical adjustment. For that reason Christian Scientists see it as being different from relying on medicine or regular medical treatment. But there are scores of records of cases where broken bones—even bad compound fractures—have been healed entirely through prayer in Christian Science.

. . .

*Why do you rely on Christian Science for the care of children?*

Perhaps I can answer that best by telling you a little about my own experience. I was raised in a home where Christian Science was practiced, and one of the things I remember most vividly about childhood healings of sickness and accidents was a sense of feeling enveloped in God's love. As I grew older I learned to face problems through prayer and saw that I didn't need to be a victim of circumstances. I began to realize that God is always present even when parents and friends may not be, and I saw that I could always depend on Him.

As parents, my wife and I raised our own children while relying on Christian Science because we wanted them to experience for themselves the immediacy of God's healing power, the reality of His love and protection. Now as grandparents we're watching them raise theirs in this same way of life.

Of course, it wasn't always easy. There were times when we were fearful. What parent isn't, sometimes? There were times when we needed to call a Christian Science practitioner to pray with us while we cared for our children, and times when we needed the help of a Christian Science nurse to bandage a wound or help us make a sick little one more comfortable through practical care.

We're grateful that these supports are there to help Christian Scientists, but over the years what has meant even more to my wife and me, and many other Christian Scientists, has been the growing sense of freedom from hurt and fear and the healings that have come as we have better understood our heavenly Father's care for His children.

---

1. John 14:12.
2. Mary Baker Eddy, *The First Church of Christ, Scientist, and Miscellany* (Boston: The First Church of Christ, Scientist, 1913), p. 4.

# 6

## The Church and

## Society

Many people today find the phrase *organized religion* a contradiction in terms. It isn't hard to understand why. The spiritual light, love, joy, and fellowship that inevitably flow from genuine worship often seem far removed from the formal religious institutions established to foster it. Yet the life of the spirit needs to be nurtured, protected, and loved, and churches continue to do that, sometimes in spite of themselves.

Mary Baker Eddy had a pragmatist's sense of both the perils of organization and the necessity for it. She wrote in 1894: "The Church, more than any other institution, at present is the cement of society, and it should be the bulwark of civil and religious liberty. But the time cometh when the religious element, or Church of Christ, shall exist alone in the affections, and need no organization to express it."[1]

It is significant that she felt humanity would *not* outgrow the need for organized churches until human character itself was fully redeemed and transformed. Convinced of the redemptive role of churches for both individuals and society, she devoted several decades of her life to structuring a church organization that would not only last but live far into the future.

The first selection in this chapter, "The Church of Christ, Scientist," is a general summary on this organization. It is reprinted from the pamphlet *Christian Science: A Century Later* and briefly surveys the Church's history, polity, and form of worship. It is followed by some broad-ranging comments on the kinds of people who are members of this Church from a chapter in the book *The Christian Science Way of Life* by DeWitt John.

---

1. Mary Baker Eddy, *Miscellaneous Writings* (Boston: The First Church of Christ, Scientist, 1896), pp. 144–145.

# The Church of Christ, Scientist

In an address given in Concord, New Hampshire, in the winter of 1899, the Founder of the Church of Christ, Scientist, spoke broadly of Christianity as "not a creed or dogma,—a philosophical phantasm,—nor the opinions of a sect. . . ." Christianity, said Mary Baker Eddy, "is the summons of divine Love for man to be Christlike—to emulate the words and the works of our great Master."[1]

This rousing, slightly unorthodox view of Christianity as a dynamic "summons . . . to be Christlike," rather than a system of "creed or dogma," may help to explain the form of the church that she had founded some two decades earlier.

On April 12, 1879, a small religious group calling themselves Christian Scientists had quietly met in Boston and voted to "organize a church designed to commemorate the word and works of our Master [Christ Jesus], which should reinstate primitive Christianity and its lost element of healing."[2]

This handful of Christian Scientists and their leader, Mrs. Eddy, could hardly have known the lasting shape that their denomination would assume over the next three decades, as its formal organization was developed. But the overriding pattern indicates Mrs. Eddy's conviction that the church organization itself is most useful when it remains secondary and of service to Christian regeneration and healing. The simple form of Christian Science branch churches, the absence of hierarchy (all officers are elected lay members), and the equal status of men and women may reflect this conviction.

*Christian Science: A Century Later* (Boston: The Christian Science Publishing Society, 1982), pp. 1–7.

She wrote in retrospect of her fervent early hopes that the established churches of the day would embrace the practice of Christian healing. But in contrast to the growing interest in healing within a number of Christian denominations today, many Christians of the late nineteenth century were apt to view healing as a special dispensation granted to Jesus and his immediate followers—a miraculous gift to be marvelled at, rather than a way of life to be emulated.

Now, more than a century after its founding, the Church of Christ, Scientist, comprised of The Mother Church, The First Church of Christ, Scientist, in Boston, Massachusetts, with its numerous branch churches and societies around the world— about three thousand in some fifty-seven countries—is still dedicated to healing. Large and small, these congregations all share in the founding purpose of the little group that met in 1879.

The Mother Church today represents not only the denomination's historical beginnings, but also the focal point of its widespread activities. The responsibilities of The Mother Church extend from the recognition of new branch churches to the publication of the church's daily newspaper, *The Christian Science Monitor*. A *Church Manual* by Mrs. Eddy sets forth the organizational framework of the movement and offers both spiritual guidance (such as the requirement that attacks on Christian Science receive "a true and just reply"[3] but be answered "in a Christian manner"[4]) and practical rules (such as requiring that membership figures not be published, in line with the Biblical injunction against numbering the people).

*Manual* By-Laws are administered by a board of five directors, while branch churches are governed democratically by their own members within the general *Manual* framework. In fact, many Christian Scientists have dual membership, actively participating in the local activities of a branch church as well as supporting the worldwide mission represented by The Mother Church and its publications.

Despite wide variances in composition of membership, branch churches share a common form of worship service. In 1894, Mrs. Eddy "ordained" the Bible and her book *Science and Health with Key to the Scriptures* as the church's "pastor." Selections from the Scriptures with related passages from *Science and Health* form the centerpiece for all Christian Science church services.

At Sunday services, following the singing of hymns and prayer, citations from the Bible and *Science and Health* are read by two lay "Readers" elected from the membership—usually to serve a three-year term. (The church has no ordained clergy.) Citations to be read are outlined in advance in the *Christian Science Quarterly—Bible Lessons.* They are studied by Christian Scientists and other interested Bible students during the week preceding the hour-long Sunday service. Branch churches around the world are thus united in considering the same Lesson-Sermon (in the language appropriate to the country and congregation). Subjects of the lessons include: God, Christ Jesus, Man, Love, Sacrament, Spirit, Matter, Reality, and so on.

Each branch church maintains a Sunday School for pupils up to twenty years old. The focus is on the Scriptures. In accordance with the *Church Manual,* "the first lessons of the children"[5] include the Ten Commandments, the Lord's Prayer, and the Sermon on the Mount. Guidance is given to help pupils live and practice Scriptural teachings in their own lives, and to learn to heal themselves and help others in the spirit of Christ Jesus' call, "Follow me."

The First Reader of each branch church selects readings for one-hour Wednesday evening testimony meetings. These brief selections from the Bible and *Science and Health* often relate to some community or world challenge on which the Scriptures shed light. Following hymns and prayer (brief silent prayer plus the Lord's Prayer), accounts of healing and gratitude are offered spontaneously by members of the congregation. Christian Scientists view this as a time to voice their appreciation for what they regard as God's blessings and care. Annual Thanksgiving Day services are conducted along similar lines.

Often found in shopping and business districts, Christian Science Reading Rooms are maintained and staffed by the local church members. Not simply a library or bookstore in the usual sense, a Reading Room represents the local church's "open door" to its community. It offers the public an unpressured and thoughtful atmosphere in which to study the Bible and Christian Science literature, including the *Monitor*. Books are also available for loan or purchase.

Although the denomination does not carry on missionary activity in the usual sense, public lectures by members of The Christian Science Board of Lectureship are familiar events in communities throughout the world. These are sponsored by local or neighboring branch churches, societies, or college organizations.

In a short Glossary of terms found in *Science and Health, Church* is defined in its highest sense as "the structure of Truth and Love; whatever rests upon and proceeds from divine Principle." (When capitalized, the Biblical terms *Truth* and *Love,* as well as the metaphysical term *Principle,* are used to signify God.) The definition continues: "The Church is that institution, which affords proof of its utility and is found elevating the race, rousing the dormant understanding from material beliefs to the apprehension of spiritual ideas and the demonstration of divine Science, thereby casting out devils, or error, and healing the sick."[6]

A Christian Scientist is likely to view "Church" as far more than a building, a form of worship, a body of doctrine, or even a group of like-minded people. Rather, he regards Church as a dynamic spiritual force in his own heart and in the community.

For many years before and after the founding of the Church of Christ, Scientist, in 1879, Mrs. Eddy wrestled with the shape of the emerging church. Despite her early hopes that no formal organization would be necessary, it gradually became apparent that some structure would be needed to support and further the church's mission. The streamlined By-Laws of the *Church Manual* (which she explained "were written at different dates, and as the occasion required"),[7] the "distinctly democratic"[8] government of branch churches, the simple form of church services, the noticeable absence of ritual and formal creed—all of these reflect to some extent Christian Scientists' conviction that Christianity is, above all, meant to be demonstrated in daily living.

1. Mary Baker Eddy, *The First Church of Christ, Scientist, and Miscellany* (Boston: The First Church of Christ, Scientist, 1913), p. 148.

2. Mary Baker Eddy, *Manual of The Mother Church* (Boston: The First Church of Christ, Scientist, 1895), p. 17.

3. *Ibid.,* p. 93.

4. *Ibid.,* p. 97.

5. *Ibid.,* p. 62.

6. Mary Baker Eddy, *Science and Health with Key to the Scriptures* (Boston: The First Church of Christ, Scientist, 1906), p. 583.

7. Mary Baker Eddy, *Miscellaneous Writings* (Boston: The First Church of Christ, Scientist, 1896), p. 148.

8. Eddy, *Manual,* p. 74.

# What Kind of People Are Christian Scientists?

It is hard to generalize about what kind of people Christian Scientists are. Their diversity is outwardly evident in their occupational backgrounds. Here is a random list of a few I know: a lawyer, a dentist, a professor of physics at a large university, a woman chemist in an atomic laboratory, a historian, a biologist; a carpenter, an automobile mechanic, a farmer, a rancher, a weigher of ship cargoes; an artist, an actor, a leading movie director; a professional football player, a dress designer, a music teacher, a cattle broker; a German baron, a lady-in-waiting in the Japanese imperial court, a British earl; a janitor, a clerk, a laborer; a banker, the president of a topflight advertising agency, a former major-general in the United States Army, a well-known corporation president, a United States senator, a university president, a former medical student.

To these might be added any number of engineers, schoolteachers, writers, housewives, businessmen, retired people, students, clerical workers, artisans, and salaried people. Here and there you will find a Christian Scientist in politics, and from time to time a figure of eminence in his chosen field.

Many who turn to Christian Science yearn to be different from what they are. They are weary of the perversities of human nature. They know they have a lot to outgrow. After all, there are a good many rough spots in human character wherever you find it.

DeWitt John, *The Christian Science Way of Life* (Boston: The Christian Science Publishing Society, 1962), pp. 1–11.

Many individuals have come to Christian Science for physical healing. Many have found it. Sometimes quickly, sometimes slowly. Yet physical healing is neither the primary purpose of Christian Science nor its main effect upon the lives of those who embrace it.

There are certain distinguishing characteristics of Christian Scientists which lie just below the surface. Let us cite a few.

Practically every Christian Scientist is a Christian Scientist because he has made a deliberate personal choice to be one.

Being a Christian Scientist is not like being an Irishman or a Texan: an Irishman is an Irishman by birth; a Texan is a Texan by geography.

Not so with the Christian Scientist. He is not a Christian Scientist by birth, by geography, or even by association with others. Nor is he one by an outward ceremony of christening or baptism. If he joins the church, it will be because he wants to; but even church affiliation, by itself, could not make him a Christian Scientist.

Even if he was born into a Christian Science family and has attended the Sunday school from infancy, there comes a time sooner or later when he has to think through its teachings for himself, and make the deeply personal decision whether or not he will embrace them.

This is not a faith one can successfully embrace in name only. It is not a religion in which, like a sponge, one can soak things up without much effort. It calls for daily effort and self-immolation. Its benefits are vast but they must be earned. The only way one can really grasp the teachings sufficiently to benefit very much from them is to make a persistent and courageous effort to live them.

Of course there are some who attend church services but have never really committed themselves to the teachings. Others, outside the church, lightly assert that they are Christian Scientists, because this suits their fancy. But this is like claiming to be a musician when one never plays music.

On the other hand, it is known, from sales of Christian Science literature, that many individuals, some of them churchgoers of other faiths, privately and even secretly study the teachings of Christian Science and try to live them.

The point is that being a Christian Scientist means adopting a way of prayer and a way of life—not merely a label. The result is that the real Christian Scientist is a worker. He studies daily. He prays—in his home and in free moments during his work. He schools himself in the art of turning to God, divine Mind, in every circumstance for guidance and inspiration.

For example, the active Christian Scientist studies daily the Christian Science Lesson-Sermon for that week, comprised of selected passages on a given subject from the Bible and from the Christian Science textbook, *Science and Health with Key to the Scriptures,* by Mrs. Eddy. To read the lesson takes about half an hour. To study it thoroughly takes more time. Many devout Christian Scientists spend an hour or more daily in study of the lesson and in prayer.

It is not uncommon for a Scientist to rise at a very early hour each morning for the sole purpose of such study before the day's activities begin. I recall one time I happened to mention this to some personal friends, a university professor and his wife. The wife's reaction was one of unrestrained merriment. She could not understand why anybody would get up early in the morning to study his religion!

But as a Christian Scientist sees it, no subject could be more important or more interesting than the nature of God, and man's relationship to Him. What we call the material universe is so vast that men often spend a lifetime studying one tiny facet of it. If one feels his religion reveals the real universe of Spirit—the Science of his own being and the answers to all his problems—then it is natural for him to think of study as a normal part of religious practice.

Outside observers have sometimes described Christian Science as an "individualistic" faith, primarily because the denomination does not carry on many of the social activities and programs common in other churches. For Christian Scientists themselves, however, the tangible warmth and fellowship of congregational life are much more than a minor "side benefit" of a theology based on God's love.

As an official of The Mother Church once commented in a letter to an inquirer asking about this point, "The absence of formalized social activities hasn't kept this love from being expressed, often in extraordinary ways. In fact, it's expressed all the more freely and spontaneously—as in a family—because it isn't mediated through formal structures. There's nothing else on earth quite like the oneness of heart and spirit this kind of fellowship makes possible."

The next three selections are included in this spirit. The profound experience of church *community* to which they point is obviously no more universal in Christian Science churches than in other denominations, but it is nevertheless real.

The initial excerpt, "Christian Scientists of the 1880s: A Reminiscence," might be called a "period piece"—a naive but heartfelt reminiscence of the fellowship among some of Mary Baker Eddy's Boston students in the early 1880s, when the church was in its infant stage. The writer, William Lyman Johnson—who was a teenage boy at the time he participated in the little scenes described—manages to convey something of the spirit of primitive Christian churches, a quality Mrs. Eddy saw as vital to the health of the Christian Church now as then. The reference in the last sentence of this excerpt is to the weekly testimony meetings that followed these informal gatherings.

# Christian Scientists in the 1880s— A Reminiscence

This old-fashioned type restaurant, which ran through to Tamworth Street, was long and narrow, always well-lighted, and always neat. It had about it an air of comfort, and here came Miss Bartlett, Mr. and Mrs. Munroe, Mrs. Colman, Mrs. Williams, Mr. and Mrs. Landy, Captain and Mrs. Eastaman, Mr. Mason, Mr. Bailey, father, mother, and myself. Miss Bartlett and the Munroes usually made up a table with us, and sometimes Mr. Mason would join in pleasant comradeship. Here, over a simple meal, the work that was laid out for the coming week and the experiences of each since they had last met would be talked over. . . .

This hour of the evening meal was filled with a wonderful sweetness. There was a free and generous exchange of thought, a simple association which bore the fruits of faithfulness and unity, while there was always a pervading perfume, since someone had seen Mrs. Eddy yesterday or today, and the few words which she had spoken opened new vistas of the truth that they must seek for and find.

There was no idolatry among these early Scientists. They were not sentimentalists for they had been tried in the fires of struggle and the battles for right. They were middle-aged people who had learned much of the world before coming into Science, and the quiet and reverent way in which they referred to the Teacher, their gentleness, and their ever-present love, spoke the impress which the spirit of Mrs. Eddy had made, a spirit that was ever with us at our meal. If things got too serious

William Lyman Johnson, in *The History of the Christian Science Movement* (Brookline, MA: Zion Research Foundation, 1926), pp. 80–81.

Mr. Munroe, who was a bit of a wag, was sure to bring everybody back to a cheerful state by saying some funny thing that did not fail to make us all smile. Then Father, who was very exacting in this regard, would invariably take out his watch and say, "Friends, it's time to be on duty and welcome friends and strangers," and so would end the evening meal, a prelude of serious thought and uplifting hope for the work that was to come.

Johnson's reference to the "work that was to come" is illustrated by "This Is Why I Am a Christian Scientist: A Testimony," a very different and much more recent reminiscence in *The Christian Science Journal*. Gwendolyn West, in a vivid family chronicle, begins with an account of the healings that led her grandparents to devote their lives to the Christian Science healing ministry, then recalls her own religious upbringing. The excerpt that follows conveys a dimension of church life not normally evident to the general public.

# This Is Why I Am a Christian Scientist: A Testimony

$B$oth [my grandparents] became dedicated Christian Science practitioners, were listed in the *Journal,* and worked for over twenty years in that capacity.

Their sons continued in Christian Science, living as if it were everything, which it was to them. Growing up the daughter of the middle son, I witnessed this total dedication. For example, I recall one Thanksgiving when I was a young teen-ager. The family and guests had just sat down to dinner after church—a rare and special together-time—when the phone rang. It was an elderly woman from our church calling to say her husband was in a serious condition and to ask if someone would please come right away. His dinner untouched, my father drove immediately to her home, some twenty minutes away. He was not a *Journal*-listed practitioner at that time, just a businessman who helped others when called upon. He rarely had a vacation or holiday, and I remember my heart sinking to see him leave, for I treasured our rare time together; but we all always knew "church comes first."

By the time my father arrived, the man had lost all color and was unconscious. My father prayed both silently and out loud, until after one hour the man stirred. My father roused him, talking to him of God. The man began to regain life and to respond. My father stayed talking with him two more hours. By now, *our* Thanksgiving was over. But our father's *real* Thanksgiving was just beginning. Three days later, Sunday at church, as I stood watching, this couple came up to my father, both taking his hands, and with tears of gratitude thanked him

---

Gwendolyn West, in *The Christian Science Journal,* October 1985, pp. 610–611.

with unforgettable expressions. I saw in that moment, as in many similar experiences, what it is to be a Christian Scientist.

In *Science and Health with Key to the Scriptures,* Mary Baker Eddy writes that "the human self must be evangelized." She says, "This task God demands us to accept lovingly to-day, and to abandon so fast as practical the material, and to work out the spiritual which determines the outward and actual."[1] Thus, to be a Christian Scientist is to sacrifice sometimes even wholesome or good human things like family get-togethers in order to work *God's* work. It is to truly put first things first. It is to serve God and man above all else. It is to have no lesser loyalties. It is wanting the Christ, Truth, *so much* that nothing else seems as important. I remember my grandmother, who had to leave home at five thirty in the afternoon, walk two miles, then ride a bus for forty-five minutes, then catch a streetcar to get to an eight o'clock Wednesday evening testimony meeting. After it was over, she didn't get home until midnight because of bus connections. In spite of all she had to go through to get there, she never missed a Wednesday or a Sunday service at church. Why? Because of *love*—love for the Christ, Truth. Because Christian Science had become the *essence* of her life. She wanted more of what healed her three sons and husband; and nothing— no inconvenience, no human activity—could keep her from getting it.

Yes, I am a Christian Scientist because of this upbringing, because of being raised where God, Christian Science, and church always came first, always healed, always guided. But every Christian Scientist must also find this way of life for himself—even if he is raised in it. He does not automatically inherit it. He must make it genuinely his own.

---

1. Mary Baker Eddy, *Science and Health with Key to the Scriptures* (Boston: The First Church of Christ, Scientist, 1906), p. 254.

The next selection is a commentary that touches more broadly on Christian Scientists' church life and the theology behind it. "Theology and the Church: A Letter," which considers Christian Scientists' church experience in a theological perspective, was included in a letter from the Church's Committee on Publication for the Canadian provinces. It is typical of the dialogue that has often been prompted over the years by discussion of Christian Science in comparative religion classes.

This selection is followed by "Individual Spirituality and the Future of Mankind," a rousing summary statement from a 1985 conference in Boston of several thousand Christian Science college students. The statement relates to the larger vision of Church shared by all Christians; it was published in *The Christian Science Journal.*

# Theology and the Church:
## A Letter

At the risk of taxing the Professor's patience, perhaps one final point might be clarified. . . .

Christian Science insists on the sacredness of each individual's relationship with God. Few other churches are more "Protestant" in that respect. This insistence has various practical consequences (i.e., the denomination's unusually strong emphasis on individual practice and study, its deep respect for individual free choice, its lay rather than clerical structure), but it does not diminish Christian Scientists' sense of what a church *as a church* means in the world. Church means infinitely more to Christian Scientists, certainly, than a congenial meeting-place for the like-minded. The individual's sacred relationship with God necessarily involves him in a sacred relationship with His children. Because sin is seen in Christian Science as a distortion indigenous to the whole mortal condition—not merely a matter of personal guilt—salvation is seen as much more than a private or "personally directed" spiritual achievement.

In traditional theological terms it involves the realization of the Kingdom. Christian Scientists differ with other Christians in interpreting the Kingdom not as an eschatological vision but as a present spiritual reality to be grasped and lived. They don't differ, however, on the role of the Church (and not just the Church of Christ, Scientist) in fulfilling this vision/reality. Their sense of a broader "socially defined" mission is reflected visibly in efforts like the publication of *The Christian Science Monitor,* but probably even more in the unheralded days and often nights their practitioners give to prayer for the people

From an unpublished letter to a Canadian college professor.

230

who come to them. As for the Church's corporate life, I recently read a description of a Christian Science college group's meeting that captures something of its spirit at least at its best:

> . . . there were only a handful of students. They were gathered in a shabby subbasement room—all that the prestigious university had been willing to grant them. They had made the room barely livable by their own labor. But what a meeting it was! Here they were, on the campus of a vast intellectual institution, each student striving to meet heavy academic demands. Each had to make quite an effort to be present. Everyone spoke from the heart, directly. It seemed like a meeting of an early Christian group. There wasn't the slightest posturing or pride. Each shared wonderfully solid healings. They genuinely loved and helped each other.[1]

I don't wish to draw a blissfully idealized picture of Christian Science congregations or of their denominational organization, which hasn't been exempt any more than other denominations' from internal discord and disagreement. It's just that, in the long run, I think it's important for both Christians and sociologists to seriously rethink the categories in which we place each other, not only in order to avoid pigeon-holing particular groups mistakenly, but also in order to understand the true theological wholeness of Christianity.

---

1. Allison W. Phinney, Jr., "The Always New and Ever-growing Church," *The Christian Science Journal,* September 1986, p. 563.

# Individual Spirituality and the Future of Mankind

$M$ary Baker Eddy wrote, "We live in an age of Love's divine adventure to be All-in-all."[1] When it comes to how wonderfully intense, how downright *engaging* life can be, the work of healing, together with the commitment to spiritual newness, is something that can't be equaled. Our spirituality is to us what the capacity to fly is to the fledgling: it's there, it's natural, its appearing is inevitable— and it takes work! It's the new birth that Mrs. Eddy says is not the "work of a moment," rather it "goes on with years."[2]

Think back to the time shortly after this great spiritual fact of being had been decisively brought to light in the life of Jesus. Perhaps it's A.D. 60 or 70. The Christian Church—*ekklēsia* in Greek, meaning "assembly" or "community"—is springing up in the Roman Empire: in Jerusalem; westward in Caesarea on the Mediterranean coast; northeastward in Damascus, and then Antioch, Asia Minor, the Greek cities around the Aegean Sea, and Rome.

There was, among many of these early Christians, a very *alive* sense of the spirit of Christ, despite the many challenges they faced from within and from without. It wasn't something they thought "about" so much as *felt,* deep in their hearts.

What a tremendous stir Jesus' life had made! It created a sort of glorious confusion—like the bursting forth of a new solar system! Imagine: hundreds of people in little groups around the Roman Empire—eventually they were from all levels of class, literacy, and importance—their hearts and minds on fire with the gospel of love and salvation.

*The Christian Science Journal,* November 1985, pp. 724–725.

Actually, when you think about it, our organizations and groups at colleges and universities often look and feel like those primitive communities in the first and second centuries. "Orgs" are informal, that's for sure! Often the members get together in rooms no one else wants; or in university buildings that aren't well maintained. But they have that same raw potential to be very alive with the light and spirit of Christ.

---

1. Mary Baker Eddy, *The First Church of Christ, Scientist, and Miscellany* (Boston: The First Church of Christ, Scientist, 1913), p. 158.

2. Mary Baker Eddy, *Miscellaneous Writings* (Boston: The First Church of Christ, Scientist, 1896), p. 15.

For Christian Scientists, a church is not only a community of faith. It must also be a healing presence in the world. The concluding two selections in this chapter elaborate this healing imperative from differing angles, historical and spiritual.

"The Social Question," a segment from Stephen Gottschalk's groundbreaking historical study, *The Emergence of Christian Science in American Religious Life,* discusses the social ethic that found expression in the establishment of *The Christian Science Monitor* in 1908. "The Church's Redemptive Mission," an article from the already cited booklet *Ecumenical Papers,* insists on the unique spiritual relevance of the churches to the massive dilemmas facing humanity.

# The Social Question

Without a solid core of devoted workers who were willing to bear the burdens of the movement in its early days, Christian Science could never have become a significant religious force in American life at all. But their spirit was by no means characteristic of the movement as a whole, and any acquaintance with its literature shows that some Christian Scientists reflected very little of their pioneering dedication. For some Christian Scientists, Mrs. Eddy's teaching was very far from a revealed truth, the establishment of which demanded and deserved unstinted sacrifice. It was, rather, a convenient method for attaining the purely human ends of health, wealth, comfort, status, and success.

The pursuit of these values—wealth, comfort, status, and success—was certainly not warranted by Christian Science teaching. But they were among the predominant values of the American middle class. The conclusion is warranted, therefore, that the class orientation of some Christian Scientists did noticeably affect their practice of its teaching. For through it, they seemed to be trying to perpetuate and protect the level of contentment to which their class aspired. The foregoing suggests only that a process of secularization was to some degree evident in the *practice* of Christian Science. It says nothing whatever about the character of Christian Science as a religious teaching—except, perhaps, that it could be distorted in this manner. It is easy enough, of course, to say that no religious teaching is practiced entirely according to its founder's intent. Yet Mrs. Eddy did

Stephen Gottschalk, *The Emergence of Christian Science in American Religious Life* (Berkeley: University of California Press, 1973), pp. 249–274.

establish clear guidelines for the practice of Christian Science—guidelines which in their rigorous demands for selflessness and dedication are not coordinate with a secular quest for a fulfilled bourgeois existence.

The greatest accomplishment of Christian Science, in terms of the religious situation into which it was projected, was the restoration of vitality to the individual spiritual experience of those who practiced it. Mrs. Eddy's teachings were clearly addressed to the redemption and healing of individual men. And one is struck, in reading the testimonies of Christian Scientists, at how complete was their conviction that divine power was at work in their own particular life-situations. Obviously, then, the social and political questions that were becoming of increasing concern to many Protestants around the turn of the century had less significance for the Christian Scientists. Articles on these problems appeared only rarely in the *Journal* and *Sentinel,* and Mrs. Eddy devotes little attention to them in her writings in proportion to her treatment of other subjects.

At the same time, the greatest danger to the correct practice of Christian Science was the spirit of secularism which is to some degree in evidence in the early literature of the movement. For this reason, the increasing social concern evident in the development of the movement in the first decade of the twentieth century is of real importance. For it reflects a significant reorientation of the thought of the movement away from the personal and private to the social and universal, a genuine broadening of the Scientists' concerns. The central event in this reorientation was, of course, the founding of *The Christian Science Monitor* by Mrs. Eddy in 1908. The importance that Mrs. Eddy attached to the *Monitor* can be gauged from the fact that she considered its establishment her greatest single achievement apart from the writing of *Science and Health*.[1]

By founding the *Monitor,* Mrs. Eddy committed the Christian Science movement in a limited way to the ideal of social concern then assuming so important a place in Protestantism. It is a curious and significant fact that the first issue of the *Monitor* came on the stands on November 25, 1908, within three weeks of the date that the Federal Council of Churches convened in

Philadelphia. Just as the publication of the *Monitor* marks the high point of social concern in the Christian Science movement, so the formation of the Federal Council of Churches marks the greatest triumph scored up to that time by the Social Gospel.

To some extent, one can draw valid parallels between Christian Science and the Social Gospel in terms of their spirit and substance. Both emerged in the soil of American culture and have been often identified as specifically American contributions to Christianity. Both claimed to cut back behind centuries of barren theology, Protestant as well as Catholic, to restore the vital meaning of the Gospel. Both proclaimed that men can be liberated from iron-bound determinism—in the Social Gospel from the laws of laissez-faire economics, in Christian Science from physical laws that bind men to sickness and death. And both represented in different ways statements of the Christian message in terms relevant to man's present life-situation.

It is understandable, therefore, that some ministers of the Social Gospel spoke approvingly of the practice of spiritual healing as yet another way in which Christianity could be made humanly relevant. Nor is it surprising that the *Sentinel* should have quoted approvingly from one of the major Social Gospel leaders, Washington Gladden, on the inadequacies of orthodoxy. Yet the major prophet of the Social Gospel, Walter Rauschenbusch, had nothing good to say of Christian Science. For he spoke of it as part of a mystical tendency within Protestantism, a form of selfish spirituality which turned its back on the world. Christian Scientists would certainly not have agreed that Mrs. Eddy's teaching encouraged either mysticism or selfishness. Yet Rauschenbusch was surely right in pointing out that Christian Science and the Social Gospel have fundamentally different concerns. For the Social Gospel, as Rauschenbusch and others described it, concentrates religious interest on the ethical problems of social life. Christian Science, however, focuses upon the ontological conditions that underlie all social problems.

In her teaching, Mrs. Eddy raised basic ontological questions about the nature of man's being which the leaders of the Social Gospel, along with most other Protestants, had regarded as settled. From her standpoint, they accepted the very errors that made social problems possible, indeed inevitable. Regarding man's finiteness as self-evident, they accepted as given the plurality of human wills, minds and interests. Their primary concerns were ethical, not ontological, and they looked upon the root of evil of human life in ethical terms. Rauschenbusch, for example, said, "Sin is essentially selfishness. . . . That definition is more in harmony with the Social Gospel than with any individualistic type of religion. The sinful mind, then, is the unsocial or antisocial mind."[2] But for Mrs. Eddy, this sin of selfishness was predicated upon a more primary error: the belief in a mind apart from God. "When we realize that there is one Mind," she wrote, "the divine law of loving our neighbor as ourselves is unfolded; whereas a belief in many ruling minds hinders man's normal drift towards the one Mind, one God, and leads human thought into opposite channels where selfishness reigns."[3]

Perhaps the best way of contrasting Christian Science with the Social Gospel in this matter is with reference to the idea of the Kingdom of God. In the Social Gospel the Kingdom is defined in social terms. Rauschenbusch called it the "Christian transfiguration of the social order."[4] But as Mrs. Eddy discussed the Kingdom, it meant in the first instance the submission of individuals to the government of God, their demonstration in their own situation of the oneness of Mind. Her "Daily Prayer" begins with the quotation from the Lord's Prayer, "Thy kingdom come." Next she goes on to deal with this idea in terms of the individual: "let the reign of divine Truth, Life, and Love be established in me, and rule out of me all sin." Finally, she extends the prayer to all mankind: "and may Thy Word enrich the affections of all mankind, and govern them!"[5] In Christian Science, this enrichment of "the affections of all mankind" will ameliorate social evils, curing the sickness of society as well as of the body; but the establishment of the Kingdom of God cannot be effected in terms of the amelioration of social conditions as such.

The two aspects of Mrs. Eddy's approach to social affairs as just discussed—her insistence that salvation is primarily individual and that meaningful reform must be predicated upon spiritual awakening—could have predisposed Christian Scientists to be unconcerned with social problems. Yet the element in Mrs. Eddy's teaching which prevented it from being practiced, except by a minority of her followers, as a metaphysical system abstracted from human affairs, was her continual emphasis upon demonstration. For her, the power of Spirit must be demonstrated in all phases of experience. Politics, economic life, and social relations must be brought under the divine government. And "human law is right," she wrote, "only as it patterns the divine."[6] Further, Mrs. Eddy did not feel that the achievement of human good was to be directly and exclusively the work of Christian Scientists. The advent of divine Science, she believed, had exerted a "leavening" effect upon the affairs of the world. The coming of Truth had affected human activities in a way of which men were not consciously aware, giving rise to reform and progress in many areas. And since the divine government had to be established in every phase of life, Christian Scientists could not ignore any evidence of progress which tended toward this end, nor any evidence of evil which obstructed its realization.

A newspaper was an ideal vehicle for the expression of Christian Scientists' social concern. For it committed them to consciousness of human affairs but not to any particular involvement with them. In this sense, the term "monitor," though it may have been suggested to Mrs. Eddy by the name of a friendly newspaper in her own city, the *Concord Evening Monitor,* was a particularly apt name for her newspaper. For a monitor is a receiving and tracking instrument. By founding *The Christian Science Monitor,* Mrs. Eddy was calling upon her followers to expand their thinking beyond their own personal lives, indeed, beyond the confines of the movement. As an article in the *Sentinel* put it a month after the first issue of the *Monitor* appeared, the effect of the newspaper "has been to lift one's eyes to an horizon far beyond one's own doorstep. The call to help in the world's thinking is no longer something that can pass unheeded, it is an imperative duty. Things we did not like to look at nor think of, problems we did not feel able to cope with, must now be faced manfully, and correct thinking concerning the world's doings cultivated and maintained."[7]

The *Monitor,* then, had great significance in terms of the orientation of Christian Scientists toward social affairs. But from another standpoint, it can be seen as an instrument of progressive reform in the field of journalism. In the years before she founded the *Monitor* Mrs. Eddy had had much experience with the press, most of it bad. The whole experience of the "Next Friends Suit" together with the muckraking attacks on her that had preceded it was one of the most difficult that Mrs. Eddy had ever undergone. But it did have one constructive effect; for it was in part responsible for her decision in the early summer of 1908 to found a newspaper. During this period she said to a student referring to the role of the *New York World* in launching the "Next Friends Suit," "Now we will show them what a good newspaper can do."[8] And in the editorial she wrote for the first issue of the *Monitor* Mrs. Eddy said that its purpose was "to injure no man, but to bless all mankind."[9] Though she made no direct reference to the *World,* the contrast between her intentions for the *Monitor* and the journalism represented by the *World* was clear enough. And it was made even clearer when in 1910, the *Monitor* sponsored a series of clean journalism meetings to attack the "yellow" press, as well as to advertise itself. Yet certainly the *Monitor* had not been founded solely in response to the *World*'s attack. In a comment on a letter from a follower written in March, 1908, suggesting that she found a newspaper, Mrs. Eddy said that she had had "this newspaper scheme" in mind for some time. Six years earlier she had referred in a letter to her intention to start a "widespread press." And the *Sentinel,* which had been founded four years before that, included several pages of news items in each issue. One can discern a growing consciousness of public affairs in Mrs. Eddy's thought from her earliest work in Christian Science through the founding of the *Monitor.*

The actual launching of the *Monitor* was a formidable task. Not until August 8, 1908, did Mrs. Eddy instruct the Board of Trustees of The Christian Science Publishing Society to begin the project, though she had informed the Board of Directors of her intentions already. Since she wanted the first issue on the stands before Thanksgiving of that year, the two boards had just a little over a hundred days to finance the undertaking, hire a staff, purchase and install a press, and put the whole thing into operation. As in the building of The Mother Church in 1894, she had set her followers a difficult goal; but in this case as before, they reached it. Other newspapers regarded the founding of the *Monitor* with great interest. Some were sympathetic to the effort, others scornful; but few expected it to succeed. Yet though the *Monitor* did pass through some difficult days, it survived to become one of the most prestigious newspapers in the United States.

The editorial policy of the paper is generally consistent with the social views congruent with Christian Science teaching, as sketched earlier. Mrs. Eddy's scattered comments on various issues furnished specific guidelines for many of the *Monitor's* editorial policies. Further, she showed deep concern with the paper's editorial policy, just as she had taken an active interest in the practical operations connected with its founding. Daily from the date the first issue of the *Monitor* appeared on the stands until her death, Mrs. Eddy carefully read over the editorials, occasionally commenting on them to the chief editor. After her death, control of the editorial policy of the *Monitor* passed to the Board of Directors. The Board by no means lays down editorial policy on every issue, though on most important questions it does. Generally, it exercises a supervisional authority and allows considerable interpretive leeway among writers for the *Monitor*—though within certain well-defined limits.

The character of the *Monitor*—its freedom from sensationalism, its broad international scope, and its high standard of reporting—has been the subject of much comment and has earned a measure of respect for the Christian Science movement that it might not otherwise have enjoyed. Yet the major significance of the *Monitor* for the movement lies in the fact that it commits Christian Scientists who wish to be faithful to Mrs. Eddy's intentions to look past their own personal destinies. And for many of them, this was indeed a crucial test.

---

1. See Robert Peel, *Mary Baker Eddy: The Years of Authority* (New York: Holt, Rinehart and Winston, 1977), p. 496, n. 66.

2. Walter Rauschenbusch, *A Theology for the Social Gospel* (New York: Macmillan, 1917), p. 103.

3. Mary Baker Eddy, *Science and Health with Key to the Scriptures* (Boston: The First Church of Christ, Scientist, 1906), p. 205.

4. Rauschenbusch, p. 3.

5. Mary Baker Eddy, *Manual of The Mother Church* (Boston: The First Church of Christ, Scientist, 1895), p. 41.

6. Mary Baker Eddy, *The First Church of Christ, Scientist, and Miscellany* (Boston: The First Church of Christ, Scientist, 1913), p. 283.

7. Quoted in Robert Peel, *Christian Science: Its Encounter with American Culture* (New York: Holt, 1958), p. 158.

8. *The Christian Science Monitor,* November 25, 1908.

9. Eddy, *Miscellany,* p. 353.

# The Church's Redemptive Mission

For centuries the Church preached otherworldliness. Heaven lay beyond the grave. Christian resignation demanded the acceptance of the inevitability of natural evil and social injustice in this imperfect world. Disasters were characterized as acts of God. Salvation had little to do with the healing of mortal ills. The Church's redemptive mission was generally seen in sacramental rather than humanitarian terms.

The eighteenth-century Enlightenment changed all that. Man as a rational animal was hailed as capable of building heaven on earth. God became an unnecessary hypothesis. Where He was retained as an object of faith, His transcendence gradually gave way to His immanence in the laws of physical nature and the energies of the human mind.

The end result of this influence on Christian faith may be today's secular Christianity—religion without God, religion as social ethics, religion as human solidarity. In such a situation the Church's redemptive mission becomes the Church's reformative mission. Its concept of healing becomes largely a concept of social surgery, its ultimate ideal barely distinguishable from that of the scientific humanist and the secular humanitarian.

There is no denying the great gains that have been made in bringing Christianity down to earth, so to speak. The mysticism that turns its back on human needs has little support in the New Testament. "He that loveth not his brother whom he hath seen, how can he love God whom he hath not seen?"[1] "Inasmuch as ye did it not to one of the least of these, ye did it not to me."[2]

*Ecumenical Papers: Contributions to Interfaith Dialogue* (Boston: Christian Science Committee on Publication, 1969), pp. 1–7.

244 · *Christian Science: A Sourcebook*

Yet from the point of view of Christian Science the question arises whether the revolution goes nearly deep enough, whether the social gospel is an adequate remedy for a discredited pietism, whether man can be reconciled to man without a much more profound reconciliation to the God revealed through Christ. Is the thisworldliness of today's popular Christianity anything more than the obverse of yesterday's otherworldliness—a shifting from the supernatural to the natural pole, when what is really needed is a renewed incarnation of the divine in the human?

As long ago as 1875, when the book now known as *Science and Health with Key to the Scriptures* was first published, its author, Mary Baker Eddy, rejected not only the hell-fire pietism of the popular religion of her day but also the bland optimism of the activist faith that was rapidly replacing it. Human life, as she saw it, could at any moment turn into nightmare so long as its material basis went unchallenged. Later, in a single phrase, she anticipated the grimmest features of the century about to unfold when she wrote of material existence as a "ghastly farce."[3]

When she started *The Christian Science Monitor* in 1908, Mrs. Eddy gave evidence of her conviction of the urgent need for Christian influence to be felt in the areas of politics, economics, and social values. But deeper even than this, according to her teaching, lay the need for a spiritual revolution in men's concept of the very universe they live in.

Behind all our fumbling, belated efforts to achieve racial justice, for instance, lies the irresistible divine fact (as Christian Science explains it) that men in their true, essential being are neither black matter nor white matter but are spiritual—made in the image and likeness of a God who is Spirit and Mind and Truth—and are therefore at one with each other as they are at one with God. This metaphysical fact, when understood in all its depth, has tremendous healing power in the human situation. Like the Copernican revolution, which may at first have seemed to have little bearing on the daily facts of men's lives but which completely transformed their relation to the physical universe, so profound a spiritual revolution in our view of man undercuts the age-old foundations of racism.

Looking at the more immediate scene, we see that society

today has thousands of instrumentalities for social action and reform. Committed Christians form the very lifeblood of many of these organizations and activities, without which the whole machinery of our modern world might well break down into hopeless chaos. The Church's direct and indirect influence in the direction of human decency can hardly be doubted. Yet the hard-bitten radical's criticism of much well-meaning religious idealism has plenty of facts to support it.

For surely the increasing magnitude of the problems confronting humanity far outstrips the capacity of even the most liberally motivated society to cope with them within present frames of reference. If the Church remains committed to purely humanist and humanitarian solutions, it may find itself eventually committed by the logic of events to "scientific" programs (in the control of population growth, for instance) that will make Orwell's *1984* look, by comparison, like 1904.

This is where we need to ask: Is it enough to believe that God has endowed men with the self-sufficiency to solve their problems through the exercise of reason, human ingenuity, and goodwill—even if augmented by heroic self-sacrifice? Is this the meaning of the life of Jesus of Nazareth?

Christian Scientists think not. They are humanist enough to believe in the necessity for reason, ingenuity, goodwill, and self-sacrifice in human affairs. They support the enlightened social reformer's goals and, as individual citizens, they may support in varying degree his methods. But they are convinced that a far more radical power is necessary to save the individual and society from ultimate disintegration—a wholly spiritual power, originating in a source not to be defined in terms of a spatiotemporal universe and a material man. This power they call the Christ.

In *Science and Health* Mrs. Eddy writes, "The divinity of the Christ was made manifest in the humanity of Jesus."[4] But the humanity of Jesus did not exhaust the Christ, as Christian Scientists understand it. That same Christ-power they see as inexhaustibly present, to be manifested in healing the world's ills just as directly as when Jesus was on earth—and just as radically.

There was nothing otherworldly about his healing of a leper

or a cripple, no mere promising of relief beyond the grave; but neither were his methods the methods of scientific humanism, operating within an acceptance of the inexorable rule of physical law. His premise was different in *kind* from the premise of meliorative human systems to which spirit is no more than an evolutionary development of matter.

To Jesus, Spirit was clearly primal substance, the causative Principle of being. It was available to men through direct apprehension, not merely through the cultivation of secondary human skills. Metaphorically speaking, this Christ-power bore somewhat the same relation to medical skills that atomic power bears to horsepower. Furthermore, Jesus promised it to all his followers, not as a miraculous dispensation but as the natural outcome of their understanding of the divine realities he had lived forth in their midst. In the account of his healing of the palsied man in Matthew 9, we read, "But when the multitudes saw it, they marvelled, and glorified God, which had given such power unto men."[5]

To the Christian Scientist this is the significance of the spiritual healing of physical disease today. It is a single instance of a divine power that cuts across the generally accepted categories of human power in a revolutionary way. As such, it offers a striking challenge to the Christian and to the Church to bring that same spiritual power to bear on all the individual and social problems of the world. The Saviour's healing of the leper and the cripple was not irrelevant to the larger needs of a leprous and crippled society. In demonstrating the power of God—a God whom the New Testament describes as Love itself—to transform and reshape the individual human being, he was demonstrating the power of that same divine Love to transform and reshape society.

"Ye are the salt of the earth," he said to his followers, "but if the salt have lost his savour, wherewith shall it be salted?"[6] If the Church allows itself to become only one more welfare or reform organization among many, then it stands to lose its unique power and may well end up committed to a program of stifling social coercion rather than of liberating social redemption—to the ethics of the ant-heap rather than of the Kingdom.

Surely the Church has a continuing commitment to awaken in its members that blazing sense of spiritual power, reality, and love which *heals*. And does this not properly begin with the healing of the Christian's own alienation from his divine source? Individual redemption remains a vital wellspring of genuine social therapy.

---

1. I John 4:20.
2. Matt. 25:45.
3. Mary Baker Eddy, *Science and Health with Key to the Scriptures* (Boston: The First Church of Christ, Scientist, 1906), p. 272.
4. *Ibid.*, p. 25.
5. Matt. 9:8.
6. Matt. 5:13.

# Further Exchanges

*How do you spread the gospel? Are you an evangelical church?*

For a Christian Scientist, spreading the gospel means primarily bearing witness to God's love for His children by following Christ Jesus in daily life as nearly as possible. Witnessing to His omnipotence means loving our neighbor in deed, healing mankind of sin and sickness. A Christian Scientist's evangelical training is his daily prayer and study of the Bible, aided by the writings of Mary Baker Eddy, the Founder of this denomination.

. . .

*How is your church governed today?*

Mrs. Eddy wrote and published a small book of By-Laws for the Church. This book, which is called the *Manual of The Mother Church,* might be termed the constitution of our movement. The provisions of the *Manual* are administered by a Board of Directors, who appoint the chief officers of The Mother Church. The branch churches, on the other hand, choose their officers by election from their own members for limited terms of office. In a way, this is a little like the federal system of government, in which The Mother Church has central authority in the affairs of the movement as a whole, but the branch churches are democratically self-governing under the *Church Manual.*

. . .

## Why don't Christian Scientists release membership statistics?

At a time when membership in this Church was growing by extraordinary leaps and bounds, its Founder, Mary Baker Eddy, introduced a rule that membership figures should not be made public. She felt strongly that numbers were not an accurate measure of genuine Christian purpose or spiritual vitality, and since then our Church has followed this rule.

While we haven't made membership figures available, there is a list of Christian Science churches and practitioners at the back of *The Christian Science Journal,* a magazine published by this Church. This provides, in effect, an easy way to count the number of churches, for anyone who needs this kind of information.

• • •

## Why don't you have ministers?

Mrs. Eddy ordained the Bible and *Science and Health* to be the pastor of her church. The Readers who read from these two books at the Sunday services are elected for that purpose by the members of each branch church from their own congregation. Christian Science practitioners, who carry on the healing ministry of Christian Science, are also lay members of our denomination who have given evidence of their fitness for this work. In a very real sense, we are a church of laymen.

• • •

## What are your church services like?

We have music and Bible readings and silent prayer and the Lord's Prayer. Then we have what is called a Bible Lesson—passages from the Bible and *Science and Health* on special subjects. These are read aloud by two Readers. Christian Scientists study this Lesson-Sermon individually during the week and try to put it into practice. Then on Sunday they share its inspiration together in a public service. On Wednesday evening there are also meetings at which people tell of healings and guidance they've received through Christian Science.

. . .

### Do you have baptism or other sacraments?

Baptism and holy communion are to us not outward observances but deeply meaningful inner experiences. Baptism is the daily purification and spiritualization of thought; communion is finding one's conscious unity with God through prayer. A beautiful "Communion Hymn" by Mrs. Eddy ends with these words:

> Strongest deliverer, friend of the friendless,
> Life of all being divine:
> Thou the Christ, and not the creed;
> Thou the Truth in thought and deed;
> Thou the water, the bread, and the wine.[1]

. . .

### Do you celebrate the Eucharist?

The Eucharist is at the very heart of Christian Science, although we don't celebrate it in the sense that we partake of bread and wine physically during our church services or have a minister or priest do so on our behalf.

We strive to partake of the Eucharist in the very midst of our daily lives. The second chapter and one of the most moving in *Science and Health* by Mrs. Eddy is called "Atonement and Eucharist." What it says is that the meaning of the Eucharist is not realized by going through the ritual but by living the kind of life Jesus showed us was possible—not that we claim any sort of equality with him. But we do understand that his mission was to live a life of such clear spiritual oneness with God that we would be able to better understand what real living is all about, what real manhood and womanhood include.

This means repenting of our own sins and omissions, recognizing our spiritual need, following in Jesus' way as best we can, studying and partaking, in a measure, in the life Jesus lived. Mrs. Eddy said, "His true flesh and blood were his Life; and they truly eat his flesh and drink his blood, who partake of that divine Life."[2] That's how we strive to celebrate the Eucharist, by partaking of the divine Life that Jesus embodied.

. . .

### What do Christian Scientists do about the poor?

Most Christian Scientists cultivate the virtue of Christian charity, as ordinarily understood. Certainly many of them contribute generously to charitable organizations. Some are engaged in social or welfare work themselves, and others are deeply concerned politically with the urgent questions of economic and social justice that affect the whole basic problem of poverty. This concern for the world and for finding healing solutions is very evident, for instance, in *The Christian Science Monitor.*

Our Church does provide substantial general relief contributions in special disaster areas—like Mexico after the earthquake and Colombia after the mudslides—and of course helps care for our local church members. We feel, however, that our primary work is to heal the root causes of poverty in the same way we heal disease—by prayer that transforms individual thinking. It's the spiritual healing—of poverty, limitation, and injustice as well as of moral and physical evils—that constitutes our unique contribution to lifting this great burden from humanity.

. . .

### How would you deal with the starving children in Africa?

Speaking for myself, I suspect if I were there I would do what you would do—I would cradle as many as I could and feed them with all the food I could lay my hands on—and in addition, while doing so, I hope I would remember to turn sincerely and expectantly to God for guidance as to how to do more—intelligently—not only to meet the immediate human needs of the multitude, but to take practical, inspired steps, for healing the fears, hates, misunderstandings, and cruelties that bring suf-

fering to humanity. It would hardly be Christian to do less! But
I'm here! And I do not feel that my geographic location can stop
my giving or silence my prayers, which include confidence in
God to heal the basic errors in human thinking that result in
war, pestilence, and starvation.

·  ·  ·

*What part does* The Christian Science Monitor *play in your outreach
to the world?*

It plays a very important part. The *Monitor* reaches more
than 140 countries throughout the world. About half its subscribers are not Christian Scientists. Many of them are journal-
ists, members of Congress or Parliament, judges, writers,
schoolteachers—people of influence in public affairs and education. Also many plain people of all sorts read the *Monitor,* and
it educates them to a wider concern for their fellow men—as
well as giving them a newspaper they can trust. That's our
aim: to tell the news with clarity, incisiveness, and integrity. In
the first issue of the paper, Mrs. Eddy wrote, "The object of
the *Monitor* is to injure no man, but to bless all mankind."[3]

As part of this effort, the *Monitor*'s shortwave news broad-
casts are now heard in many countries throughout the world.
And beginning in 1988, the *World Monitor* nightly TV newscast
in the United States has carried the *Monitor* tradition of thoughtful journalism into the television medium.

·  ·  ·

*What does your church do for the community?*

Its biggest contribution is its healing work—and by that we
don't mean only the healing of physical disease. We mean the
healing of the fears and disorders and frustrations that plague
the individual *and* the community.

Many Christian Science lectures, as well as articles published
in our Church's periodicals, focus on just this sort of much-
needed healing of community problems.

This kind of healing is the best way we can demonstrate that the Christ is always present in human affairs to satisfy men's deepest needs and yearnings. If people learn, through healing, the infinite power of the Christ-spirit, they're going to take this new sense of spiritual power and love out into their community activities. You'll find Christian Scientists engaged in all sorts of community projects and humanitarian work—you might call it an overflow of their conviction of God's loving care for all His children.

.   .   .

## What does it do for young people?

If you listen to the testimonies given by young people in our churches, or read what they write in our periodicals, you may be struck by one thing: religion is something they spontaneously relate to their school studies, their social life, their sports, their temperamental hang-ups, their family problems and intellectual doubts. Not in a pious or preachy way, but as a vital source of joy and inspiration and healing. Our various youth activities aim to make religion practical in their lives.

.   .   .

## What youth activities do you have?

Most important are our Sunday Schools; they lay a foundation for fruitful living. Then there are our college organizations, which are more than a youth activity since they include faculty members and others in the academic community. Through these organizations the members are helped in their application of Christian Science to the problems of campus life. At headquarters in Boston, our youth divisions give constant care and attention to the needs of young Christian Scientists all over the world. From time to time, regional conferences in various countries and large-scale conferences in Boston bring together thousands of students to share their experiences and inspiration.

.   .   .

*How does Christian Science help to solve problems like racism, poverty, war?*

You might say that it points to the root error from which these destructive ills arise. This error, as we see it, is the belief that man is cut off from God—that he is a finite mortal, the product of random material forces. From this belief, accepted as the basis of thought and action, come all the things that divide us, all the limitations and barriers of human life. But as one learns to accept his spiritual unity with God—the infinitely loving Father of us all—this begins to unfold his true unity with his fellow men. Then follows the gradual healing of those elements of thought—like selfishness, pride, and intolerance—which lie behind racial and economic injustice and cause war. As a person's affections become more unselfed and universal, he's also led to support enlightened human measures to combat the ills of society. Christian Scientists participate as individuals in all sorts of activities directed toward this end. And the *Monitor* keeps them well aware of the world's needs!

· · ·

*What does your church say about homosexuality?*

Our church has always regarded homosexuality as something that calls for compassion, spiritual regeneration, and healing, rather than condemnation of persons on the one hand or acceptance as a Christian way of life on the other. This church has a very strong conviction of the worth and dignity of all the children of God. Our dedication to Christian healing rests on our conviction that to learn what it really means to be the child of God is to find freedom from ills, fixations, abnormalities, and compulsive behavior patterns never imposed by God on His children.

The student of Christian Science tries his or her best to take seriously primitive Christianity—the teachings and example of Christ Jesus. Jesus talked a lot about morality, and those lessons teach us all much. In the case of the adulterous woman, for example, he spoke to her with the mingled forgiveness and healing power so typical of true Christian morality. "Neither do I condemn thee: go, *and sin no more*."[4] This is the position accepted and established for our church by its Founder, Mary Baker Eddy.

•  •  •

### What about living for others, which is so central to Christianity?

Christian Science makes very strong, life-changing Christian demands on its followers; it certainly doesn't encourage a casual or superficial attitude toward religion. Its theology does emphasize a strongly practical approach—living Christianity instead of theorizing—but the primary emphasis is on healing of sin. Mary Baker Eddy, who discovered and founded Christian Science, once wrote, "It demands less cross-bearing, self-renunciation, and divine Science to admit the claims of the corporeal senses and appeal to God for relief through a humanized conception of His power, than to deny these claims and learn the divine way,—drinking Jesus' cup, being baptized with his baptism, gaining the end through persecution and purity."[5] The whole thrust of Christian Science is to become sufficiently free of sin and selfishness oneself in order to help others.

---

1. *Christian Science Hymnal*, Nos. 298–302.

2. Mary Baker Eddy, *Science and Health with Key to the Scriptures* (Boston: The First Church of Christ, Scientist, 1906), p. 25.

3. Mary Baker Eddy, *The First Church of Christ, Scientist, and Miscellany* (Boston: The First Church of Christ, Scientist, 1913), p. 353.

4. John 8:11 (italics added).

5. Mary Baker Eddy, *Retrospection and Introspection* (Boston: The First Church of Christ, Scientist, 1891), p. 54.

# 7

# Historical Perspective on Mary Baker Eddy

$M$any religious movements come and go, briefly visible like yesterday's news. For those movements that come to stay, the development of mature scholarly perspectives on their early history can be a slow process. There are often legends to be put aside; biases, pro and con, to be honestly recognized; facts to be carefully sifted from the available evidence.

The result is a much more balanced view, but by no means necessarily a history written in grays! A United Methodist scholar recently made the point that the primary impetus behind early Methodism was its determination to be a church like the early Christian Church. In the case of Christian Science, too, the maturing of historical scholarship has brought fresh understanding to the profound commitment to New Testament Christianity that impelled its beginnings.

The sources collected in this book are not predominantly academic. It would be misleading not to include several examples, however, representative of the serious historical work that has appeared in the past several decades on Christian Science and its Founder, Mary Baker Eddy.

For readers seeking a comprehensive biographical portrait of the Founder, the most definitive study remains Robert Peel's trilogy, *Mary Baker Eddy: The Years of Discovery, The Years of Trial,* and *The Years of Authority* (New York: Holt, Rinehart and Winston, 1966, 1971, 1977)—a work described by University of Chicago historian Martin Marty as one that "breaks down the barriers between apologists and critics." Rather than excerpt from those volumes, this chapter includes portions from shorter but similarly "barrier-breaking" articles on specific historical issues.

The first selection comes from a 1980 article in *The New England Quarterly* entitled "Historical Consensus and Christian Science: The Career of a Manuscript Controversy." Written by Thomas C. Johnsen, then in the Graduate School at Johns Hopkins University, the article examines a sadly protracted document scam that for many years left widespread misunderstanding about both the origin of Christian Science and the nature of its teaching.

The controversy stemmed from a highly publicized charge of plagiarism—an allegation that part of Mrs. Eddy's major work, *Science and Health with Key to the Scriptures,* came from a manuscript on the philosopher G. W. F. Hegel by a nineteenth-century German-American, Francis Lieber. The supposed "source" manuscript was published by a clergyman in 1936 and later became the focus of a series of polemical attacks on Christian Science by a fundamentalist writer. In the academic community, the charge was also initially presumed true, but as the document began to receive closer scrutiny, the discrepancies in it proved glaring and obvious. The bubble finally burst in 1955, when a Baptist seminary professor produced a book-length study showing the document to be a crude forgery.[1]

*The New England Quarterly* article traces the forgery to the minister who originally published it. It shows that the purported Lieber document was never written by Lieber and did not in fact exist until it was concocted by Walter Haushalter as part of a scheme to extort money from The Mother Church. The article also traces Haushalter's protracted campaign to bring the book to the attention of the public once this scheme had failed. While the full details on the perpetration of the fraud are available in the published article, the following summary paragraphs draw some of the broader lessons to be gathered from the episode.

---

1. Conrad Henry Moehlman, *Ordeal by Concordance: An Historical Study of a Recent Literary Invention* (New York: Longmans, Green & Co., 1955).

# Historical Consensus and Christian Science: The Career of a Manuscript Controversy

The plagiarism accusation has had a wide popular circulation in the large body of polemical literature on Christian Science published by writers of other denominations, such as Walter Martin's *The Kingdom of the Cults*. References like this are significant in that they bring us back to the problem of consensus myths and the tendency of such myths to shape perceptions. In this case, while a fresh examination of Mary Baker Eddy's theology would extend beyond the scope of this essay, her own emphasis on the Protestant roots of her thought contrasts markedly with the view of Christian Science embodied in the [Walter] Haushalter essay. The acceptance of the fraudulent document rested on the assumption that Christian Science could be understood essentially without reference to Christian sources. This assumption had behind it a long tradition, first, of orthodox and fundamentalist polemics, and second, of what a recent *New York Times* review termed "prosecutorial journalism," academic as well as popular, which portrayed Christian Science in non-Christian and essentially reductionist terms. Only recently have scholars begun to remove some of the traditional interpretative blinders and consider the movement in the context of the Christian culture in which it grew.

The situation is further complicated by the existence of two opposing traditions of biography on Mrs. Eddy herself—in the words of one commentator, as "rose-colored" and "black." Thus, a 1973 monograph on the movement noted, while "not a

Thomas C. Johnsen, in *The New England Quarterly,* vol. 53, no. 1 (March 1980), pp. 20–22.

few" of Mrs. Eddy's followers made her into a "plaster saint," critics at the same time "vied for epithets to denounce her" on levels as diverse as the street-corner reportage in the *New York World* and the Brahmin discourse in the *North American Review.* Again, it is only within the past decade that a major study has attempted to resolve the disparity, taking her seriously as a religious figure while reducing her neither to hollow saint nor inspired mountebank. As historian Martin E. Marty has remarked, the time seems finally ripe for such reappraisal.

More broadly, the episode dramatizes the special force with which distorting myths sometimes operate in the study of minorities or negative reference groups, whether racial or religious. In this light, the lack of real questioning in the initial reception of the Haushalter document may have larger implications than the fact of the forgery itself. The predominant assumptions underlying conventional scholarly assessments of Christian Science have not only led to dubious conclusions, but have in many instances prevented the most useful questions from even being asked.

$M$ary Baker Eddy's own cultural roots were in New England Puritanism. She joined the Congregational church as a teenager and remained a member for nearly four decades, until the year she published *Science and Health*. This religious background helps to explain a great deal about her teaching, including its Calvinistic bluntness about the problem of human sin.

It also helps to explain why Mrs. Eddy insisted that there was such a profound difference between healing in Christian Science and the therapeutic practices of Phineas P. Quimby, the benign "magnetic" healer from Portland, Maine, whom she at one time regarded as a mentor. For Mrs. Eddy, the issue was not personal but theological—the difference between authentic Christian healing and (as it might be described today) a psychological therapy based on suggestion. As historian Stephen Gottschalk makes clear in "Mrs. Eddy and Quimby," an excerpt from an extended entry in *The Encyclopedia of the American Religious Experience,* the long controversy over Quimby's "influence" on Mrs. Eddy has tended to obscure this basic religious difference.

# Mrs. Eddy and Quimby

$E$ddy's contact with Quimby appears to have been one of those moments, apparent in other careers as well, in which previously disparate elements are drawn into sudden unity, opening further channels for investigation. Specifically, her encounter with Quimby related her medical experiments and her Christian preoccupations by suggesting that the mental basis of disease pointed to a science underlying Jesus' healing works. On the specific nature of this science Eddy's ultimate thinking differed radically from anything Quimby wrote. But the idea that there could be such a science operated as a catalyst in her experience, giving specific focus to her nascent desire for a more spiritually and physically liberating Christianity.

Well before meeting him, she had reached conclusions of her own as to the mental causation of disease through experiments with homeopathy, a medical system that holds that a patient's ability to fight an illness is stimulated by the administration of minute doses of a drug that, in healthy persons, produces symptoms of the disease being treated. While some mid-nineteenth-century advocates of homeopathy had strong affinities with Swedenborgianism, the system's significance to Eddy lay in its empirical bearing on the mental origin of disease. Sometime during the 1850s she concluded that it was the patient's faith in the drug rather than the drug itself that was responsible for the substance's apparent effects. This conviction, which was in con-

---

Stephen Gottschalk, "Christian Science and Harmonialism," in *The Encyclopedia of the American Religious Experience,* ed. Charles H. Lippy and Peter W. Williams (New York: Charles Scribner's Sons, 1988), vol. 2, pp. 901–916.

sonance with Quimby's own views on the role of belief and "explanation" in causing and curing disease, helps explain why on first writing to him Eddy professed "entire confidence" in his philosophy—which she soon came to see had even greater religious implications than she had thought.

From the first Eddy projected onto Quimby an intensity of religious interest that was as native to her as it was foreign to him. Whereas he connected his healing technique only intermittently with religion, she did so consistently, referring to it in her first newspaper tribute to him as "a very spiritual doctrine" and praising him publicly upon his death in a poem on "Dr. P. P. Quimby, Who Healed with the Truth that Christ Taught." As Fisher wrote, Quimby "held that religious beliefs were founded in deception. Mrs. Patterson was an earnest advocate of the view that religion was all in all." The assessment of the matter by the eminent German church historian Karl Höll is hard to fault: "That which connected her with Quimby was her conviction that all disease in the last analysis has its roots in the mind, and that healing therefore must be effected through mental influence. But it was her earnest Puritan faith in God that separated her from Quimby from the beginning."[1]

That Eddy may have had an inkling of this disparity is suggested by her question in a letter to Quimby in 1864, "What is your truth if it applies only to the evil diseases which show themselves?"[2] implying a far broader vision of the religious implications of his therapeutics than he entertained. This prodding question addressed to Quimby when his influence on her was supposedly at its height tends to confirm her later claim that the influence ran both ways. Horatio Dresser's mother, Annetta, recalled well after the controversy over Quimby's influence on Eddy had erupted that "those interested would in turn write articles about his 'theory' or 'the Truth,' as he called it, then bring them to him for criticism."[3] But as Eddy's biographer, Robert Peel, notes, Quimby's son George's recollection of Mrs. Patterson "talking with [Quimby], reading his Mss., copying some of them, writing some herself and reading them to him for his criticism" is the only record of anyone's having done this.[4]

Certainly the basic principle—or Principle as Eddy would have it—of Christian Science cannot be traced to Quimby's writings, nor is there any evidence that he would have agreed with it. The testimony of George Quimby is relevant on this point. He insisted that Eddy got "her inspiration and idea"— that is the concept "that disease was a mental condition"—from Quimby. But he also stated categorically, "The *religion* which she teaches certainly *is hers,* for which I cannot be too thankful; for I should be loath to go down to my grave feeling that my father was in any way connected with 'Christian Science.' "[5] If Eddy's "inspiration and idea" was simply "that disease was a mental condition," she might well have owed this to Quimby— though her own experience had already led her toward this conclusion. But the "inspiration and idea" of Christian Science as a theology and a metaphysic was something far different—so different that George Quimby was exceedingly anxious to dissociate himself and his father from it. To what, then, did she owe the "inspiration and idea" of Christian Science itself?

## *"A Woman of One Idea"*

To Eddy this "inspiration and idea" was in one sense the fruit of the many years of struggle and searching through which, as she put it, God had been "graciously preparing" her to receive Christian Science. Specifically, she associated its "discovery" with a moment of spiritual illumination gained while reading a Gospel account of one of Jesus' healings. That illumination, she claimed, brought about her immediate recovery from the severe effects of a fall in February, 1866, less than three weeks after Quimby's death. The details of the incident have been much disputed, the crux of the matter being the conflict between what the attending physician was reported by a newspaper at the time as saying about the gravity of her injuries and his downplaying of the incident years later. Eddy's turning to the Bible for healing, however, fits well with the pattern suggested by other evidence and in the long run is more historically significant than the degree of her injuries.

Abundant evidence of her activities over the next several

years shows her deeply preoccupied with exploring the Scriptures, in which she believed she was discovering the science underlying Christian healing. By the autumn of 1866 she was deeply immersed in an intensive analysis of Genesis intended to be the first volume of an ambitious but uncompleted work to be called "The Bible in Its Spiritual Meaning." Other contemporary testimony leaves no doubt of her increasing conviction, in the words of one who knew her at the time, that she "had cognition of certain great principles in the life and teachings of Christ which were not well understood or properly set forth by religious teachers."[6]

What Eddy felt she had discovered through her exploration of Scripture was a radically new and enlarged concept of God that correlated with her own deepest religious experience. In this respect the numinous quality of the language in which she describes her healing is itself revealing. "That short experience," she wrote in 1896, "included a glimpse of the great fact that I have since tried to make plain to others, namely, Life in and of Spirit; this Life being the sole reality of existence."[7]

For her this true sense of Spirit meant that God was real, sovereign, and absolute in a way that contradicted materialistic assumptions far more radically than traditional Christian theology had ever conceived. Given Eddy's strong religious background, it would simply never have occurred to her to question that God was the intelligent, loving Father to whom Christians prayed. But she held too that the full promise of Christianity could not be realized until God was seen as the Life, Soul, and ordering Principle of all being, which must like him be spiritual—until it was understood that there could be no actual life, substance, or intelligence apart from him.

This was the fundamental idea that Eddy fleshed out over the nine years after 1866 into the theology and metaphysics of Christian Science. It was basic to both that one infinite God must be unconfinable in the forms he creates. In the chapter "Recapitulation" from *Science and Health,* which she had adapted from a series of questions and answers originally prepared for classroom use in 1870, she wrote: "This is a leading point in the Science of Soul, that Principle is not in its idea. Spirit, Soul, is not confined in man, and is never in matter."[8] Mortality itself, she contended, proceeded from and operated within the sinful sense of the one Soul or Life as fragmented and divided into a multiplicity of human personalities, each with a finite mentality and body expressing it. She used the terms "personal sense" and later "mortal mind" as shorthand for this false sense or basic error, eventually adopting the phrase "animal magnetism" to indicate the hypnotic nature of its operation.

The whole meaning of Jesus' saving mission, she contended, lay in the fact that his healing works and overcoming of death broke through the false concept of existence built up by mortal mind on its mistaken premise of life apart from God. The virgin birth of Jesus, Eddy held, enabled him to live man's spiritual sonship with God in the midst of human experience. She believed that this sonship, or true status of man in Christ, was uniquely embodied in the life and person of Jesus yet not confined to him. For her Jesus' healing as well as his crucifixion and resurrection were historical events of supreme importance, revealing that authentic spiritual being is inseparable from God and therefore triumphant over suffering and mortality.

It was to open the possibility of achieving this authentic spiritual being to all men that Jesus struggled and sacrificed on humanity's behalf. As Eddy wrote in her short work *No and Yes:*

> The glory of human life is in overcoming sickness, sin, and death. Jesus suffered for all mortals to bring in this glory; and his purpose was to show them that the way out of the flesh, out of the delusion of all human error, must be through the baptism of suffering, leading up to health, harmony, and heaven. . . .
>
> Love bruised and bleeding, yet mounting to the throne of glory in purity and peace, over the steps of uplifted humanity,— this is the deep significance of the blood of Christ. Nameless woe, everlasting victories, are the blood, the vital currents of Christ Jesus' life, purchasing the freedom of mortals from sin and death.[9]

In contradistinction to the theory of the substitutionary atonement, Eddy maintained that "Jesus spares us not one individual experience, if we follow his commands faithfully; and all have the cup of sorrowful effort to drink in proportion to their demonstration of his love, till all are redeemed through divine Love."[10] This true Christian discipleship, she insisted, must include Christian healing if it is to make good on the meaning of Jesus' mission. Her discovery of Christian Science, she felt, had elucidated this healing and the science that made it possible; and its conscientious practice had resulted empirically in the radical healing of both sickness and sin. But the purpose of physical healing for her was entirely secondary to the healing of sin. Far from merely improving human existence, it was intended to prove that spiritual being was not, as Christian orthodoxy would have it, a condition belonging to some heavenly realm in the beyond. Rather, it was the Kingdom of God to which ordinary material sense is blind but which is nevertheless present to be brought to light. From this standpoint the materiality that appears so palpable to the senses really represents only a limited or uninspired grasp of spiritual reality. In the Christian terms that came so naturally to her, Eddy saw matter as "the flesh" opposed to "the Spirit" and the belief in its reality as a denial of her basic conviction of "Life in and of Spirit, this Life being the sole reality of existence."[11]

As a Unitarian minister who interviewed Eddy just after she moved to Boston observed, ". . . she is a woman of one idea, almost to the point of wearisomeness."[12] This conviction of "Life in and of Spirit" well expresses that "one idea." Eddy's contact with Quimby was an important aspect of the process whereby she arrived at it and provided her with some working concepts and useful language to define the operation and effects of "mortal mind." But nothing in Quimby accounts for the idea itself. It was not Quimby adapted or Quimby Christianized; it was simply a different idea. And it was her one great theme from 1866 onward.

---

1. Karl Höll, "Der Szientismus," *Gesammelte Aufsätze zur Kirchengeschichte* (Tübingen: J. C. B. Muhr, 1921–1928), vol. 3, pp. 463–464.

2. Mary Baker Eddy, Letter, April 24, 1864, Archives of The Mother Church.

3. Robert Peel, *Mary Baker Eddy: The Years of Discovery* (New York: Holt, Rinehart and Winston, 1966), p. 180.

4. *Ibid.*

5. George Quimby, From Phineas Parkhurst Quimby, in *The Quimby Manuscripts,* ed. Horatio W. Dresser (New York: Thomas Y. Crowell, 1921). (Italics added.)

6. Peel, *Mary Baker Eddy: The Years of Discovery,* p. 210.

7. Mary Baker Eddy, *Miscellaneous Writings* (Boston: The First Church of Christ, Scientist, 1896), p. 24.

8. Mary Baker Eddy, *Science and Health with Key to the Scriptures* (Boston: The First Church of Christ, Scientist, 1906), p. 467.

9. Mary Baker Eddy, *No and Yes* (Boston: The First Church of Christ, Scientist, 1891), pp. 33, 34.

10. Eddy, *Science and Health,* p. 26.

11. Eddy, *Miscellaneous Writings,* p. 24.

12. Robert Peel, *Christian Science: Its Encounter with American Culture* (New York: Holt, 1958), p. 115.

Mary Baker Eddy once wrote, in reply to the sardonic criticism of Mark Twain: "What I am remains to be proved by the good I do."[1] For Twain and many of his contemporaries, the fact that she was a woman in a public role then normally reserved for men quite obscured other perspectives on what she achieved.

Jean A. McDonald assesses the implications of this fact in her article "Mary Baker Eddy and the Nineteenth-Century 'Public' Woman: A Feminist Reappraisal," which originally appeared in the *Journal of Feminist Studies in Religion.* The article examines a large body of evidence showing how Mrs. Eddy was stereotyped by male detractors who resented her for intruding, as they saw it, into privileged male domains of serious thought, theology, and medicine. This stereotyping, McDonald shows, in turn colored the very academic perceptions of Mrs. Eddy upon which feminist historians have often uncritically relied. The ironic result has been that *their* portrait of her is strikingly similar to conventional male views of women who have left their "proper sphere" and intruded into male territory!

Only as feminism itself has matured have feminists begun to assess more positively Mrs. Eddy's place in a strong tradition of Christian spirituality, including her deeply felt emphasis on the motherhood as well as the fatherhood of God.

---

1. Mary Baker Eddy, *The First Church of Christ, Scientist, and Miscellany* (Boston: The First Church of Christ, Scientist, 1913), p. 303.

# Mary Baker Eddy and the Nineteenth-Century "Public" Woman: A Feminist Reappraisal

It is plain that members of predominantly male professions applied to Eddy stereotypical definitions of women in general. However, if we are indeed uncovering male bias in the traditional portrait of Eddy, we should find that not only the definitions, but also the motives assigned to her for ignoring those definitions, are reflected in the motives assigned to women in general. In contrast to the high-minded purposes they assigned to themselves and their friends, nineteenth-century men responded to public women by disparaging their activities, belittling their efforts, trivializing their significance and achievements, and reducing their motives to a struggle for personal power, dominance, and glory, to envy of maleness and wishing to be a man. They did this in terms which strikingly match the vocabulary they used in discussing the motives of Eddy and her followers. . . .

Clearly, this vocabulary could have been lifted directly from the clerical, medical, or academic portraits by Eddy's contemporaries. For these depicted her as motivated not by a search for truth—a biological impossibility—but by envy of maleness, ambition for personal glory, power, and dominance.

"What's Christyan Science?" asked Mr. Hennessy.
"Tis wan way iv gettin' the money," said Mr. Dooley.[1]

Eddy was aggressive, "a pope in petticoats," "the Lydia Pinkham of the Soul," a Kaiser, a czar, so greedy for money and power that the whole purpose of her queendom was "to build to

---

Jean A. McDonald, in *Journal of Feminist Studies in Religion,* vol. 2, no. 1 (Spring 1986), pp. 100–111.

the sky the glory of the sovereign, and keep it bright to the end of time." Christian Science was not a religion but a business, a gigantic "conspiracy" that Eddy had organized of "enterprising American ladies who are making a fat living out of the weak-minded and credulous," thus rating themselves a position in life other than as the "kitchen hands and servants" with whom they really belonged.[2]

What is most striking about this last statement and the many others of which it is representative is the degree to which its substance parallels the consensus among contemporary feminist scholars . . . : that Eddy and her followers gravitated into Christian Science because of its personal utility to them in compensating for their otherwise low status in a male-dominated society. Indeed, the contemporary feminist consensus is in essentials so close to that of male contemporaries of Eddy and the early Christian Science movement that it may be regarded as little more than a sophisticated restatement of it. . . .

Feminist scholars have to a large degree accepted the judgment of Eddy's contemporaries that Christian Science was a woman's movement. Yet this organization reputedly made up of enterprising American "kitchen hands" in fact included a considerable body of *men:* senators, congressmen, governors and mayors, clergymen, physicians, judges and lawyers, university professors and writers, artists and actors, businessmen and society leaders, often writing and speaking publicly on behalf of the movement to enormous audiences.[3] While women were numerically predominant in the Christian Science movement, men played an extremely prominent role in its expansion as well as in the running of the church—a point that has been largely ignored both by nineteenth-century male commentators and by a surprising number of later academic writers.

Could this be because, perceived through the lens of prevailing male stereotypes, a woman-led movement could not possibly be taken seriously by men? If so, those men who appeared to be taking it seriously could be written off as not "real" men. Psychologically, if a woman develops a secure place in masculine space, that ipso facto diminishes the "manly" nature of that space and hence the manly image of the man who occupies the space. As [an

Anglican archbishop] put it, as late as 1968, "If the Church is to be thrown open to women, it will be the death knell of the appeal of the Church for men."[4] But men could reduce the threat posed to men by Christian Science by ignoring the fact that the new movement was attracting both women and men, and by characterizing it as a movement by, for, and about women, having in consequence no logic, no sense, no significance—nothing to contribute to men and men's sphere.

A search through the mass of articles, speeches, verses, cartoons, and reports on Christian Science at that period reveals that this was indeed what men were doing. The movement had to be merely a woman's movement, and therefore, occasionally "presumably," but usually categorically, so it was. The members, men announced, were "*presumably* of the weaker sex," "persons . . . still in the childhood of mental development," "mostly people with . . . disease of the generative organs," "principally of the feminine gender," "the majority" of them "women of queer nervous constitution, when not strictly on the make," "fatuous women" and only "senile gentlemen."[5]

*Men* were the true scientists, writers, intellectuals, thinkers, so, as a woman's movement, Christian Science was by contrast everything that was feminine—unscientific and unintellectual, ludicrous and illogical. When men dramatized this "lunacy" in cartoons, verses, drawings, and articles, their stock characters were sagacious males exposing the comedic and/or the mercenary nature of the movement to the simpleton females who were duped by it, for, explained the celebrated Mr. Dooley, "not manny men is Christyan Scientists, but near all women is, in wan way or another." The simpletons were of the ignorant servant class, in ragged clothes, or schoolmarms and formidable battleaxes, hair tightly pinned, determined backs stiffened, hands archly poised, sharp noses supporting the inevitable spectacles, hard jaws, and lips either pursed dogmatically, or ferociously grinning at their woebegone dupes. . . .[6]

Not only does the actual role of men in the Christian Science movement fly in the face of this picture, but the reason the movement attracted substantial numbers of both men and women undermines the interpretation of it as woman's quest for status and power in a male-dominated society. What was the reason? What was indeed motivating Eddy's followers—those "millions" of "good paying and intelligent patrons" whom we saw earlier had "been deceived" into accepting Christian Science?

The tendency of traditional male historians to rely predominantly on secondary sources for their studies of women's lives—a casual approach men have not pursued when studying men—means that we are unlikely to find there the reasons for women's behavior. Surprisingly, feminist scholarship on Eddy is also based largely on secondary sources rather than on original sources that allow women to interpret their own experience. Turning to the original evidence will give us not only better scholarship but better *feminist* scholarship.

One of the best original sources of information on the motivation of Eddy's followers is the collection of testimonial letters by converts to Christian Science, appearing in each issue of *The Christian Science Journal*.[7] These letters give us clues as to why people were attracted to Christian Science, what they thought Eddy was teaching them, and what value they felt her teaching had. Moreover, the collection allows us to assess Eddy's own motivations.

A randomly selected volume of *The Christian Science Journal*[8] contains 156 letters, one-third of which were from men.* Notably, there is no perceptible difference between women and men letter writers in terms of what appears to have drawn them to the Christian Science movement. Looking past the sometimes florid style typical of the period to the content of the letters, we find clear indications that, next to healing (the most frequent motive), what both the women and the men had most sought, what they had not found elsewhere, and what they were finding in Eddy's teaching, was a satisfying concept of God.

Both women and men confessed previous anguished doubts about orthodox Christian teachings and about many parts of the Bible. They had yearned to "understand" but were instead told by clergymen and friends that they "must have faith and believe" and "not try to comprehend" (woman, pp. 206–207;

---

*Subsequent references to this volume will appear by page number in the text.

men, pp. 273, 268). Some, unable to "have faith," or because of their encounters with agnostics, had left organized religion altogether (men, pp. 205, 266–67; women, p. 540). Others had obediently tried to follow instructions but found no change in their experience as a result, so then had lost heart. "I used to say that I could do the works which Jesus did if I only had his faith. I tried to gain faith, and gladly listened to sermons on that topic, but they were disappointing. They neither showed me the way nor gave me the inspiration I needed. I could not trust the promises of the Master and be healed, and I did not see that others around me fared any better" (woman, p. 131).

If such individuals were disillusioned by the theologically orthodox "have faith and believe" school, they were equally alienated by the philosophically orthodox "be cheerful and optimistic" view. In common with many others of their day, they found that they could not reconcile the concept of a "good" deity who yet "caused" suffering, sent it, or "permitted" it. "As long as I believed that God made me sick, what right had I to hope for health, even though the doctor emphasized continually that I must not allow myself to become discouraged? The advice to maintain a hopeful state of mind is certainly fatuous unless a reasonable ground for such hope be given at the same time" (woman, p. 202; see also women, pp. 58, 128, 130, 199). Disillusioned theologically, medically, philosophically, they tended to discard the Bible as mysterious, contradictory, and impractical (women, pp. 348, 615) and to turn instead to psychology, poetry, philosophy. But still their "hunger for God increased" (women, pp. 57, 206, 277, 409); intellectual searching only intensifying their dilemmas and doubts.

However, when they read *Science and Health* they were "held" by it (women, pp. 540, 615). Even if at first put off by its style, they kept coming back to it (woman, p. 199). "I was eagerly reading the pages of Mrs. Eddy's book . . . looking for its substance" (man, p. 198). "I continued my reading in almost breathless expectancy," fearful that it might not measure up to the hopes raised. "It often contradicted my previous religious doctrinal instruction, but never once did it contradict the Bible! My questions were all answered" (woman, p. 540). They found that it stressed an understanding of God but rejected the concept of belief, at which point they could finally say, "I have . . . at last found a God whom I can understand and worship" (men, pp. 269, 273; women, pp. 57, 206, 270), have been brought "nearer and nearer to God" (man, p. 472), and have "a better understanding of the Bible" (women, pp. 414, 277, 348, 745; man, p. 273).

Their comments on Eddy's concept of God help explain much about the movement's appeal. Perhaps most essential to converts was Eddy's radical insistence that God absolutely is not the cause of evil in any form. Rather, the letters said, he is "a God who does not afflict" (p. 202) "but who is in very truth infinite, omnipresent good" (p. 199). To many converts, Eddy opened the full meaning of the Bible by showing God as Mind—the infinite consciousness or intelligence—fully manifested in the life of Jesus. A Jewish convert wrote that she had had "an innate aversion" to the name of Jesus until finding the explanation of the Messiah in *Science and Health.* Now, she said, "I . . . pray that I may be found worthy to follow in his footsteps and that I may reflect more fully that Mind 'which was also in Christ Jesus,' the Exemplar and Wayshower" (p. 807).

Expanding on Jesus' use of the term "Father" for God, Eddy held that God could be known as Mother as well. Many converts touched on their greater sense of nearness to a God who was also a "tender Father-Mother" (p. 613). They expressed satisfaction at finding a God whom they could "at last" understand because the proof of His reality and power in healing showed that He is not just a supernatural person to whom one can pray, but is the divine Principle of all being, and "this Principle is ever perfect and harmonious, ruling men now" (p. 198).

Although these letters claimed that their new concept of God had healed them of diseases, the effects of accidents, and various other difficulties,[9] the appeal of a new understanding of God was so compelling that most converts expressed more appreciation for that than for the physical relief. "All this physical help is, however, as nothing beside the knowledge that I have found God, that I have not sinned away my day of grace; that I am not a lost soul!" (woman, p. 620). "I am more thankful that I now have some knowledge of Him whom to know aright is life eternal" (man, p. 268), a "spiritual understanding of Life as God" (woman, p. 211). The healings "pale" before "the wonders of Spirit and the spiritual regeneration now going on," "the great spiritual uplift experienced" (men, pp. 551, 621, women, pp. 208, 614), the "wonderful light" (woman, p. 687), the Bible now "indeed becoming a 'light unto my path' " (woman, p. 545).

In some cases the appeal of physical relief had even been counterproductive:

> The first time a friend spoke to me of [Christian Science], telling me her husband had been healed through its application, I doubted, and never gave it another thought. Had she told me that he was healed through the right understanding of God and His spiritual laws which govern man, I might not have been so skeptical. . . . [Later my] friend told me that through reading [*Science and Health*] she was learning to understand the Bible; that she had never before cared to read it, except from a sense of duty. . . . I too wanted to read the book for I wanted to know more about God. . . . [Since then] there have been no unanswered "whys" (woman, pp. 745–747; see also women, pp. 58, 59, 61, 128, 130, 474, 545; and man, p. 612).

These letters do not provide even hidden evidence for the motivations traditionally assigned to public women—the thirst for money and power; rather they testify to a great need to *know*. For these women and men the passion for certainty, their hunger for reality, had not been stemmed but deepened by the metaphysical explosions set off by Darwinism and the undermining of religious faith by other secular influences. Why then has their theological hunger been ignored for so long? Why have their health problems been documented, but almost never their intellectual and spiritual search?

One answer may lie in the stereotype that while men seek religion to satisfy their sense of reason and truth, women seek religion to satisfy their emotional needs. Thus even if the women in the letters *say* that they were attracted to Christian Science because it satisfied their sense of reason and truth, the stereotype suggests that it would not be valid scholarship to believe them. . . .

From Anne Hutchinson's time to that of Mary Baker Eddy and her followers, women as well as men were troubled by religious doubt. Eddy's contemporary, Harriet Beecher Stowe, pointed out that philosophical and theological discussion and questioning was a principal outlet for every nineteenth-century New England farmer during intervals at hoeing, *and also* for every woman and girl at loom or washtub. Stowe's own theological questioning after the death of her son found its way into the tormenting "whys" of the woman character in one of her novels—a character whose agonized questioning stands out with searing immediacy against the bland piety of the rest of the book. Like future converts to Christian Science, this character contemplates "in desperate moments" giving up the Bible. Yet she is able to make no sense of the nineteenth century's alternative deity, since "Nature," like God, was also inexplicably both beneficent and cruel. . . .[10]

If we accept these converts' own words and the genuineness of their existential and religious dissatisfaction with the nineteenth-century theological status quo, then we have to concede to them a genuine religious motivation at least equal to the other motivations put forward to explain their attraction to Christian Science. Equally to the point, we have to concede two further needs: the need to reassess the theological content of a book that so satisfied the *theological* hunger of these converts, and the need to reassess the motivations of its author. Can we accept as genuine the converts' own accounts?

Support for their genuineness can sometimes be found in unlikely places. For among Eddy's severest critics are those who, like the converts, view *Science and Health* as indeed a book about God, a book accepting some traditional concepts of the deity while also contributing new ones. . . .[11]

Ironically, further testimony on the theological motivations of Eddy and her followers, and the theological appeal of her book is provided by many clergymen who were deeply concerned about defections to Christian Science. If their own members were turning away from their traditions unsatisfied, what, they asked, might be deficient in their own presentation of Christian truth? The Christian Scientists were giving the people "light," while we gave them "the husks and doctrines." . . .[12]

And so we return to our initial question: is Mary Baker Eddy's history that of a typical power-frustrated nineteenth-century woman who found satisfaction through commercial status and power? Or, because the match between the traditional portrait of Mary Baker Eddy and the stereotype of the public woman is so close, might this portrait of her be grounded in defensiveness rather than in fact? To extend a question Carl Degler raised in 1974,[13] is there a history of women who have contributed useful insights to the history of ideas, and is Mary Baker Eddy one of them?

This study obviously does not attempt to do more than raise the question. But in that process enough evidence has come to light to suggest a possible answer in favor of a nontraditional appraisal, and to point to the need for further research in the same direction. The evidence suggests that in their scholarship on Eddy, feminists may well have been heading in an inappropriate direction, one contrary to their own deepest concerns and, ironically, congruent with a traditional male perspective.

---

1. F. P. Dunne, "Mr. Dooley: On the Practice of Medicine," *Harper's Weekly*, vol. 45 (July 13, 1901), p. 698; Rev. Gregory, "More Suggestions Touching 'Christian Science,' " *Homiletic Review*, vol. 39 (April 1900), p. 378.

2. "Mrs. Eddy the Aggressor," *Journal of the American Medical Association*, vol. 33 (December 16, 1899), p. 1560; Rev. R. Heber Newton, quoted in Charles M. Oughton, M.D., *Crazes, Credulities, and Christian Science* (Chicago: Colegrove, 1901), p. 35; Mark Twain, "Christian Science—III," *North American Review*, vol. 176 (February 1903), p. 178; *American Medicine*, vol. 12 (July 1906), p. 181; H. V. Sweringen, "Christian Science," *Cincinnati Lancet-Clinic* n.s. 47 (July 20, 1901), pp. 55–61; George F. Shriady, "Christian Science Viewed through the Spectacles of a Lay Writer," *Medical Record*, vol. 59 (May 25, 1901), p. 817; *Medical Record*, vol. 62 (October 4, 1902), p. 541; Editorials in *New York Times*, November 14, 1902, p. 8, col. 4, and June 11, 1900, p. 6, col. 4; and *St. James Gazette* (London), in *Literary Digest*, vol. 17 (December 24, 1898), p. 757.

3. Prominent among these were United States Senator Moses E.

Clapp of Minnesota; Johns Hopkins University professor Hermann S. Hering, son of the founder of homeopathy; Judge Hickman, professor of law, University of Minnesota; Attorney-General Clarence A. Buskirk; former successful businessman Edward A. Kimball; Charles Klein, popular author of long-running Broadway plays; Howard Chandler Christy, artist and creator of the famous "Christy girl"; and Lord Dunmore of England.

4. Quoted in Eva Figes, *Patriarchal Attitudes* (London: Faber and Faber, 1970), p. 54.

5. Shriady (italics added); S. L. Jepson, "Human Suggestibility," *West Virginia Medical Journal,* vol. 5 (September 1910), p. 76; Robert T. Morris, M.D., "On Faith Cures," *Medical Record,* vol. 59 (May 4, 1901); Frank E. Fee, "Wanted—A New Name for a New Form of Insanity," *Cincinnati Lancet-Clinic* n.s. 40 (March 5, 1898), p. 233; "Christian Science and the Church in England," *Medical Record,* vol. 68 (December 9, 1905), p. 944; and Editorial in "Science or Faith," *Medical Standard,* vol. 22 (April 1891), p. 123.

6. Dunne, p. 698. And see illustrations in *Life,* September 4, 1902, p. 193, and March 17, 1904, p. 264.

7. I have been able to find only three other studies that have used this source: Stephen Gottschalk, *The Emergence of Christian Science in American Religious Life* (Berkeley: University of California Press, 1973), pp. 222–238; R. W. England, "Some Aspects of Christian Science as Reflected in Letters of Testimony," *American Journal of Sociology,* vol. 59 (March 1954), pp. 448–453, and vol. 60 (September 1954), pp. 184–185; and Penny Hansen, "Woman's Hour: Feminist Implications of Mary Baker Eddy's Christian Science Movement, 1885–1910" (Ph.D. diss., University of California, Irvine, 1981).

8. *The Christian Science Journal,* vol. 28 (1910–11), the year of Eddy's death.

9. Both men and women listed release from difficulties such as heart, kidney, and stomach troubles, malignant growths, and alcoholism. But in addition, men listed industrial injuries, hernia, and epilepsy; while women listed ovarian problems, breast cancer, and childbirth that was "markedly easier and quicker" than previous occasions under medical treatment (p. 132). The fact that both women and men so often valued the theological satisfactions above even these rather remarkable cures tells us something about the depth of their spiritual hunger.

10. Harriet Beecher Stowe, *The Minister's Wooing* (1859; reprint, Hartford: The Stowe-Day Foundation, 1978), pp. 24, 87, 334, 341, 343–346, 356. Madonna Kolbenschlag, "Women's Fiction: Redefining Religious Experience," *New Catholic World,* vol. 224 (November–December 1981), pp. 252–256, is an analysis of contemporary feminist fiction as a chronicle of women's experience in terms of a "spiritual search." See also Carol P.

Christ, "Margaret Atwood: The Surfacing of Women's Spiritual Quest and Vision," *Signs,* vol. 2 (Winter 1976), pp. 316–330; and the response by Judith Plaskow on pp. 331–339. These also discuss the tendency of some contemporary women theologians to consider nature as deity and the virtues and dangers of this trend.

11. Susan L. Lindley, "The Ambiguous Feminism of Mary Baker Eddy," *Journal of Religion,* vol. 64 (July 1984), pp. 318–331, is a feminist scholar who has picked up on Eddy's new concept of God as "Mother" while overlooking Eddy's more numerous images of God as "divine Mind" and "Principle." Thus Lindley argues that Eddy was attempting to develop a compensatory "feminist theology," a truly feminist church, but the attempt was "ambiguous," and so it failed. In view of the evidence above, however, it would seem more likely that the attempt appears ambiguous because there was no such attempt. Although one may adopt the position that the only legitimate pursuit for a woman was advocacy of the feminist cause, this was not Eddy's position, and it can be argued that holding her to this standard has the ironic effect of doing to Eddy what men have traditionally done to women. It takes her out of her own framework ("the search for truth") entirely and defines her in male terms ("a woman is uninterested in truth").

12. G. Frederick Wright, "Christian Scientists," *Bibliotheca Sacra* (Congregational), vol. 56 (April 1899), p. 381; the sampling of similar clerical views from various other denominational journals in *Current Literature,* vol. 41 (December 1906), pp. 679–680; Rev. J. A. Milburn in *Indianapolis Star,* in *Christian Science Sentinel,* February 17, 1904, p. 392; and Rev. Holland, canon of St. Paul's Cathedral, London, in M. Carta Sturge, *The Truth and Error of Christian Science* (London: Murray, 1903), p. xvi.

13. Carl N. Degler, *Is There a History of Woman?* (Oxford: Clarendon Press, 1975).

Jean McDonald's almost passionate insistence on "genuine religious motivations" in Mary Baker Eddy and her followers is ultimately not a feminist insight but a spiritual one. The religious questions Mrs. Eddy struggled with were and are universal, however unconventional her response. This insight is amplified in "Mary Baker Eddy in Perspective," a 1982 church commentary published in *American Heritage—The Magazine of History*. It was written in response to an earlier "psychohistory" by Dr. Julius Silberger, Jr. The commentary summarizes the fuller, but by no means saccharine, picture of Mary Baker Eddy that emerges from the scholarly evidence now available on her life.

# Mary Baker Eddy in Perspective

One thing on which Mrs. Eddy's admirers and critics agree is that she was a "remarkable" woman. The fact that she founded a major American religious movement in an age and at an age when she might have been expected, in her own ironic words, to be a little old lady in a lace cap, justifies at least that much of a generalization.

But remarkable people are more often than not complex. And when their lives are as long as Mrs. Eddy's was (she lived from 1821 to 1910) they often change in remarkable ways, becoming virtually several different people in the course of their evolving experience. This makes it all the more necessary to avoid winding the threads of such a life onto the single spool of one's own interests and assumptions.

As a practicing psychiatrist, Dr. Silberger naturally tries to account for Mrs. Eddy's life and motivation in terms of psychological factors of professional interest to him. Such a sketch expectably conveys the impression of a woman driven by personal and emotional needs against the background of nineteenth-century American social conditions. But it is important to remember that these conditions included strong religious influences—especially in rural New England where the Puritan spirit was still very much alive during Mrs. Eddy's youth. The evidence bearing on her religious motivation is both plentiful and essential.

One need not be a believer in her teaching or even in Christianity itself to see that realism in biography does not, cannot,

*American Heritage—The Magazine of History,* vol. 33, no. 2 (February–March 1982), pp. 110–111.

exclude the religious dimension of human life. That was the attitude of the facile iconoclasm in biographical writing which flourished a half-century or more ago (the period, incidentally, when there first appeared the "debunking" accounts of Mrs. Eddy's life upon which later psychobiographers have drawn). But an interdisciplinary approach generally opts for some understanding of the fuller dimensions of the subject.

With an insight into the human spirit born of his own experience as a survivor of Auschwitz, psychiatrist Viktor E. Frankl has written, ". . . humanity has demonstrated ad nauseam in recent years that it has instincts, drives. Today it appears more important to remind man that he has a spirit, that he is a spiritual being." Frankl is not speaking of preoccupation with religion in the conventional sense but of that profound concern with the meaning of life which is an irreducible part of the human spirit.

Mrs. Eddy's wrestlings with this question simply cannot be excluded from any meaningful account of her life and struggles. The problem of evil presented itself to her in girlhood in terms of the stark Calvinist doctrine of predestination, against which she rebelled with all the force of her youthful nature. It confronted her anew in the form of the loss and desolation that overshadowed her middle years. And through the whole first half of her life it pressed itself upon her intermittently in the physical sufferings and nervous debility to which she was so often subject. Decades of adversity forced her to consider the question in a way that far transcended the limits of her personal experience and broke radically with the conventional theology of the day.

No less a psychologist than Gordon Allport has warned against the "error of the psychoanalytic theory of religion" which locates "religious belief exclusively in the defensive functions of the ego." Mrs. Eddy's real achievement was not to have made a personal "success" of a life that for the first forty-five years brimmed over with disappointments. Rather, it was to have found in the Bible a transforming insight into the meaning of life that enabled her to develop a practical theology which grappled with the age-long problem of evil.

Long before Auschwitz, acutely troubled souls had been asking, "Can God really be good—can there even be a God at all—
when emptiness, agony, and human brutality are so often the
human lot?" The answer that Mrs. Eddy found in the life of
Jesus Christ was that evil of every sort was no part of God's
creative will, no part of the true spiritual order of His universe,
and that this truth understood could begin at once to lift the
burden of evil from experience.

However, she insisted that such an understanding could be
incorporated into living only through radical Christian discipleship; it was, she held, a far cry from the exercise of will power,
blind faith, or a manipulative mental technique. To the end of
her days she counted herself (as she figuratively put it) a "willing disciple at the heavenly gate, waiting for the Mind of
Christ."[1] Her writings refer frankly to the intense struggles she
went through in carrying out what she felt to be her mission,
and nowhere did she claim to be humanly perfect or the equal of
Jesus. Certainly it's untrue to say that she expected not to die,
whatever some of her overzealous followers may have hoped
for.

No more than the life of a Jonathan Edwards, a Mother Mary
Seton, or a Martin Luther King, Jr., can Mrs. Eddy's life be
separated from the religious purpose that dominated it. Indeed,
it is only by transcending their own purely personal concerns
and involving themselves passionately with man's quest for
meaning that any such figures attain the status which history—
sometimes reluctantly—grants them.

---

1. Mary Baker Eddy, *Science and Health with Key to the Scriptures* (Boston: The First Church of Christ, Scientist, 1906), p. ix.

Perhaps the most fitting postscript to this chapter can be found in a comment by religious historian Martin Marty from the biographical film documentary "Mary Baker Eddy: A Heart in Protest":

> There's no doubt that in one sense she is doing what everyone from atheists like Sartre to intense believers like Pope John XXIII are doing; they are putting their banner up against the forces of meaninglessness and saying, I defy them; I don't have to be merely passive. Whether people can follow where her banner would lead is a very different question; but I think one has to say, Here's a steadfast, decades-long attempt not thus to be overwhelmed.

# Further Exchanges

*Mrs. Eddy said that her discovery of Christian Science occurred as a result of her healing from the effects of a fall on the ice in 1866. What about the charge that she invented or exaggerated the account of this experience?*

The historical evidence for her account of this event rests on far more than one person's word! Actually, the known details of the incident come from a variety of sources, including a newspaper report, other witnesses (not Christian Scientists), and a letter from that same period. Two days after the fall, to cite one piece of evidence, the local newspaper reporting the accident described her condition as "critical." Neighbors and friends were called to help; her minister was sent for; and her husband, who was away on business, was also sent for by telegram. Many years later the physician involved did make several statements downplaying the whole thing, but at the time of the accident, according to the newspaper report, he "found her injuries to be internal, and of a very serious nature."[1]

. . .

*Was there anything unusual or miraculous in Mrs. Eddy's life?*

Like other religious leaders in history, Mrs. Eddy had a revolutionary experience that could be called "unusual." This was the overwhelming conviction that came to her at the time of her healing in 1866 that God and His perfect spiritual creation are the only realities. But the healing itself she didn't regard as a miracle, though it may have been unusual. Instead, she saw it as completely in line with God's law. For the next forty-five years

she explored and taught Christian healing on exactly that basis.
Of course, it might be considered miraculous that a woman of
her day could found and establish a worldwide religion.

. . .

*What about the charge that Mrs. Eddy had a telephone placed in her
tomb so that she would be able to remain in touch with her church!*

Absurd as it is, this canard has made the rounds for years,
giving rise in some instances to the charge that Mrs. Eddy
believe in spiritualism, when the exact opposite is the case. The
useful little volume *Rumor!* published by Penguin Books, contains this trenchant comment on the origins and falsity of the
"telephone in the tomb" myth; first it repeats the rumor then
gives the facts that disprove it:

> *Not true.* The construction of Eddy's white marble tomb at
> Mount Auburn Cemetery in Cambridge, Massachusetts, was so
> involved that a telephone was installed at the site to keep the
> workers in close touch with their home office. This apparently
> sparked the rumor, though the phone was taken out as soon as
> the memorial was finished. Workers at Mount Auburn say they
> still get plenty of questions about Eddy's phone—more than
> seventy years after her death.[2]

. . .

*What about the view that Christian Science and its healing practice
are really just an expression of the American tradition of positive
thinking or human optimism?*

I think that sometimes people who are not acquainted with
Christian Science conjure up some image of it that really doesn't
fit the way it feels to the Christian Scientist. Healing comes
continually in the life of a Christian Scientist. He also sees it
with his children; he sees it in his relationships with others; he
sees it in major healings of serious, so-called fatal illness among
his friends and fellow church members. There is a lot in these
healings that draws us on, that compels us to feel that Christian

Science is substantial, that it's real, that there's a Principle of being to be learned and to become committed to. Now, I don't think that anybody who has his wits about him is going to tell you that human existence is a bowl of cherries. Human experience is *rough,* and Christianity has known it was rough from the very beginning. The Bible says that the last enemy that shall be destroyed is death. So it isn't on the basis of looking at the world through rose-colored glasses that Christian Scientists commit themselves to spiritual healing. They find that in Christian Science there is more than enough to draw them on and to give them a sense of being sustained and of being deeply grateful to this power that has come into their lives.

. . .

*Haven't some scholars spoken of Christian Science as a prime example of the American positive thinking and success psychology?*

This has been the case, but this view by no means reflects the best or most recent scholarship on the subject. As several recent studies show, Christian Science—like other religious teachings— has to some extent been distorted in practice. Specifically, some of its adherents have lost sight of its tough demand for thoroughgoing Christian regeneration, regarding Christian Science instead as a means for realizing purely human values of health, wealth, and success. But to the degree that this has happened, the result can no longer be called Christian Science.

Mrs. Eddy had a very tough and realistic view of the human condition and a very definite conviction that evil on the human scene can be neither ignored nor glossed over. Her theology insists that it be *faced* and overcome on the basis of the absolute power and love of God. She saw this power and this love as practically provable through healing works. But the purpose of these works, she held, was not primarily therapeutic but redemptive.

So, no, Christian Science is far, both in its theology and in the spirit of its genuine practice, from any sort of positive thinking and success philosophy. As Mrs. Eddy once put it, ". . . success in error is defeat in Truth."[3] What's more, these points have become clearer in recent scholarship, which has decisively separated Christian Science from other traditions that have been confused with it for far too long.

1. Quoted in Robert Peel, *Mary Baker Eddy: The Years of Discovery* (New York: Holt, Rinehart and Winston, 1966), p. 195.

2. Hal Morgan and Kerry Tucker, *Rumor!* (New York: Viking-Penguin, Penguin Books, 1984), p. 30.

3. Mary Baker Eddy, *Science and Health with Key to the Scriptures* (Boston: The First Church of Christ, Scientist, 1906), p. 239.

# Towards a Scientific

# Christianity

What is *unique* about Christian Science? How should its meaning for the religious life of our time be assessed? The very term *Christian Science* itself suggests the answer. Mary Baker Eddy saw her teaching as proving the scientific means of demonstrating—realizing in practice—the full transforming power of Biblical Christianity.

From this standpoint, true Christianity is not in conflict with the physical sciences as useful human pursuits. But it *is* in conflict with materialistic conclusions that some have mistakenly drawn from physical science—conclusions that regard man as organized matter and matter as determining the conditions of life.

"Christianity and Science," a section from the concluding chapter of *A Century of Christian Science Healing,* explores this point.

# Christianity and Science

Our present age is sometimes characterized as the post-Christian era. For good or for ill, the natural sciences wield much of the intellectual authority that once belonged to the historic Church.

On the one hand atomic physics has made possible the total extinction of the human race; on the other hand molecular biology has made plausible the indefinite prolongation of human life. In this situation the implications of spiritual healing have a great deal more importance than may be recognized at first.

If man is mere organized matter, governed in the last analysis by laws of physics and chemistry, then his position in the universe is a very precarious one indeed. Inhabiting a planet which itself is the merest mote of dust in astronomical space, chance product of a blind evolutionary process, he faces the eventual annihilation of his whole kind in the inevitable death of the solar system, if not by some earlier man-made catastrophe.

This is the cosmic destiny which awaits the most ambitious hopes and achievements of the scientific materialist. This is the sense of ultimate meaninglessness which haunts even his jauntiest assurances. Beyond tomorrow's scientific utopia lies the shadow of ultimate cataclysm.

To this existential situation Christian Science brings a radical but reasoned conviction that Life is Spirit, eternal and indestructible. This is something different from the traditional religious hope in a heaven beyond the grave. The three-decker universe implied in older conceptions of heaven was one of the early

*A Century of Christian Science Healing* (Boston: The Christian Science Publishing Society, 1966), pp. 251–255.

casualties of modern science. The kingdom of heaven announced by Christ Jesus and revealed by Christian Science is the presence of Spirit here and now; it is the infinite order and harmony of the universe created, maintained, and beheld by divine Mind. It is spiritual reality as opposed to material appearance, immortal being as opposed to temporal self-delusion.

In the context of today's physics, matter eludes understanding by the ordinary layman. Its seeming solidity dissolves into a shadowy whirlpool of energy which he finds himself unable to comprehend or to imagine. He is told that matter can only be understood mathematically, and he knows that this mathematical understanding enables the physicist to control it far more effectively than when it was regarded as impregnable substance. He knows that what his forebears would have regarded as miracles are now achievable by what those same forebears might have regarded as mathematical magic, but with unhesitating faith he accepts these miracles as the natural result of scientific understanding.

The Christian Scientist goes a step farther. As he sees it, a metaphysical understanding of matter—derived from the recognition of Spirit as true substance—confers a power over material appearances surpassing anything achieved by natural science. For, metaphysically understood, matter is seen to be an impossible limit on the power of Spirit, an insubstantial belief that substance, or being, is finite and mortal. It is a false mode of consciousness, with no more power than belief gives it. Viewed in this light, material limitations inevitably yield before spiritual understanding.

Such a view is not to be confused with traditional forms of philosophical idealism. Plato and Hegel can rescue man from the tyranny of phenomenal appearances only by theory, never by healing, and a merely theoretical rescue is no rescue at all. To find one's roots in the Life that is Spirit is something quite different from taking a philosophical stance on the primacy of ideas.

Christianity has always been a way of life, not merely a way of thinking. Christian Science, as its very name implies, draws life and thought together.

This, as the Christian Scientist sees it, was the way of Jesus of Nazareth. His purpose, he said, was to bear witness to "the truth," and the truth, he promised, "shall make you free."[1] Truth *acts*. Through every act of his earthly ministry Jesus brought the truth of spiritual being to bear, precisely and predictably, on the error of material appearances.

Of his healing work Mary Baker Eddy writes: "Jesus beheld in Science the perfect man, who appeared to him where sinning mortal man appears to mortals. In this perfect man the Saviour saw God's own likeness, and this correct view of man healed the sick."[2]

A child who sees a straight stick lying halfway in a puddle and halfway out may believe that the stick is bent at the point at which it enters the water. A better informed adult is able to explain that the stick is not really bent, for he "looks" not at the visual image of the stick but at his scientific knowledge regarding the refraction of light. Then he lifts the stick out of the water to prove his point.

This rough analogy suggests something of the way in which a Christian Scientist looks beyond the temporary evidence of the physical senses into what he calls the Science of Being for a true explanation of man. He does not wishfully imagine a perfect human being where a sick and sinning mortal seems to be, but he thrusts beyond all material appearance to the truth of spiritual being. To perceive the truth of any situation is to have that situation grasped by Truth. To perceive man as the expression or idea of Spirit is to reshape human experience closer to the spiritual idea.

The healing of physical disease is one of the most concrete proofs that can be offered of the substantiality of Spirit. It is not of itself conclusive, and in the nature of things it cannot be offered under the conditions of controlled experiment. But in conjunction with all the other evidences of spiritual power furnished by Christianity understood as Science it offers a substantial challenge to materialistic assumptions.

In the nature of things the propositions of Christian Science cannot be affected by new developments in natural science—for instance, the possible discovery of other forms of life on other planets or the synthetic creation of human life on this planet. For if reality is pure Spirit, material existence at best can be only a series of attempted approximations of reality. As Mrs. Eddy puts it, "Whatever seems to be a new creation, is but the discovery of some distant idea of Truth; else it is a new multiplication or self-division of mortal thought, as when some finite sense peers from its cloister with amazement and attempts to pattern the infinite."[3]

Christian Science rests on an absolute premise, even though it appeals to verification by experience. Christian Scientists often speak of prayer as "knowing the truth," and Truth itself towers far above any particular instance of its power. The worship of God is in its highest sense an absolute commitment to Truth, regardless of the consequences to oneself.

This is illustrated in the testimony of a woman who turned to Christian Science after the doctor told her he could do no more for her.[4] Suffering from an internal growth, totally blind, almost completely paralyzed, and finally in a semicoma, she heard her husband say to the practitioner who had been called in, "If Christian Science heals my wife, I'll be the best Christian Scientist you have in your organization." The practitioner answered: "Don't say that. If Christian Science is not the truth, you do not want it, even if it heals her. If it is the truth, you want it, even if she is not healed." Suddenly, as the woman later explained, "the fear of dying left me in my realization that what I really wanted was to know God better—to know Him as He actually is—to know the truth." The same night she was instantaneously healed.

This is an example of the scientific spirit, the love of truth for its own sake, though the practical proof was "added." That Christian Scientists who are working in the physical and biological sciences have been able to improve the quality of their contributions to these sciences through their understanding of Christian Science is not without significance. There is no hostility between their religion and the scientific spirit, but Christian Science operates from a position beyond the calculations and categories of material sense.

"The kingdoms of this world," we read in Revelation 11:15,

"are become the kingdoms of our Lord, and of his Christ; and he shall reign for ever and ever." The sciences of this world caught up into the universe of Mind are transmuted into that spiritual Science of Being which lies beyond all finite questionings.

---

1. John 8:32.

2. Mary Baker Eddy, *Science and Health with Key to the Scriptures* (Boston: The First Church of Christ, Scientist, 1906), pp. 476–477.

3. *Ibid.,* p. 263.

4. Lois B. Estey, Geneva, New York, in *The Christian Science Journal,* December 1955, and the *Christian Science Sentinel,* March 23, 1957.

$A$t the 1985 meeting of young Christian Scientists at The Mother Church referred to in chapter 4, a student spoke of a striking overnight healing of a broken collarbone. "Such healings," he said, are "part of a crucial spiritual struggle with materialism that's being fought and won on what matter says is its own turf—everyday life. . . . Every healing we have . . . is cutting through material belief. It's proving for all humanity that our life is in God and not in matter. And that's why the healing of the body is inseparable from the moral and spiritual regeneration that's at the heart of Christianity."[1]

Certainly spiritual healing has profound implications not only for Christian faith but for the physical sciences as well. Twentieth-century physics has revolutionized scientific concepts of time, space, and matter. Many are beginning to explore the implications of this revolution for religion. The subject has been of particular interest for Christian Scientists, whose views on "time, space, and matter" may seem both less unusual and more readily understandable in today's post-quantum universe.

The following selection, however, cautions against simplistically equating the developing insights of contemporary physics, provocative as they are, with a particular religious viewpoint. "Keeping a Spiritual Perspective on the New Physics" was written by a Christian Science practitioner and appeared in *The Christian Science Journal*. In insisting on the far-reaching metaphysical implications of *Christianity*, it reflects Mary Baker Eddy's simple (but not simplistic) statement "Jesus of Nazareth was the most scientific man that ever trod the globe."[2]

---

1. Scott F. Preller, "Spiritual Healing as the Cutting Edge of the Future," *The Christian Science Journal*, October 1987, pp. 15, 16.

2. Mary Baker Eddy, *Science and Health with Key to the Scriptures* (Boston: The First Church of Christ, Scientist, 1906), p. 313.

# Keeping a Spiritual Perspective
# on the New Physics

When Mary Baker Eddy wrote in the Preface to her book *Science and Health with Key to the Scriptures,* "The time for thinkers has come,"[1] she was talking about far more than the need for a new intelligentsia. The thinkers she was looking for would come from all walks of life and have varied educational backgrounds. But they would all have one thing in common: a deep discontent with the materialism of the age and a willingness to live their lives in a totally new light—in the light of spiritual realities.

For Christian Scientists there must always be more to being a thinker than having mere intellectual curiosity about the admittedly fascinating—and sometimes disturbing—ideas and developments of late twentieth-century science, theology, and medicine.

As *Science and Health* observes:

> In the material world, thought has brought to light with great rapidity many useful wonders. With like activity have thought's swift pinions been rising towards the realm of the real, to the spiritual cause of those lower things which give impulse to inquiry. Belief in a material basis, from which may be deduced all rationality, is slowly yielding to the idea of a metaphysical basis, looking away from matter to Mind as the cause of every effect.[2]

To the author of *Science and Health,* the questions of what constitutes reality, substance, causality, time, space, mind, matter, and energy were not merely topics of intellectual or philosophic interest. They were the very stuff of everyday life. They had to be understood in the light of a new view of reality—a

---

Steven L. Fair, in *The Christian Science Journal,* July 1988, pp. 19–23.

view of reality that results in a revitalized, scientific, *healing* Christianity.

It's hard not to notice that something remarkable, even extraordinary, has been going on in modern physics. Our language has become sprinkled with exotic terms for even more exotic objects and happenings—things like black holes, quasars, quarks, antimatter, and the "big bang." What's it all about? It's about a revolution in human thinking as important as any in scientific history: the quantum theory of matter and energy.

Generalizing about quantum physics—the physics having to do with the structure and behavior of molecules, atoms, and their constituents—can be tricky. Even in the scientific community there are many interpretations about its ultimate meaning. But if one were to summarize the dominant interpretation of the nature of matter, it would probably be this: there is no reality below or behind the surface appearance of matter; the *appearance itself* is the reality. To put it another way, in quantum physics mathematical *description* is the only knowable reality.

The new physics tells us that when we encounter matter at its most elementary level—the quantum—we are dealing with effects without knowable causes. It says we are dealing with ephemeral entities, if they can even be called entities, about whose ultimate nature we can say nothing except that we know them *only* as mathematical descriptions and as the *effects* on the instruments of the observer who is measuring them. In fact, in a certain sense, by observing and measuring quantum events we actually "create" their reality as phenomena.

The physicist tell us, for example, that the unobserved electron is not a "thing" but exists *only* as a nonphysical set of probabilities (called the wave function). The electron doesn't really exist in any particular place *until we look at it and measure it.* So far as physics can say, there is no actual electron until it is observed and measured! The phenomenon we call "electron" is created by our looking at it. In the words of the father of quantum physics, Niels Bohr: "*There is no quantum world. There is only an abstract quantum description.*"[3]

These remarkable conclusions show why quantum physics represents a shift in human thinking every bit as fundamental as those brought about by the Copernican or Newtonian revolutions. The physicist has been compelled to admit that when physics deals with the basic components of matter—electrons, protons, neutrons, and whatever apparently makes them up—it is no longer dealing with "objective reality" as such. It is dealing with observer-dependent, observer-created phenomena—with shadows and symbolic descriptions, and not with *things.*

As the discoverer of quantum wave mechanics, Erwin Schrödinger, comments, "Please note that the very recent advance [of quantum and relativistic physics] does not lie in the world of physics itself having acquired this shadowy character; it had [this character] ever since Democritus of Abdera and even before, *but we were not aware of it; we thought we were dealing with the world itself.*"[4]

These admissions of the new physics are of great interest. While they are not statements of Christian Science, they do indicate the breaking up of material beliefs, a kind of "mentalization" of mankind's view of matter. And yet as startling as all these admissions are, one should be careful of jumping to conclusions about what they actually mean.

They *do not* mean, for example, that quantum physics itself is shadowy, vague, or inexact. The mathematics of quantum mechanics describes matter's behavior with an accuracy that gives physical scientists unprecedented predictive ability, as witnessed in the many modern inventions based on quantum theory. Nor does this new view of matter mean physicists as a whole have concluded that the world around us is a dream, or that the world of the senses isn't real, or that it doesn't actually exist.

Physicists generally believe the world we see around us is real enough, but they have been forced to admit that they don't know what, if anything, underlies matter or even if there *is* a "deep" reality beneath matter's surface appearance. As quantum physicist Nick Herbert comments in his highly regarded and informative book *Quantum Reality,* "One of the best-kept secrets of science is that physicists have lost their grip on reality."[5]

A startling statement! And yet despite these developments, the physicist's basic belief that matter/energy ultimately is real and indestructible has changed little, if at all. What has changed is that the physicist's *description* of matter is more mental and abstract than ever before in history, and consequently the concepts of substance and reality have largely lost any everyday, readily understandable meaning.

What does this mentalization, this abstraction of matter into mathematical probabilities, mean? Does it mean that quantum physics shows physical science converging with the teachings of Christian Science in its views of matter? Does it mean that modern physics tends to support a spiritual or metaphysical view of reality, as some have argued? Let's see.

In an article in *The American Scholar* physicist and author Jeremy Bernstein critiques a book (one of many popular ones) which strongly implies that the insights of modern quantum physics show a scientific basis for Eastern mysticism. Citing the changeability of material science, he warns, "To hitch a religious philosophy to a contemporary science is a sure route to its obsolescence."[6]

Despite this obvious danger, some writers and books have also tried to demonstrate that the new physics all but "proves" or substantiates Christian Science, arguing that physicists are virtually saying or are on the verge of believing what Christian Science says about matter and reality.

There are several reasons why this belief is ill-advised, both from the standpoint of modern physics and from the standpoint of Christian Science. The most obvious is the danger Bernstein alludes to: if a physical theory or interpretation of reality ever "proved" or "verified" a religion, then the collapse of that theory would surely "disprove" the religion. And few things are more changeable than present-day theories of matter and cosmology.

Given the difficulty and profundity of the concepts of quantum physics, let alone its mathematics, perhaps it is understandable that similar-sounding statements could lead people to assume there are similarities with Christian Science where none actually exist. Yet if one examines modern physics *on its own terms* and *understands* what the physicists really are talking about, it soon becomes evident that quantum physics and Christian Science are not saying the same thing at all.

Not one of the major founding scientists of modern physics—Heisenberg, Schrödinger, de Broglie, Planck, Pauli, or Einstein—believed that the new physics either refuted *or* supported a spiritual view of reality (although most of them had deep religious convictions). When physicists talk *as physicists* about matter's "unreality" or "nonexistence" (when it's not being observed or measured), they are not echoing or "confirming" the metaphysical concepts of Christian Science. They aren't talking metaphysics at all. They are talking about the *limitations of material knowledge* that physical science and the human mind encounter when matter is examined at its smallest, most basic level. The thing to remember is that similarities in *wording* do not necessarily mean similarities in *meaning*.

The fact is, today's quantum physics no more "proves" or illustrates the truth of Christian Science than the Newtonian physics of Mrs. Eddy's time "proved" or illustrated it. And when today's physics is superseded by new theories, they won't "prove" (or disprove) Christian Science either. They can't. Why? Because human theories can never bridge or leap the gap from matter to Spirit. As *Science and Health* explains:

> Physical science (so-called) is human knowledge,—a law of mortal mind, a blind belief, a Samson shorn of his strength. When this human belief lacks organizations to support it, its foundations are gone. Having neither moral might, spiritual basis, nor holy Principle of its own, this belief mistakes effect for cause and seeks to find life and intelligence in matter, thus limiting Life and holding fast to discord and death. In a word, human belief is a blind conclusion from material reasoning. This is a mortal, finite sense of things, which immortal Spirit silences forever.[7]

For a Christian Scientist, nothing could make clearer the great divide between the limited conclusions and material reasoning (however refined) of material science and the grand revelations of unchangeable divine Science. And yet, having said all this, and having drawn these crucial distinctions, we would be missing the point if we were to conclude that these intriguing developments in modern thought are of no significance and should be casually dismissed or ignored.

All of these revolutionary changes in human belief indicate that mankind's faith in matter's substantiality and objective "thing-ness" has been shaken to its very foundation. And is it surprising to the Christian Scientist that this revolutionary change has all occurred in the hundred or so years since the discovery of Christian Science?

The mentalization, even in a degree, of this area of human thought can be seen as welcome evidence of the leaven of divine Science, bringing about progress even as it shows up the limitations and pitfalls of material methods and thought systems. Mrs. Eddy felt such signs of leavening were important. While they do not "prove" Christian Science, they illustrate the powerful effect of Truth on the illusory belief of life in matter and thus help turn thinkers to the consideration of mental and spiritual causation.

This is not to deny or denigrate the role of modern science in its efforts to improve the human condition. Nor is it to ignore the higher motives of those devoting themselves to the advancement of human knowledge. When moral and spiritual values are not trampled upon or ignored, the Christian Scientist welcomes this advancement of knowledge and supports the honest effort to put off material limitations. Likewise, through prayer and spiritualization of thought, the Christian Scientist who works in the sciences can help leaven them, bringing safety, wisdom, and a deep, spiritually based humanity and vision to scientific progress.

What the Christian Scientist objects to is the scientific materialism that resists the very idea that Spirit exists or that spiritual healing is possible. Because Christian Science healing overturns conventional suppositions about health, substance, life, law, cause and effect, materialism either ignores it or else tries to explain it away as the effect of the human mind on the body. Failing to do that, materialism tries to convince the public that such healing is unreliable, "dangerous," and should be outlawed.

Considering the limits of material observation and knowledge that even modern physics has come to admit, we can see how far ahead of his time Jesus was when he said, "The kingdom of God cometh not with observation: neither shall they say, Lo here! or, lo there! for, behold, the kingdom of God is within you."[8] Reality, as Jesus defined it, can never be known through material observation or physical theory, however powerful or refined. Reality is not in matter to be observed but in Spirit to be discovered and brought to light through demonstration.

How encouraging it is to the student of Science that the Master of physics and metaphysics, Christ Jesus, *proved* matter and so-called material law not to be what they appear! As *Science and Health* says, "He plunged beneath the material surface of things, and found the spiritual cause."[9]

When Jesus went about doing physically "impossible" things, like walking on water, instantly healing the blind and lame, and raising the dead, he wasn't performing "miracles," in the usual sense of that word. He was giving mankind a glimpse of the true nature of reality. He was revealing Spirit's allness and man's wholeness and goodness and perfection as the very image of Spirit.

1. Mary Baker Eddy, *Science and Health with Key to the Scriptures* (Boston: The First Church of Christ, Scientist, 1906), p. vii.

2. *Ibid.*, p. 268.

3. Niels Bohr, quoted in Nick Herbert, *Quantum Reality: Beyond the New Physics* (Garden City, NY: Doubleday, Anchor Press, 1985), p. 17.

4. Erwin Schrödinger, quoted in Ken Wilber, *Quantum Questions: Mystical Writings of the World's Great Physicists* (Boston: Shambhala Publications, New Science Library, 1984), p. 9.

5. Herbert, p. 15.

6. Jeremy Bernstein, "Out of My Mind: A Cosmic Flow," *The American Scholar,* vol. 48, no. 1 (Winter 1978–79), p. 8.

7. Eddy, *Science and Health,* p. 124.

8. Luke 17:20, 21.

9. Eddy, *Science and Health,* p. 313.

The title of the final selection in this chapter, "Christian Science—A Time for Reappraisal," speaks for itself. It also points to a conclusion that could be drawn from many of the sources in this book. Written by Richard J. V. Robinson for a British university periodical, *Four Elements,* the commentary calls for fresh consideration not only of "scientific" Christianity but of the broader spiritual situation of our time.

# Christian Science—A Time for Reappraisal

A recent leading article in *The Economist* on the Jonestown massacre made an arresting prediction. It may be, it said of the world's current spiritual turmoil, "if things go well," that the time between now and the twenty-first century will rival in importance for the development of the human consciousness such periods as the fifth century B.C., the first century A.D., and the Renaissance, and lead to "a possible pacification of the long war in inner space" between the scientific, and the instinctive, feeling elements of the human mind.

It's easy to respond unsympathetically to the growing religious ferment, much of it taking place at the moment outside the churches, and dismiss it as a reaction against the increasingly scary elements of modern life, the instability of western societies, the sense of powerlessness in the face of inexorable forces that are not understood. Perhaps the toughest blow of all, because it strikes closest to home, has been dealt by genetics, which would hang round our necks the verdicts of inherited patterns from which, the inference is, there is no escape, and within which our freedom of manoeuvre may be negligible.

For those who confidently equate transcendence with superstition, such dismissal is no doubt the only honest response, but those who have no such certainties will welcome the grass, to use *The Economist*'s vivid phrase, that has begun to force its way up through the cracks in the agnostic concrete.

Experience seems to indicate that if there were new paths to follow which might lead to answers of a radically new kind they

Richard J. V. Robinson, in *Four Elements* [Preston Polytechnic], Summer 1979, pp. 47–56.

are unlikely to be mere deductive extensions of existing lines of thought. Leaps into the dark, bold conceptual challenges to universally accepted attitudes have traditionally characterised major changes in our understanding of how things work.

Although the majority had doubts as to whether she landed on terra firma, the propositions with which Mary Baker Eddy confronted the religious thought of her time and ours, when considered fairly on their own merits (an important proviso in view of the steam that has been generated around them) certainly had all the outward signs of such a leap. There are ideas that have lain largely unrecognised in its teaching which I believe have a significant contribution to make to the present state of affairs and something particularly to say about the way forward for Christianity.

When Christian Science came on the scene in the 1870s religion and science were in direct confrontation. That aspect of "the long war in inner space" was at its height, and for the most part it was religion that was in retreat and an ever more sceptical eye was turned on the attempts to reconcile a merciful creator with arbitrary suffering, eternity with death, foreknowledge with free will.

For centuries such questions had taxed to the utmost the ingenuity, not to say the reason, of the religious thinker. But it was simply not possible, Mrs. Eddy said, to reconcile the purposeless miseries of so much of this life—what she came to call "the ghastly farce of material existence"[1]—with any reasonable concept of God, whether defined as a beneficent First Cause or a loving, omnipotent Father who made all things.

Mrs. Eddy's response to these dilemmas, which was progressively clarified between 1875 and 1910 in successive editions of her book *Science and Health with Key to the Scriptures,* proved as controversial as any religious issue in that supremely controversial half-century. The phenomenal growth of adherents after 1875, including too high a proportion of ministers, doctors, and academics for the comfort of their respective professions, is largely forgotten today. The unique aspect of this growth was that it neither stemmed from the preaching of a dynamic personality (Mrs. Eddy progressively withdrew from the public eye to write), nor from a powerful authoritarian organisation, but from a book, and specifically from the ameliorative and liberating effect of the book on the lives of its readers.

*Science and Health,* the Christian Scientists claimed, threw a new light on the Bible, reaffirming its centrality in the twentieth as in previous centuries and it brought a wholly fresh perspective to bear on the healing practised by Jesus and his disciples. It maintained that God, Spirit, was the only reality; that the physical senses were unable to testify to or understand this reality; that nevertheless mankind had access to such understanding; and that a radical transformation of human lives as the direct result of spiritual vision was a present possibility.

As mere theory such radical assertions would soon have been forgotten, but the element of verification represented by spiritual healing was the crucial bridge which Mrs. Eddy regarded as an inevitable consequence of knowing God as all-powerful, ever-present Love. It is this aspect which challenges the adequacy of a purely semantic treatment of the subject.

Such healing in its fullest and purest form was exemplified in the life-work of the Master. He was not, they believe, merely making a prophecy about an after-life, but a promise about the liberating effect of spiritual-mindedness in this life as well when he declared, "Ye shall know the truth, and the truth shall make you free."[2] Healing then, is less significant as the removal of symptoms, whether of illness, of lack, of grief or whatever the afflictive condition may be, the common denominator being a sense of alienation from God, than as the evidence of individual spiritual progress drawing us closer to God and bringing a deeper understanding of why we are here and where we are going.

So frequently is its teaching on the unreality of matter used as a stick to beat Christian Science with (usually coupled with the inference that it involves turning one's back on human suffering) that it's worth taking a little space to quote an extract from an article by one of Mrs. Eddy's closest students to whom she entrusted special responsibilities for seeing that Christian Science was accurately presented to the world, Alfred Farlow. The article appeared in the *Boston Times* in 1904. Referring to the proposition "there is no matter" as an abstract statement, "a rather remote conclusion which is neither understood nor acceptable to the individual unless he first has some knowledge of the premise upon which it is based," Farlow went on,

> The statement, 'there is no matter,' standing alone and independent of any qualification, seems to mean that everything that we see,—the entire creation,—is non-existent, while in truth Christian Science teaches that all things, from the least to the greatest, are real, though not what they seem to the peculiar sense of those who have not yet learned to perceive them as God made them and as they really are. . . . When we are correctly informed as to what God's creation is we can understand what it is not.

A sentence of Mrs. Eddy's, and many could be instanced, expresses the same idea in the Christian terms of the new birth: "With the spiritual birth, man's primitive, sinless, spiritual existence dawns on human thought,—through the travail of mortal mind, hope deferred, the perishing pleasure and accumulating pains of sense,—by which one loses himself as matter, and gains a truer sense of Spirit and spiritual man."[3]

Challenges to the objective independence of matter, the notion that "things aren't what they appear to be" is as old as Plato, though too often debased by simplistic analogies about mirages and railway lines not really meeting on the horizon. But no one in modern times had moved beyond speculation as to what things weren't to a demand for proof as to what they really were, and had related the whole subject to the meaning and significance of the mission of Jesus Christ. "She was discerning enough," writes [Robert] Peel in the prologue of *Mary Baker Eddy: The Years of Authority,* "to recognize that Christian authority must rest not only on the truth of its message but also on its validation by practical, repeatable results. This involved a new concept of both revelation and demonstration."[4]

It also involved, if Mrs. Eddy was right, the breakthrough in the impasse between religion and science. Although what she was saying about the nature of matter was, as the Farlow quotation indicated, far from being the heart of her teaching it was still significant that if matter behaved in fact as the theory predicted it would, then religion could be known in terms of law: the empirical priorities of the twentieth century would be honoured. The bitterest lesson of all was to find that world opinion didn't respond in that way, and that the entrenched certainties of material-mindedness, as she saw the resistance, fought at every point, by their very nature, the claims of spirituality.

Yet the evidence of the efficacy of what she taught was not lacking. Although the achievements of Christian Scientists are modest in comparison with the unparalleled example of Jesus Christ and his immediate disciples, they still constitute after one hundred years as impressive a body of testimony to effective spiritual healing as exists in this century. Critics have tended to dismiss the data without studying it, generally as some form of psychotherapy appropriate only to psychosomatic disorders, but this falls far short of accounting for the record.

It also fails to account for the subjective experiences of Christian Scientists who, stereotypes notwithstanding, have no less than the average proportion of normal and intelligent people in their midst. Even more significant to them than the outward evidence of healing is the profound sense that accompanies it of enlarged perception of their intact spiritual identity, a largely inarticulable awareness of closeness to God.

This is not a mystical condition, in fact a feature of such experience is a sharper comprehension of the outward circumstances of life. A key factor, and one that has perhaps a special significance today, when the question is uppermost of how religion can be directly relevant to an overmastering and headlong world, is that this teaching is essentially thisworldly, though nonmaterial; that is to say, it challenges sense testimony as the determinant of valid experience, while recognising as of crucial importance the ebb and flow of human consciousness in its upward struggle towards liberation. It was this aspect of her teaching which underlay Mrs. Eddy's founding of *The Christian Science Monitor,* a much respected newspaper, "to injure no man but to bless all mankind"[5] and which explains its specific role as a part of the spiritual mission of her church.

The urge to confine consciousness within the orbits of the five senses is more than anything else the bar to authentic spiritual experience. We all possess, the Christian Scientist would say, a spiritual sense, and it is through the acknowledgement and enlargement of this spiritual sense that we are able progressively to exercise our dominion over the conditions of material living and the verdicts of its laws. This is not just a faculty of the religious man; every step forward towards greater tolerance, freedom, and creativity is a direct manifestation of it.

If this religion has a contribution to make at the present crossroads it certainly will not lie in merely raising titillating philosophical questions about the relationship of sense data to reality, useful as such discussion may be in opening thought, but in affirming the great religious truths of God's allness, of His love for man and the unbounded promise and power that the vision of that love has to transform and heal the human condition. These truths in the last resort, Christian Scientists would say, are not for intellectual rationalization; they are articulated less by words than by being lived, and in meeting the human need. And if Mrs. Eddy was right, the possibilities are different, not just in degree, but in kind from what can be accomplished from a basis of a life bounded by the physical senses.

The acknowledgement of any conceptual breakthrough that may bring order to the present confusion and despondency is likely in practice to be gradual, rather than a single overnight reversal, visible to all, of some hitherto dominant premise. No doubt the established churches will discover new moral and spiritual energies which will adjust the emphases apparent at the moment, and play an increasingly important part. But it seems to me at least possible that the ideas that I have been discussing, propounded one hundred years ago, and obscured as they have been by events that followed, may now be about to receive closer examination than they have yet had, and found to provide unsuspected food for thought.

---

1. Mary Baker Eddy, *Science and Health with Key to the Scriptures* (Boston: The First Church of Christ, Scientist, 1906), p. 272.

2. John 8:32.

3. Mary Baker Eddy, *Miscellaneous Writings* (Boston: The First Church of Christ, Scientist, 1896), p. 17.

4. Robert Peel, *Mary Baker Eddy: The Years of Authority* (New York: Holt, Rinehart and Winston, 1977), p. 4.

5. Mary Baker Eddy, *The First Church of Christ, Scientist, and Miscellany* (Boston: The First Church of Christ, Scientist, 1913), p. 353.

# Sources on Christian Science
## Referred to in the Text

Andrews, David Brooks. "The Future of Christian Healing: Fresh Convictions and Spiritual Realism." *The Christian Science Journal,* June 1988, pp. 30–33.

*A Century of Christian Science Healing.* Boston: The Christian Science Publishing Society, 1966.

*Christian Science: A Century Later.* Boston: The Christian Science Publishing Society, 1982.

"Christian Science and Community Medicine." *The New England Journal of Medicine,* vol. 290, no. 7 (February 14, 1974), pp. 401–402.

"Christian Science and Spiritual Healing Today: A Conversation with the Reverend Paul Higgins." *Christian Science Sentinel,* October 6, 1986, pp. 1857–64.

*Christian Science Hymnal.* 1932 ed. Boston: The Christian Science Publishing Society, 1932.

Christiansen, Stig K. Letter in *Update: A Quarterly Journal on New Religious Movements,* vol. 9, no. 3 (September 1985), pp. 61–62.

*Dialogue with the World.* Boston: The Christian Science Publishing Society, 1972.

*Ecumenical Papers: Contributions to Interfaith Dialogue.* Boston: Christian Science Committee on Publication, 1969.

Eddy, Mary Baker. *Manual of The Mother Church.* Boston: The First Church of Christ, Scientist, 1895.

—————. *Miscellaneous Writings* (1896) and other works contained in *Prose Works Other than* Science and Health. Boston: The First Church of Christ, Scientist, 1925.

—————. *Science and Health with Key to the Scriptures.* Boston: The First Church of Christ, Scientist, 1906.

Fair, Steven L. "Keeping a Spiritual Perspective on the New Physics." *The Christian Science Journal,* July 1988, pp. 19–23.

Flower, B. O. *Christian Science as a Religious Belief and a Therapeutic Agent.* Boston: Twentieth Century, 1909.

Gottschalk, Stephen. "Christian Science." *Encyclopaedia Britannica.* 15th ed., 1984.

———. "Christian Science." *The Encyclopedia of Religion.* Ed. Mircea Eliade. New York: Macmillan, 1986.

———. "Christian Science and Harmonialism." *The Encyclopedia of the American Religious Experience.* Ed. Charles H. Lippy and Peter W. Williams. New York: Charles Scribner's Sons, 1988.

———. "Christian Science Today: Resuming the Dialogue." *The Christian Century,* vol. 103, no. 39 (December 17, 1986), pp. 1146–48.

———. *The Emergence of Christian Science in American Religious Life.* Berkeley: University of California Press, 1973.

———. "Mary Baker Eddy." *The Encyclopedia of Religion.* Ed. Mircea Eliade. New York: Macmillan, 1987.

———. "Update on Christian Science." *Theology Today,* vol. 44, no. 1 (April 1987), pp. 111–115.

Höll, Karl. "Der Szientismus." *Gesammelte Aufsätze zur Kirchengeschichte,* vol. 3. Tübingen: J. C. B. Muhr, 1921–1928, pp. 460–479.

"Individual Spirituality and the Future of Mankind." *The Christian Science Journal,* November 1985, pp. 724–725.

John, DeWitt. *The Christian Science Way of Life.* Boston: The Christian Science Publishing Society, 1962.

Johnsen, Thomas C. "Christian Scientists and the Medical Profession: A Historical Perspective." *Medical Heritage,* vol. 2, no. 1 (January–February 1986), pp. 70–78.

———. "Historical Consensus and Christian Science: The Career of a Manuscript Controversy." *The New England Quarterly,* vol. 53, no. 1 (March 1980), pp. 3–22.

Johnson, Lee Zeunert. Interview, "Christian Healing—'Indispensable.' " *Christian Science Sentinel,* February 3, 1986, pp. 191–196.

"Mary Baker Eddy: Another View." *American Heritage,* vol. 33, no. 2 (February–March 1982), pp. 110–111.

McDonald, Jean A. "Mary Baker Eddy and the Nineteenth-Century 'Public' Woman: A Feminist Reappraisal." *Journal of Feminist Studies in Religion,* vol. 2, no. 1 (Spring 1986), pp. 89–111.

Murphy, Carol. "The Image That Heals." *Pastoral Psychology,* vol. 22 (February 1971), pp. 37–42.

Nelson, Robert. "Focus on Christian Science." *Catalyst for Youth,* vol. 4, no. 9 (May 1973), pp. 2–6.

O'Brien, Lois. "Prayer's Not a Gamble." *U.S. News & World Report,* April 28, 1986, p. 81.

Peel, Robert. *Christian Science: Its Encounter with American Culture.* New York: Holt, 1958.

———. "The Christian Science Practitioner." *Journal of Pastoral Counseling,* vol. 4, no. 1 (Spring 1969), pp. 39–42.

———. *Mary Baker Eddy: The Years of Discovery.* New York: Holt, Rinehart and Winston, 1966.

———. *Mary Baker Eddy: The Years of Trial.* New York: Holt, Rinehart and Winston, 1971.

———. *Mary Baker Eddy: The Years of Authority.* New York: Holt, Rinehart and Winston, 1977.

———. *"Science and Health* and the Bible," in *The Bible and Bibles in America.* Ed. Ernest S. Frerichs. Atlanta: Scholars Press, 1988, pp. 193–213.

———. *Spiritual Healing in a Scientific Age.* San Francisco: Harper & Row, 1987.

Phaup, R. Graham. *My God.* Ed. Hayley Mills and Marcus Maclaine. London: Pelham Books, 1988, pp. 56–57.

Phinney, Allison W., Jr. "Mary Baker Eddy: Her Influence upon Theology." In *Mary Baker Eddy: A Centennial Appreciation.* Boston: The Christian Science Publishing Society, 1966, pp. 89–95.

———. "The Spirituality of Mankind." *Christian Science Sentinel,* September 3, 1984, pp. 1529–33.

*Prayer and Spiritual Healing.* Boston: The Christian Science Publishing Society, 1967.

Preller, Scott F., et al. *The Bible: Our Fountain of Living Water.* Boston: The Christian Science Publishing Society, 1987.

Robbins, Pam, and Robley Whitson. "Mary Baker Eddy's Christian Science." *Sign,* vol. 59, no. 10 (July–August 1980), pp. 16–21.

Robinson, Richard J. V. "Christian Science—A Time for Reappraisal." *Four Elements* [Preston Polytechnic], Summer 1979, pp. 47–56.

"Spiritual Healing as the Cutting Edge of the Future." *The Christian Science Journal,* October 1987, pp. 13–19.

Talbot, Nathan A. "The Position of the Christian Science Church." *The New England Journal of Medicine,* vol. 309 (December 29, 1983), pp. 1641–44.

West, Gwendolyn. "This Is Why I Am a Christian Scientist." *The Christian Science Journal,* October 1985, pp. 610–611.

*Sources in <u>Christian Science: A Sourcebook</u> of
<u>Contemporary Materials</u>*
Published by The Christian Science
Publishing Society

A Century of Christian Science Healing
Answers to Questions
The Bible: Our Fountain of Living Water
Christian Science: A Century Later
Christian Science and Legislation
Christian Science Hymnal
The Christian Science Journal
The Christian Science Monitor
Christian Science Quarterly
Christian Science Sentinel
Dialogue with the World
Ecumenical Papers: Contributions to Interfaith Dialogue
Mary Baker Eddy: A Centennial Appreciation
Mary Baker Eddy: The Years of Discovery, The Years of Trial,
    The Years of Authority
Prayer and Spiritual Healing
We Knew Mary Baker Eddy

*Sources in Christian Science: A Sourcebook of Contemporary Materials*
# Published by The First Church of Christ, Scientist, in Boston, Massachusetts (works by Mary Baker Eddy)

Christ and Christmas
The First Church of Christ, Scientist, and Miscellany
Manual of The Mother Church
Message to The Mother Church for 1900
Message to The Mother Church for 1901
Message to The Mother Church for 1902
Miscellaneous Writings
No and Yes
The People's Idea of God
Pulpit and Press
Retrospection and Introspection
Science and Health with Key to the Scriptures
Unity of Good

# Index

Biblical inerrancy, 57. *See also* Bible
*Bibliotheca Sacra,* 282n
blind faith, 150, 157; in contrast with
   Christian discipleship, 286; systematic practice of Christian healing
   more than, 120–121, 157. *See also*
   faith healing
Board of Directors. *See* The Christian Science Board of Directors
Board of Trustees of The Christian
   Science Publishing Society, 240–
   241
Bohr, Niels, 304, 309n
Bok, Derek, 173n
"born again," a definition of, 81
*Boston Post,* 173n
*Boston Times,* 173n, 313
Bow, New Hampshire: Mrs. Eddy's
   birthplace, 25
branch churches (of Christian Science church), 11, 25, 50; democratic government of, 218; listed
   in *Christian Science Journal,* 249;
   "*Manual* framework," 216. *See
   also* The Church of Christ, Scientist; *Manual of The Mother Church*
broken bones: Christian Science care
   of, 209–210; healings of, 302
Buber, Martin, 98
Bultmann, Rudolph, 86

Calvinism, 5, 98, 263
cancer: healing of, 124
carnal mind, 126; divine Mind and,
   126; Mary Baker Eddy's statements on, 108; Paul on, 108, 113n,
   150, 160; sickness and sin as products of, 150
*Catalyst for Youth,* 3, 25, 320
Catholic and Catholicism, 3, 14, 18,
   20, 22–23; Christian Science view
   of (response to), 207–208, 210n
celibacy, 22–23
*A Century of Christian Science Heal-*

*ing,* xii, 124, 126n, 144, 145, 165–
166, 295, 297, 319
*charisma,* 152, 155n
charismatic(s), 117, 198
children: care of, 182, 210; healings
   of in Christian Science, 170, 183,
   191; of God, 126, 210, 254; spiritual education of, 11; Sunday
   School, 217, 253
Christ, 8, 18, 21, 28, 40, 42, 52, 53,
   56, 57, 58, 63, 69, 70, 73, 80, 81,
   86, 87, 88, 96, 103–104, 105, 107,
   192, 244, 250, 267; as Truth, 53,
   228; Christian Science view of, 8,
   52–53, 80, 102–104, 105, 106,
   107, 110–111, 245; divinity of,
   52–53; Mary Baker Eddy's statements on, 18, 53, 63, 86, 109, 111,
   112, 151, 154, 194, 196n, 215,
   245, 267; healing and, 42, 76, 96,
   152, 160, 205; Messiah, 53; mind
   of, 47, 48, 286; mission of, 151,
   154n; power of, 75, 151, 245, 246;
   salvation in, 107; saving work of,
   80; significance of blood of, 112,
   113n; spiritual authority of, 75.
   *See also* Jesus Christ
*Christ and Christmas,* 41, 42n. *See also*
   Eddy, Mary Baker
Christ Jesus. *See* Christ; Jesus Christ
*The Christian Century,* 85, 85n, 86,
   320
Christian experience, xiv–xv, 21, 43
*The Christian Faith,* 67, 71n
Christian healing. *See* Christian Sci-
   ence healing; healing; spiritual heal-
   ing
"Christian Healing—
   'Indispensable,' " 187, 193–196,
   320
Christian Science, 57, 96, 128, 137,
   190, 194–195, 201, 316; as reli-
   gious movement, 5; as Science of
   Being, 146, 154n; as way of life,

"Christian Science and the Care of
Children: The Constitutional Issues," 181–186
"Christian Science and the Church
of England," 281n
*Christian Science as a Religious Belief
and a Therapeutic Agent,* 23, 173n,
319
The Christian Science Board of Directors, 11, 19; administer By-
Laws, 216, 248; appoint chief officers of The Mother Church, 248;
launched *The Christian Science
Monitor,* 240–241
Christian Science church. *See*
Church of Christ, Scientist
Christian Science healing, 117–162,
203; as worship, 148; contribution
to renewal of healing in mainstream churches, 199; demands of,
147–148; in contrast to manipulation, 149, 263; in contrast to pastoral counseling, 150–151; instances
of failure, 130–131; William James
on, 170; long-time record of, 174,
176–177, 183; not faith healing,
159, 176, 184; not positive thinking, 289–291; purpose of, 145–
148; reality and, 148; salvation
and, 145–151; spiritual significance of, 145, 246; what it is and
what it is not, 157, 206, 267. *See
also* Christian Science practitioners; Christian Science treatment;
healing; spiritual healing
*Christian Science Hymnal,* 255n, 319
*Christian Science: Its Encounter with
American Culture,* 111, 113n, 242n,
270n, 321
*Christian Science: Its Legal Status,*
169, 173n
*The Christian Science Journal,* xii, 12,
72, 142, 183, 191, 197, 198, 226,
227, 229, 231n, 232, 236, 249, 275,

281n, 301n, 302, 302n, 303, 319,
320, 321
*The Christian Science Monitor,* 11, 15,
19, 230, 234, 236–242, 242n; editorial policy of, 241; establishment of,
11, 26, 234, 236, 239, 240, 242, 315;
Founder (*See* Eddy, Mary Baker);
journalistic reform and, 240; meaning of name, 239; public respect for,
15, 241; purpose of, 11, 26, 236–
242, 244, 251, 252, 254, 315; responsibility of The Mother Church for,
216; subscribers, 252. *See also* Eddy,
Mary Baker
Christian Science movement, 12–13,
166; historic composition of, 273,
274; organization and structure of,
216; reasons for joining, 275–276.
*See also* Christian Scientists;
Church of Christ, Scientist
Christian Science nurse: description
of duties, 210
"The Christian Science Practitioner," 135, 137–141, 321
Christian Science practitioners, 12,
137–141, 170, 227–228, 302; description of, 50, 133–134, 137–
138, 142–143, 150, 158, 235–236,
249; listed in *Christian Science Journal,* 249; New Testament standard
for, 138, 138–139, 140, 209; not
counselors, 150–151; relation to patient, 209, 230–231; religious vocation and ministry, 138; training,
138. *See also* Christian Science healing; Christian Science treatment
*Christian Science Quarterly,* 43, 50,
204n
*Christian Science Sentinel,* xi, xvn, 87,
89n, 128, 169, 169–170, 173n,
183, 187, 188, 191, 193, 236, 240,
301n, 319, 320, 321
"Christian Science Today: Resuming
the Dialogue," 85, 86, 320

organization, 215; redemptive mission of, 207, 213, 218, 230, 243–247; revival of healing in, 152–154. *See also* Christianity; Church of Christ, Scientist; healing
*Church and State,* 180, 181
Church of Christ, Scientist, 10–13, 18–19, 138, 215–219, 249; aid to community, 251–254; Bible Lesson-Sermons, 11, 19, 21, 51, 201, 217, 249; branch churches of, 11, 25, 50, 216, 218, 248, 249; challenge of secularization, 12; The Christian Science Board of Lectureship, 218; Christian Science practitioners, 137–141, 249 (*See also* Christian Science practitioners); college organizations, 233, 253; ecumenical involvement, 63–64, 85–92; fellowship, 223–231; Founder (*See* Eddy, Mary Baker); goals and functions of, 10–13, 27, 50, 200, 209, 215, 247; government of, 251–254; healing principle characteristic of, 193, 206–207, 208, 215, 216, 247; history of, 25–26, 50, 215–219; lectures, 218, 252; membership composition, 10–11, 27, 215; membership figures, 19, 206–207, 216, 249; The Mother Church, 50, 194; pastor of, 27, 50, 216–217; periodicals of, 166, 252 (*See also The Christian Science Journal; The Christian Science Monitor; Christian Science Quarterly; Christian Science Sentinel*); Readers, 51, 217, 249; Reading Rooms, 217, 218; Sunday school, 20, 217, 253; what attracts members to, 275–276; worship services of, 11–12, 19, 27, 51, 216–217, 249–250
Church of England, 152, 154n
church organization, 215, 216. *See also Manual of The Mother Church*

"The Church's Ministry of Healing" (the Archbishop's Commission of the Church of England), 154n
"The Church's Redemptive Mission," 234, 243–247
*Cincinnati Enquirer,* 185–186
*Cincinnati Lancet-Clinic,* 280n, 281n
Clapp, Rodney, 204n
class legislation, 188
Colman, Janet F., 224
comforter, 194, 196n; as Holy Spirit, 66, 70
Committee on Publication, 132, 229, 319
communion, 19; Christian Science understanding of, 250–251; Mary Baker Eddy's view of, 251
"Communion Hymn," 250. *See also* communion; Eddy, Mary Baker
compassion, 140–141, 178; definition of, 140; prayer and, 140
*Concord Evening Monitor,* 239
Congregational church and Congregationalism, 15, 263, 282n
consciousness, 125–126, 135, 145; as related to Christian Science healing, 145; of disease, 135
Constitutional issues regarding healing practice, 180, 181–186
Copernican revolution, 244
Cox, Harvey, 85, 85n
*Crazes, Credulities, and Christian Science,* 280n
creation, 66, 78, 80–81, 88; spiritual creation, 80. *See also* Genesis
creed, Christian Science view of, 98, 215
crucifixion, 28, 73, 86, 92, 105; Christian Scientist's understanding of, 105. *See also* Jesus Christ

"Daily Prayer," 238. *See also* prayer, in Christian Science

quantum physics, 110, 302, 303–
309; and Christian Science, differ-
ent views, 306–309; theory of mat-
ter and energy, 304–305
*Quantum Questions: Mystical Writings
of the World's Great Physicists,* 309n
*Quantum Reality: Beyond the New
Physics,* 305, 309n
*Quarterly. See Christian Science Quar-
terly*
Quimby, George, 265, 266, 270n
*The Quimby Manuscripts,* 270n
Quimby, Phineas Parkhurst, 6, 263,
270n; association with Mary
Baker Eddy, 263, 264–266, 269

racism, 224, 244, 254
Rauschenbusch, Walter, 237, 238,
242n
Readers, 51, 217, 249; elected lay
members, 217; First Reader, 51.
*See also* Church of Christ, Scientist, worship services of
Reading Rooms (Christian Science
Reading Rooms), 217–218
reality, 6–7, 9, 16–17, 43, 81, 82, 95,
96, 178, 195, 269; appearance vs.,
81, 298; as Jesus defined, 308–309;
Christian Science perspective on,
6–7, 17, 39, 303–304; experience
of, 96; God and, 7, 38, 103, 288,
313; healing and, 87–88, 139, 145,
148, 172, 300, 313; in quantum
physics, 304–305; matter and, 95,
300; physicists' view of, 305, 307;
use of terms "real" and "unreal,"
109, 148, 303
reason, 95
rebirth. *See* "new birth"
"Recapitulation," 267–268. *See also
Science and Health with Key to the
Scriptures*
reconciliation, 244. *See also* atonement

redemption, 47, 52, 106, 135, 142;
creation and, 80–81; Mary Baker
Eddy's teaching on, 241, 268–269;
from sin, 106; healing and, 135.
*See also* atonement; Jesus Christ;
salvation
reform, power for, 194–195
regeneration, 7, 16, 19, 30, 39, 83;
demand for, 83; healing and, 50,
124, 137
"The Relation of Christian Faith to
Health" (adopted by 172nd General Assembly of the United Presbyterian Church in the U.S.A.),
98–99, 154
religion: perception of in the 1870s,
312; psychoanalytic theory of,
285–286
religious freedom, 169, 190; rights
and responsibilities of, 169. *See
also* Constitutional issues regarding healing practice; laws and legislation
"Religious Healing in the United
States: 1940–1960," 155n
repentance, 153. *See also* Jesus
Christ; regeneration; salvation
responsibility: Christian Science parental rights and, 169; ethic of, 185
resurrection, 28, 64, 82, 86; as pivotal in human history, 86, 105;
and ascension as revelations of reality, 82–83; Christian Scientists'
view of, 72–77, 86, 92, 111; connection between physical healing
and, 75, 111; demythologizing
view of, in contrast to Christian
Science view, 74–75; meaning to
disciples, 76. *See also* Jesus Christ;
salvation
"The Resurrection of Jesus," 72–77
*Retrospection and Introspection,* 13n,
204n, 255n. *See also* Eddy, Mary
Baker

Next

April 15th to May 1st

8th & April 1st

finish (9000
MO

Apr to MAY 1st

2...
4)9000